Flying Star
Feng Shui

OTHER FENG SHUI BOOKS BY STEPHEN SKINNER

The Living Earth Manual of Feng Shui: Chinese Geomancy (1976)
Feng Shui: The Traditional Oriental Way to Enhance Your Life (1997)
Feng Shui for Modern Living (2000)
Feng Shui Before and After:
Practical Room-by-Room Makeovers for Your House (2001)
K.I.S.S. Guide to Feng Shui (2001)

Flying Star Feng Shui

Stephen Skinner

TUTTLE Publishing

Tokyo | Rutland, Vermont | Singapore

Published in 2003 by Tuttle Publishing, an imprint of Periplus Editions (HK) Ltd

www.tuttlepublishing.com

Copyright © 2003 Stephen Skinner

Library of Congress Cataloging-in-Publication Data
Skinner, Stephen, 1948–
    Flying star feng shui / by Stephen Skinner.—1st ed.
      xv, 239 p. : ill. ; 24 cm.
    Includes bibliographical references (p.) and index.
    ISBN 0-8048-3433-4 (pbk.)
    1. Feng shui. I. Title.

  BF1779.F4 S5783 2003
  133.3/337—dc21   2002044373

ISBN 978-0-8048-3433-9

Distributed by

North America, Latin America, and Europe
Tuttle Publishing
364 Innovation Drive
North Clarendon, VT 05759-9436
Tel: 1 (802) 773-8930
Fax: 1 (802) 773-6993
info@tuttlepublishing.com
www.tuttlepublishing.com

Asia Pacific
Berkeley Books Pte. Ltd.
3 Kallang Sector #04-01/02
Singapore 349278
Tel: (65) 6741-2178
Fax: (65) 6741-2179
inquiries@periplus.com.sg
www.tuttlepublishing.com

Japan
Tuttle Publishing
Yaekari Building, 3rd Floor
5-4-12 Osaki, Shinagawa-ku,
Tokyo 141-0032
Tel: (81) 3 5437-0171
Fax: (81) 3 5437-0755
sales@tuttle.co.jp; www.tuttle.co.jp

First edition
23 22 21   7 6 5

Design by Jill Feron, Feron Design
Diagrams by Linda Carey
Printed in Malaysia   2104VP

Acknowledgments

Some years ago I casually suggested to Joey Yap that he and I collaborate on a book on Flying Star feng shui. If that collaboration had happened, this present book might have been that much richer. Perhaps the most thorough and practical work specifically on Flying Star currently available is Joey's excellent Xuan Kong home study course, available through www.dragon-gate.com.

I also owe a debt of gratitude to Derek Walters, whose seminal work, *Chinese Astrology* (which has just been reprinted in 2002), provides the most complete English language source for much of the Chinese astronomical and astrological background to the Flying Star system.

Contents

List of Figures

List of Tables

A Note on Transliteration

Feng shui is a Chinese art or science, so we need for a moment to consider how its concepts have been rendered in English. Chinese, as you probably know, is written with a series of characters, which are sometimes almost pictorial. This helps in understanding their meaning. Often the oldest ideas are the simplest characters. For example the Chinese character for tree looks a little like a pine tree with downward sloping branches 木, but its sound conveys nothing to an English speaker.

Again the Chinese character for Earth 土 is rather like a sprout coming up through a flat line of the soil. This character is written as "*ti*" in English, so that although we have its sound almost right, the additional meaning of fertility conveyed by the form of the character is lost. So we lose much more meaning in translating Chinese to English than translating for example French or German to English.

In a subject like feng shui we have to be particularly careful not to lose too much of the meaning in translation. Even more important, we must also be careful of meanings *added* to words accidentally by translators. An example of this is *lung. Lung* is the Chinese word that was translated by the early translators as "dragon." So a *lung* must be a fire-breathing, cave-dwelling, treasure-guarding defiler of maidens.

Wrong! A *lung* is just the opposite. It is a creature of water and wind, and a key creature in feng shui. It lives in the sea, in rivers, and in the clouds on mountaintops. It does not breathe fire, and it certainly doesn't expect to be hunted or killed by saints or knights on horseback!

Written Chinese is over 3,000 years old, thousands of years older than either spoken or written English. There are two main ways of showing or transliterating Chinese characters into English. Both are imperfect, as neither really portray the sound of Chinese entirely correctly, and of course neither show the shape of the original Chinese character. The oldest popular system, Wade-Giles, is named for its inventors, Sir Thomas Wade and Herbert Giles, and it was the most commonly used until the 1950s when the government of the People's Republic of China introduced another system called *pinyin.*

The *pinyin* system of writing Chinese characters in the Roman/English alphabet was first devised with scholarly help from Albania. Some of the stranger bits of this system derive not from Chinese, or even from English, but from Albanian pronunciation!

Most books on traditional feng shui adhere to the older Wade-Giles system, while some modern books (especially BHS-style feng shui) use *pinyin.* In this guide we will use Wade-Giles so that many of the earlier traditional books on feng shui still remain understandable.

The *pinyin* system is also associated with simplified Chinese characters (also introduced in the People's Republic of China in the 1950s). Because feng shui was suppressed in mainland China in 1927 (and still is frowned upon), not much original material on feng shui has been written in these characters, and definitely none of the Chinese language classics of feng shui were written in simplified characters. For both of these reasons I avoid using *pinyin* transliteration in this book.

I Say "*Pa Kua*," You Say "*Bagua*"

An example of the confusion brought about by the use of two different systems is the Chinese words for "eight trigrams." In Wade-Giles the words are *pa* (eight) and *kua* (trigrams). In *pinyin* the words are *ba* (eight) and *gua* (trigrams). Say them out loud, roll them around your mouth, and you will see that they are essentially the same sound, something like "bar kwar."

But when "ba gua" is shortened to "bagua," and non-Chinese readers start pronouncing it "bag-you-ah," and have even forgotten that it is in fact two distinct words and treat it as a single noun, then we have traveled many miles from the original meaning. At that point bad transliteration starts to interfere with meaning, and in turn, with our understanding.

You don't have to *learn* Chinese to understand feng shui. It's only important to recognize words that are key feng shui concepts. Perhaps the most obvious one is *ch'i* (Wade-Giles), which is pronounced "chee." In *pinyin* however, it is written as "qi," but of course is still pronounced "chee." You can easily see why we will be using Wade-Giles throughout this book!

In this book there are a lot of apparently ordinary English words used in a special sense. For example, "Stem" means one of the ten Chinese star Stems. To distinguish it from the botanical stem of a plant we have capitalized it. Another key example is Element. If used with a lower case it has its usual chemical meaning. But if Element is capitalized then it means one of the five Chinese Elements, which are more like types of energy than the substances you can pick up and handle.

Introduction

Feng shui is the Chinese art or science of improving the quality of life by making specific changes to the arrangement of a landscape, a city, your house, or even individual rooms. Everyone knows that redecorating a house or a room can have an uplifting effect on the people living in it. The ancient Chinese knew that this result occurred not just for psychological reasons, but because the life energy flowing in the room had been changed. They evolved specific and detailed rules for changing this energy, which they called *ch'i*.

Feng Shui is concerned with the flow of ch'i energy. Notions such as ch'i are sometimes considered fanciful, but they are no more fanciful than radio waves that nobody has ever seen, touched, or smelled. How do we know that radio waves exist? We only know of their existence from their effects. We only know of the existence of ch'i from its effects, many of which can be demonstrated. As such, the existence of ch'i is easier to demonstrate than the existence of radio waves, which depend on the use and construction of complex equipment to prove and detect them.

The flow of ch'i is affected by six things: direction, alignment, water, the 5 Elements, timing, and the Earth's magnetic field. It is fairly easy to set up a simple experiment to demonstrate this and hence to demonstrate the existence of some kind of energy, which we might as well call ch'i, as the Chinese have been doing for thousands of years. For example, practitioners of *ch'i kung* (or *qi gong* if you prefer) are able to demonstrate amazing physical feats dependent upon the accumulation of ch'i in their bodies. However, ch'i also accumulates in our environment, in the buildings and rooms in which we live and work.

To put it crudely, feng shui enables us to make precise changes to the ch'i in our environment, which will change our relationship with the world, even help head off periods of bad luck, and amplify periods of good luck.

I deliberately use the word "luck," which to Western ears may sound strange and unscientific. We often confuse "luck" with "chance." Chance is mathematical and governs things like the chance of winning the lottery. Luck is the availability of beneficial opportunities. Luck, for the Chinese, is seen like a commodity that can be accumulated, can be lost, and can even be stolen. Feng shui is about correcting our subtle environment in order to increase our luck, or if you like, our ability to attract and take advantage of opportunities.

Feng shui is a proactive thing. Once you have set up the correct feng shui environment, you will find many opportunities coming your way—opportunities for love, business opportunities, opportunities of promotion, and so on. It is up to you to accept and take advantage of these possibilities. People who lie in bed all day bewailing their lack of luck will not be helped by even the best feng shui. Conversely, people who correctly stimulate *all* the feng shui points in their home will find themselves rushed off their feet in a whirlwind of activity.

The usefulness of Flying Star feng shui is that it takes away the apparent random distribution of good and bad luck over time and enables you to pinpoint causes of variations in luck. It also allows you to change such bad luck, which manifests in ill health, bad relationships, and even poverty. The physical things used to make these changes are often referred to as "cures" or "remedies" by feng shui practitioners. This comes as a bit of a shock to the average Westerner who is used to thinking of luck as chance. Likewise, anyone who is tempted to lump feng shui with divination is wrong. Divination is a passive attempt at determining what is in store for you; feng shui is an active practice to find out why you have the luck you have—and to change it.

This book explains feng shui in a simple, step-by-step manner, so that you can change the energy patterns in your home or office to improve:

- Your relationships with the people around you—from friends, family, and co-workers to your romantic interests
- Your career and finances—for better work and investment opportunities
- Your health and well-being—and that of your immediate family.

Until now, most books in English on feng shui have concentrated on the 8 Mansion School of feng shui, or interior decoration, and simple, rule-of-thumb alignment feng shui, which is known to many Chinese with traditional upbringing. These work well enough, over a period of time, but Flying Star techniques, which are another part of feng shui, often provide more dramatic, far reaching, and sometimes almost immediate changes.

FLYING STAR FENG SHUI

"Flying Star" is simply a picturesque term for changing types of subtle ch'i energy present in our living environment, our homes, and our workplaces. Flying Star feng shui is concerned with ch'i quality, direction, and flow, particularly over time. This timing is measured by the Chinese solar calendar, which is, from a seasonal and cyclic point of view, rather more accurate than the Western calendar. The location or direction of entry of ch'i is also important and is measured with a compass. This is not just an ordinary Western trekking compass, but an intricate precision instrument, called the *lo p'an*, or Chinese compass, which predated the use of the Western compass in navigation by hundreds of years.

Flying Star feng shui is the essence of feng shui. It explains the *timing* element, which is missing from all the simpler feng shui styles currently known in the West. Flying Star explains why our luck changes over time and how we can stay one jump ahead of it.

Flying Star feng shui has often been referred to as Advanced feng shui in books in English, because there have been very few sources of information about it in English. However, Flying Star is an important part of any thorough feng shui diagnosis—some would say, the most important part.

Flying Star assumes there is a very real link between the present time, the time a building was built or occupied, its directional orientation, and the consequent changing luck of its occupants.

The 9 Flying Stars are essentially ch'i energy configurations that move from location to location inside a building, changing position over time. The essence of Flying Star feng shui is to make sure that important functions like sleeping, eating, and studying are done in rooms or parts of the building with favorable Flying Star configurations. Where this configuration is not favorable, Flying Star feng shui offers techniques for improving it.

When a potentially bad Flying Star combination arrives or "flies into" an important room, we use our knowledge of the cycles of the 5 Chinese Elements to modify, reduce, or defeat these effects. Conversely, beneficial Flying Star combinations can be further energized by appropriate Element placement. Often, the impressive effects of such work occur very rapidly.

On a technical note, Flying Star feng shui is known as *fei hsing* in Chinese, and is a part of *Hsuan Kung* feng shui (sometimes spelled *Xuan Kong*). This in turn is one of the approximately 9 major Schools of feng shui, many of which are unknown in the West, but include schools such as the *San Yuan* (Three Period) and *San He* (Three Combination or Form) School. A summary of these schools is found in appendix 7.

Chapter 1

Theory of Feng Shui

Those of you who are new to feng shui will have to learn a few basic concepts, the alphabet of feng shui if you like, before you'll be able to appreciate the specific techniques of Flying Star feng shui. Once you do, you'll learn some truly amazing techniques for improving your life by adjusting your surroundings. It will not always be obvious how these concepts fit in, but it will become clear when I explain how to apply them in the later chapters.

Even those of you who are familiar with feng shui, should review the basic concepts—like the interrelation of the 5 Elements—so that you do not have to keep referring back to earlier chapters.

This chapter is by its nature a very compact introduction to the whole subject of feng shui, before the book settles down to concentrate specifically on Flying Star feng shui. This is meant to be a quick summary, rather than a full exposition of the whole of classical feng shui.

We will very quickly run through basic feng shui concepts to make sure that you have the necessary background before embarking on Flying Star feng shui. If this is all familiar stuff, then pass rapidly on to the next chapter.

Numbers are very important in feng shui, just as they are in mathematics or accountancy. In this chapter we will examine the main feng shui numbers, which includes the 4 seasons, 5 Elements, 8 directions, 12 Branches, 24 main divisions of the compass, and so on. These numbers help us to measure time and the flow of ch'i energy.

1. SHAN AND SHUI: MOUNTAINS AND RIVERS

First we need briefly to touch upon geography and introduce a few basic Chinese language terms. Feng shui is an art that has been derived from the landscape, from observing the flow of ch'i energy in the land. In fact its ancient name was *ti li*, which today is the word used in modern China for the subject of geography.

The ancient Chinese observed how ch'i can be cradled and accumulated in a well protected hollow, or dispersed on a windy ridge. They observed that large bodies of water can pool ch'i energy, but a rapidly flowing stream will disperse it. They analyzed various landforms, in just the same way as a modern geographer might, and they reduced all landforms to just two Elements: mountains and water.

If you think about it, there is nothing else. Modern geographers understand that huge cycles of geological time see the upthrust and buckling of the Earth's crust into mountain ranges. These mountains are then eroded by wind and water to form silt floodplains of winding rivers, rich deltas, and fertile fields from which all life derives. Left behind by this erosion are mountains, valleys, chasms, and gorges—in fact, every other geographical phenomenon.

If we translate this into Chinese, the mountains (*shan*) are upthrust and then eroded by wind (*feng*) and water (*shui*) to provide the entire physical environment we live in. Let us group those terms. *Shan shui* (or mountain-water) is the Chinese name for landscape. *Feng shui* (or wind-water) is the Chinese name for the art of managing the subtle side of this environment for the benefit of man.

Shan and shui are perhaps the two most important words we will learn in our study of feng shui. It is important to understand that these terms are firmly rooted in the realities of geography, because later in this book we will discover that shan and shui are also applied to technical matters like the 24 directions of the compass and to types of energy resident inside buildings.

Feng shui takes this further and deals with the movement of ch'i energy not only through the landscape but also in our homes, offices, and even our bodies.

2. WHERE IT ALL BEGAN: YANG AND YIN

Yin and yang are two more important Chinese concepts. The ancient, literal meaning of yin implies "shady north side of a hill" and yang means the "sunny south side of a hill." Immediately you have a direct geographical application not only to the surface of the earth but also to the idea of complimentary pairs. Many books on feng shui state that yang and yin are hot and cold, male and female, or light and dark. Be careful to remember that it is the *relationship* which is yin/yang, not the thing. The relationship between hot and cold is the relationship between yang and yin. Cold, by itself, is not yin. Hot, by itself, is not yang.

Creation is made up of opposites, the light (yang) and dark (yin). Yin governs the Earth, all that is negative, female, dark, water, soft, cold, deadly, or still; while yang governs Heaven and all that is positive, male, light, fiery, hard, warm, living, and moving. The combination and permutation of the yang and the yin forms the rest of the universe, the life and breath of the universe is ch'i, which is formed by the interaction of yin and yang.

Yin and yang are represented in the Chinese classic, the *I Ching*, as a whole line (yang) and a broken line (yin). As the whole line is one thing and the broken line is two things, yang is equated to one and yin to two: it follows that all odd numbers are symbolically yang and all even numbers are symbolically yin. Therefore the mating of odd-

and even- numbered ch'i flows is a beneficial combination. This piece of binary arithmetic becomes very useful when evaluating the numerical value of the 9 Flying Stars.

3. The Three Primes: Heaven, Man, and Earth

Chinese civilization sees the whole of creation as made up of the Three Primes: Heaven, Man, and Earth. Heaven and Earth's influences both affect Man, or humankind. Man lives on Earth below Heaven. Man is therefore influenced by both Heaven and Earth from the moment he is born. He cannot easily alter what fate he receives from Heaven, but by using feng shui he can affect the luck he receives from Earth.

4. The Four Seasons, 4 Celestial Animals, and 4 Compass Directions

Yin and yang apply at every level, from cosmological through geographical down to the human condition. Even the seasons are capable of being organized in the light of yin and yang. Summer, the hottest season, is the most yang. Winter, the coldest season, is the most yin. Direction can also be organized in a yin/yang way. Hot yang summer is attributed to the hot South, while cold yin winter is attributed to the cold North. Spring is hot yang arising out of the cold yin of winter and is found in the place of the rising Sun, the East. Autumn is waning yang and ascribed to the West, which is also the place of the waning or setting Sun.

Thus the four seasons follow a cycle of waxing and waning yin and yang. The day follows the same pattern. The Sun rises in the East (spring), reaches its peak in the South (midsummer), sets in the West (autumn), and is dark in the North (midwinter). Consequently the seasons are attributed to the four quarters as follows:

> Spring – East (waxing yang)
> Summer – South (maximum yang)
> Autumn – West (waxing yin)
> Winter – North (maximum yin)

Feng shui also gives a Celestial (or symbolic) Animal to each of these four quarters:

> East – the Green Dragon
> South – the Red Bird
> West – the White Tiger
> North – the Black Tortoise

In feng shui, one of the purposes of these 4 Celestial Animals is to act as landform markers in the environment around a house or building and to mark the 4 cardinal points N, S, E, W.

5. THE 5 ELEMENTS—*WU HSING*

One of the most important enumeration systems used in feng shui is the division of things into the 5 Elements. These are basic to Chinese thinking and are used in Chinese medicine, geology, philosophy, and even psychology. First we will look at the names of the 5 Elements, then we will look at how they connect up with the 4 compass directions. Then we will look at how the 5 Elements interact with each other.

The 5 Elements of the Chinese are different from the ancient Greek Elements of fire, air, earth, and water, for the Chinese Elements include Wood (which symbolizes all growing vegetation, not just trees) and Metal (which symbolizes to a certain extent things fabricated or purified from the Earth).

The 5 Elements are:

Water ....shui 水
Fire...........huo 火
Wood ....mu 木
Metal........chin 金
Earth ....t'u 土

Interestingly, air (*feng*) is left out although water (*shui*) is present.

It is a little misleading to refer to these as the "5 Elements," for the Chinese word *hsing* indicates movement, so perhaps the "5 Moving Energies" might be a more appropriate name. This would certainly reinforce the idea that they generate and destroy each other in a continually moving cycle; however, we will continue to use the word "Element" as so many other books in English use the same translation of *hsing*.

The 5 Elements can be allocated to the 4 seasons and hence to the 4 compass directions and the 4 Celestial Animals, as seen in figure 1.1.

Note that the arbitrary convention of European and American map making is to put North at the top. The Chinese convention and that of feng shui books generally (which is much older) is to put South at the top. However it does not matter which way up this diagram is put, as the relative positions are still the same.

If you have trouble with this, then simply turn the book around and look at the illustration from the opposite direction. North will then appear at the top, and every direction will be in its "normal" position. The point I am making is that it does not matter which direction you use to look at it, because the compass points are still in the same relative position. All books on feng shui use the Chinese convention, which states that the south is the warmest and hence most beneficial, and is therefore shown at the top. This convention incidentally pre-dates the Western north-oriented map-making convention by more than a thousand years.

By placing Water in the north and Fire in the south, these two Elements are opposed to each other. Likewise Metal in the west opposes Wood in the East. Let us look more closely at the relationships between all of the 5 Elements, not just these simple pairs of opposites.

Fig. 1.1 *The Four Directions with Corresponding Elements and Celestial Animals*

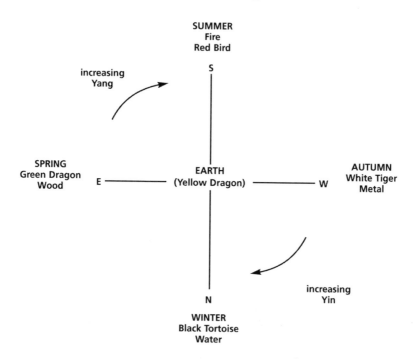

The most important thing is the mutual relationship between these Elements, and this is often expressed in cycles of Production and Destruction. As one commentator once put it, "In a card game, it is not the individual cards that matter, but their relationship to other cards in the hand." Make sure that you grasp the following cycles, as they will become essential knowledge as you start to apply feng shui remedies.

6. ELEMENT PRODUCTION, DESTRUCTION, AND REDUCTION CYCLES

The Elements *produce* each other in the order shown in figure 1.2. In this cycle, Wood burns to produce Fire, which results in ash (or Earth) in which Metal may be found. Metal is also found in the veins of the earth, from which (according to Chinese thought) sprang the underground streams (Water), which nourish vegetation and in turn produce Wood. And so the cycle goes on.

Each Element also destroys another in the Destruction or Controlling sequence shown in figure 1.3. Here Wood is destroyed by Metal implements, which are melted by Fire, which is quenched by Water, which is dammed by Earth, whose nutrients are extracted by Wood or vegetation. And so this cycle returns to the beginning again.

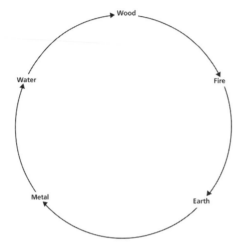

Fig. 1.2 *The Production Cycle of the Elements*

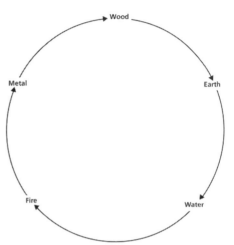

Fig. 1.3 *The Destruction Cycle of the Elements*

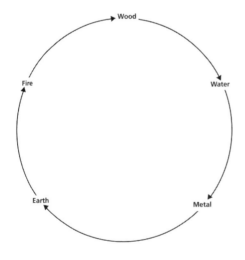

Fig. 1.4 *The Reduction Cycle of the Elements*

The third cycle, the Reduction (or Weakening) Cycle (figure 1.4), is the exact reverse of the Production Cycle. In the Reduction Cycle, each Element is weakened by its predecessor. In a sense, the Reduction Cycle is more useful than the Destruction Cycle. For example, if you wish to destroy or weaken the energy symbolized by Wood, it is easier to use Fire than Metal (the axe). This Cycle works by using the produced Element to weaken its parent Element. An easy way to remember this is to consider how a mother can be worn out by her children. So Wood (which produces Fire) can be "worn out" or drained by Fire.

The Production, Destruction, and Reduction Cycles provide the theoretical background for generating Flying Star feng shui remedies, and so they are very useful to know by heart. We revisit these Cycles in chapter 15.

Fig. 1.5 *The 4 Cardinal and 4 Inter-cardinal Directions*

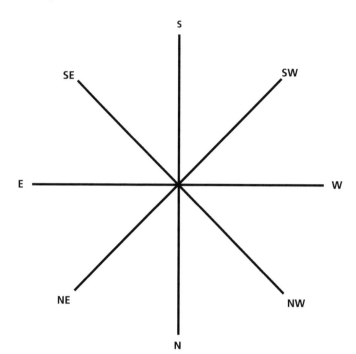

7. THE 8 DIRECTIONS

Feng shui is about direction, and so we expand our basic compass of 4 directions to one showing 8 directions. It is a basic requirement of any feng shui analysis to identify which of the 8 directions a building faces.

Let us continue our discussion of 8-fold things by looking at one of the most fundamental symbol sets in the whole of Chinese civilization: the 8 trigrams.

8. THE 8 TRIGRAMS OF THE *I CHING*

The *I Ching* is a Chinese classic based on a binary system of divination derived from the two basic units yin and yang, respectively, the female broken line (- -) and the male unbroken line (—).

A trigram is a three-tier combination of yin and yang lines: consequently there are 2^3, or 8, trigrams. Trigrams are called *san yao kua* (or gua) in Chinese (meaning "3-line kua"), or *kua* for short. Read each kua from the bottom line upward. The Ch'ien trigram with all 3 yang lines is the most male, the Father. The K'un trigram with all 3 yin lines is the most female, the Mother, as shown in column 7 of table 1.1. Interestingly, in the same

Table 1.1: *The 8 Trigrams, or Kua, with Correspondences*

Trigram	Element	Associated Animal	Geographical Reflection	Associated Season	Interpretation	Family Member
Ch'ien	Metal	Dragon, Horse	Heaven	Late Autumn	Creative, strength, roundness, vitality	Father
K'un	Earth	Mare, Ox, Cow	Earth	Late Summer, Early Autumn	Receptive, yielding, nourishment	Mother
Chen	Wood	Galloping Horse, Flying Dragon	Thunder	Spring	Movement, arousal	Eldest Son
K'an	Water	Pig	Moon and Water	Mid-Winter	Curved objects, flowing water, danger	Middle Son
Ken	Lesser Earth	Dog	Mountain	Early Spring	Steadiness, stillness, gates, fruits, seeds	Youngest Son
Hsun	Lesser Wood	Hen	Wind	Early Summer	Gentleness, penetration, growth, vegetative growth	Eldest Daughter
Li	Fire	Pheasant	Sun and Lightning	Summer	Adherence, dependence, weapons, drought, brightness	Middle Daughter
Tui	Lesser Metal	Sheep, Goat	Lake and Seawater	Mid-Autumn	Joy, serenity, reflections and mirror images	Youngest Daughter

Note that the Father has all yang lines, the Mother has all yin lines, the sons have just one yang line, and the daughters one yin line.

column, the three sons all correspond to a trigram with only one yang line, while the three daughters correspond to trigrams with only one yin line.

In this way a hierarchy can be built up extending from Ch'ien (the most yang kua with 3 yang lines) to K'un (the most yin kua with 3 yin lines). Looking at it another way, in each trigram, or kua, the bottom line represents Earth, the middle line Man, and the top line Heaven.

In table 1.1 the first column shows the trigram, and its name, while the sixth column gives an indication of the general nature and action of the trigram. The second column shows its Element. Note that Wood, Earth, and Metal have 2 trigrams each, while Fire and Water only have one trigram each. The third column gives the traditional animal association. The fourth column clearly shows the geographical roots of trigrams. The fifth column gives us the key to relating the trigrams to figure 1.1, as it shows the seasonal correspondence of the trigrams.

To make the connection between feng shui and the trigrams, we must relate the trigrams to the compass directions. The 8 trigrams are attributed to the 8 points of the compass in two distinct and separate arrangements. These two arrangements are referred to respectively as the Former Heaven Sequence (allegedly devised by Fu-Hsi circa 2800 BC) and the Later Heaven Sequence (identified with King Wen circa 1027 BC, the first ruler

Fig. 1.6 *Former Heaven Sequence of the Trigrams*

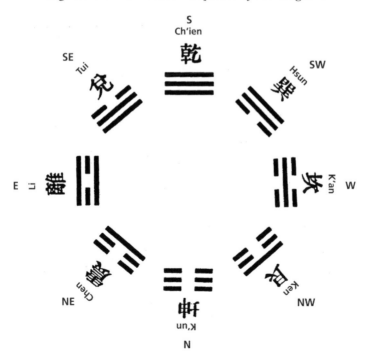

of the Chou dynasty). Although the history behind these two arrangements need not concern us, the fact that the two arrangements are radically different is important. The two Sequences are shown in figures 1.6 and 1.7. Read these diagrams from the bottom up, or on the circle, from inside outwards. The lines of the trigrams closest to the center of the circle are the lowest lines and are counted as the first line.

We will mostly be interested in the Later Heaven Sequence of trigrams, as this is associated with the world as it is now, and so it is this one that you should attempt to learn. Remember that when recognizing the trigrams, they are drawn from the bottom to the top, the inside of the diagram to the outside: the upper line is outermost.

The 8 trigrams are combined one with the other to make 8 x 8 = 64 hexagrams, which are the basic figures used in the Chinese classic the *I Ching*.

In Chinese, hexagrams are called *ta kua*, or big kua, to distinguish them from san yao kua, the 3-line kua or trigrams. You will be relieved to learn that for basic Flying Star feng shui the hexagrams are not important, and we need only concern ourselves with the 8 trigrams. But it is useful to know that the figures of the *I Ching* do relate directly to feng shui (and in fact are the basis of another school of feng shui — see appendix 7).

Fig. 1.7 *Later Heaven Sequence of the Trigrams*

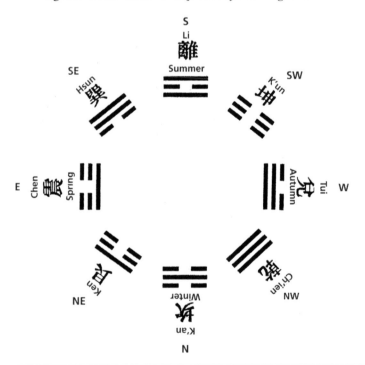

9. LO SHU MAGIC SQUARE

The *Lo Shu* is one of the most ancient tools of feng shui. It is a sort of tic-tac-toe grid of 9 chambers. In its basic form it holds 9 numbers:

4	9	2
3	5	7
8	1	6

This is the Basic, or Earth, form, but not the only form. There is a different permutation of numbers within the grid for each of the 9 Periods. These are shown in full in appendix 4. The Lo Shu is called a magic square because whichever way it is added up, even diagonally, it still totals 15. This same magic square appears also in Europe where it is associated with the Earth and the planet Saturn.

Lo Shu literally means "Lo map or diagram." The Lo Shu magic square was first seen as a collection of dots representing the above numbers written on the back of a turtle emerging from the banks of the Lo river around 2205 BC. It was seen by the Emperor Yu, who had a reputation for controlling the disastrous floods of ancient China. And so the Lo Shu has always been associated with the control of water and hence with feng shui.

The 9 numbers in the 9 squares form the basic diagram. We need to fit some of the other symbols we've learned on this base. We will start with the 8 trigrams.

Fig. 1.8 *The Lo Shu Turtle As Seen by the Great Yu*

烏龜背書（洛書）

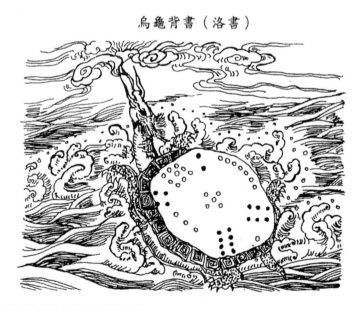

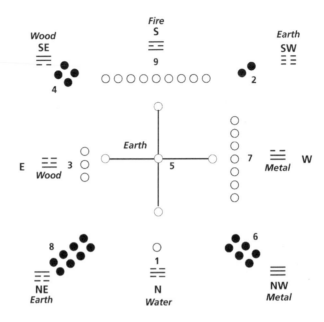

The Lo Shu neatly coincides with the Later Heaven Sequence of the trigrams. Because there are 9 chambers in the Lo Shu, it is natural that the 8 trigrams should be equated with the outer cells of the Lo Shu. Nine is considered the most yang number (being odd and the largest integer). South is the hottest or most yang direction. Therefore, in the Basic Lo Shu, the cell containing "9" is orientated to the South. When compass points and the 5 Elements have been added in, you get the figure 1.9.

If we simplify this a little and add in the colors usually associated with the numbers, we get the figure 1.10.

Each of these key feng shui elements are stressed to a different degree by the various schools of feng shui that have developed over the last few millennia. Essentially they all use the elements I have discussed in this chapter, but with a different emphasis, to a more or less degree.

One of the main differences between 8 Mansion School of feng shui and the Flying Star School of feng shui is the treatment of the Lo Shu. The 8 Mansion School only uses the above Basic form of the Lo Shu. The Flying Star School discovered that the energies represented by these numbers were not frozen in time, but moved around over time. It is this movement that we are going to look at in this book.

Remember that the numbers in the Basic Lo Shu add in every direction (even diagonally) to 15. Check it now for yourself. In later chapters we will show how these numbers move around the Basic Lo Shu to form different permutations.

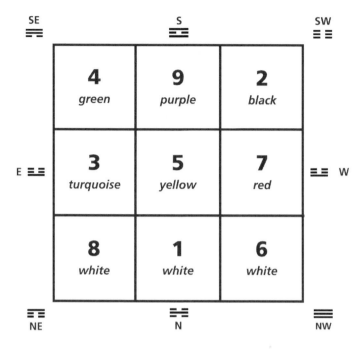

Fig. 1.10 *The Colors, Directions, and Trigrams of the Lo Shu*

Look quickly at appendix 4, and you will see all 9 different Lo Shu arrangements. If we want to identify one specific arrangement we call it by the number in the center square. Thus the fifth permutation has "5" in the center square, the sixth has "6" and so on.

We have already noticed that in the "standard" Lo Shu (see above) every column and row and diagonal adds to 15. This is also true of the "5," "2," and "8" Lo Shu permutations.

Table 1.2 shows the totals generated by each of those permutations. Notice that each of these permutations has a "signature" total.

These numbers are *very* significant, and although we will not go into them in detail, it is sufficient for you to note that the signature total for each Lo Shu permutation indicates a lot about the qualities of that Lo Shu. A simple example of the importance of these signature totals is that all Lo Shus that add to 15 are considered to be Earth Lo Shus.

The practice of feng shui has developed over thousands of years and has separated into a number of Schools that emphasize different things in their practice. (See appendix 7 for more details of these schools.)

We have now covered the simplest sets of feng shui terms. The 5 Elements and 8 trigrams are used time and time again in more complex calculations. It may be worth reviewing this chapter a few times before moving on—just to make sure you understand

Table 1.2: *The Totals Generated by the Lo Shu in Different Permutations*

Period	totals signature	
2	15	⎫
5	15	⎬
8	15	⎭
1	21 and 12	⎫
4	21 and 12	⎬
7	21 and 12	⎭
3	18 and 9	⎫
6	18 and 9	⎬
9	18 and 9	⎭

these key concepts. Base your review around the compass points. The least you need to know is:

- The 4 cardinal compass points N, S, E, W and how they relate to the 4 seasons, the 4 symbolic Celestial Animals, plus the intervening directions of SE, NE, SW, NW.
- The 5 Elements, and how they relate to the 4 compass points plus center.
- The 3 Cycles of Production, Destruction, and Reduction, in other words, how to produce one Element from another, and how to destroy one Element by using another. (How you apply this theory in practice will become apparent in chapter 15 on feng shui remedies.) Make sure you know how to look them up—you will find them easy to learn as you work with them.
- The 8 trigrams, and the fact that they relate to the compass points in two different ways—the Former and Later Heaven Sequences. You don't need to commit both these Sequences to memory. Just be aware they exist, and know that the Later Heaven Sequence is the most important from our point of view (when dealing with interior house feng shui).
- The Basic Lo Shu square (with a "5" in its center) and its 9 numbers. Be aware that 9 permutations exist, but don't try to learn them.

Chapter 2

Time Dimension

Luck changes over time, and feng shui therefore, has a time dimension: what is lucky for you today may not be so in twenty year's time. To understand time dimension feng shui you need to understand how the Chinese measure time.

Before we get down to how to maximize your luck using the correct timing, we have to look at the nature of time itself. The Chinese have a longer history of astronomical observation and written record keeping than any other civilization in the world, and their view of history is so long-term that they count in epochs of 3,600 years and list the rise and fall of their dynasties as far back as 2852 BC. As you might expect, their calendar is in many senses more complex than the Western calendar. The simple animal signs of popular Chinese astrology comprise only the tip of a very large and interesting iceberg. To start, the Chinese have two calendars: a lunar calendar (based on the Moon cycles) and a solar calendar (tied very closely to the seasons and the rotation of the Earth around the Sun).

The measurement of date and time has always been linked with the movement of the heavenly bodies. Unfortunately these bodies do not move in a way that is arithmetically simple. In all calendars the day is related to the rising and setting of the Sun. The day is the most obvious unit of time. The West divides the day into twenty-four hours, but the Chinese divide it into twelve hours, each with 120 Western minutes. The Chinese use these "double hours" even today. Most, but not all, calendars also use the time it takes for the Earth to go round the Sun as a second unit of time, the year. Finally many cultures divide the year into twelve or thirteen months or "Moons."

In North America, Europe, and a multitude of other countries, there is only one calendar. It is a solar calendar, meaning it is linked very closely with the rotation of the Earth around the Sun. In fact this calendar was devised by Julius Caesar (in 46 BC), and modified by Pope Gregory (in AD 1582). One of the problems with a solar calendar is that the period of rotation of the Earth around the Sun is not an even number of days. In other words, there is no exact number of days in the year. This number is in fact close to 365.242199 days.

Other calendars have used the Moon as their timekeeper. These calendars are called lunar calendars, from the Latin *luna*, meaning "Moon." Islamic countries use a lunar calendar. With a lunar calendar, three problems arise:

1. There isn't an even number of days in one Moon cycle (approximately 29.53059 days).
2. There isn't an even number of Moon cycles in the year (approximately 12.36826).
3. There are at least three ways of measuring the length of the Moon cycle: including from one new Moon to another or from one full Moon to another, each giving different measurements.

The usual cure for these problems is to pop in an extra lunar month every now and then, which is not a very satisfactory solution.

Although our Western calendar is a solar calendar, it still uses the Moon for religious dating: for example, every year Easter falls on a different date determined by the phases of the Moon. This is a little bit of lunar paganism left over and used to define a Christian festival. As the Western calendar is a solar calendar, it should mainly keep track of the seasons, but nowadays you would be lucky to find any city dweller who could instantly give you the commencement dates of each of the seasons.

THE CHINESE SOLAR CALENDAR

The Chinese, however, are very aware of the heavens and have both a lunar and a solar calendar. Fortunately feng shui uses the more logical of the two, the Chinese solar calendar.

Although Chinese New Year festivities and popular Chinese astrology are governed by the lunar calendar, for feng shui and agricultural purposes we must use the more precise Chinese solar calendar to measure the seasons and actual tides of ch'i that are so important to feng shui. Many books on feng shui in English get the two calendars rather mixed up. One writer on Flying Star feng shui, who accidentally used the lunar calendar in her first book on the subject, finished up with the embarrassment of an occasional 13th lunar month ruining her calculations.

The Chinese solar calendar is called the *Hsia* calendar (pronounced "she-ah"), or farmers' calendar, and it regulates agriculture because the Sun determines the seasons. The solar year starts precisely with the beginning of Spring, which falls on either February 4 or 5. The reason why there are two possible dates is not due to any uncertainty in the Chinese calendar, but because the Western calendar "wobbles" (due to the insertion of an irregular extra day during leap years).

THE 24 *CH'I CHIEH* SEASONS

Because time is an important part of Flying Star feng shui, we need to look at how the Chinese divided up their year—not into 12 months, but into 24 mini-seasons.

The seasons are basic to the solar calendar because the Sun governs the progress of the seasons. Four seasons are enough for city folk. But four seasons are really too simple for the average farmer, who wants to know exactly when the last frost will occur and when he should plant his grain. It is far too imprecise to simply say, "sometime in spring," when "sometime" is a three-month period. So the Chinese solar agricultural calendar divides the year into 24 divisions, which are called *ch'i chieh* or mini-seasons.

The 24 ch'i chieh (sometimes spelled *jia qi*) seasons also have to fit with the solstices and equinoxes, those all-important days marking each season. The two equinoxes mark the middle of spring (around 21 March) and the middle of autumn (around 21 September), when we have equal hours of night and day (hence "equi-nox," which means "equal night"). The two solstices mark the middle of summer (around 21 June) and the middle of winter (around 21 December). (The last two statements are true for the Northern Hemisphere. The reverse is true in the Southern Hemisphere.) One of the calendar mistakes that we make in the West is assuming that the solstices and equinoxes mark the *beginning* of seasons, when in fact they mark the *middle* of each season. (The ch'i chieh relate to the 24 divisions of the compass that we will come to in a later chapter.)

The seasons in turn relate to the 5 Chinese Elements as in table 2.1.

Table 2.1: *The Seasons Related to the 5 Chinese Elements*

Spring	Wood
Summer	Fire
(center of the 4 seasons)	Earth
Fall/Autumn	Metal
Winter	Water

Beyond the calendar year there is an important cyclical side to Chinese time keeping. This is expressed in words that use plant metaphors. Heaven is measured by the 10 Heavenly Stems, and Earth is measured by the 12 Earthly Branches.

10 HEAVENLY STEMS

We have to look at two more cycles, which appear over and over again in time keeping and on the feng shui lo p'an compass. Initially, it's enough to know that they exist. Don't try to memorize them. You can refer back to this discussion later.

The 10 Heavenly Stems are simply the two aspects of each of the 5 Elements run through twice. Everything is either yin or yang and the Elements are no exception, so the Stems are 5 x 2 = 10 in number. The 10 Heavenly Stems are a very old set of symbols, and apart from an oblique connection with the stars of the Milky Way, their names do not really mean much to modern Chinese anymore. The 10 Heavenly Stems were at one point looked upon as literally the stems upon which the stars were seated, although this may simply have been a poetic interpretation. They are described as lucky or unlucky according to their yin/yang balance.

Table 2.2: *The 10 Heavenly Stems, or T'ien Kan*

Number	Name	Element	yin/yang	lucky/unlucky
1	chia	Wood	yang	U
2	i	Wood	yin	U
3	ping	Fire	yang	L
4	ting	Fire	yin	L
5	wu	Earth	yang	-
6	chi	Earth	yin	-
7	keng	Metal	yang	L
8	hsin	Metal	yin	L
9	jen	Water	yang	U
10	kuei	Water	yin	U

Note the alternation of yin and yang and that each Element is therefore represented twice. Note also that the order of the Elements is that of the Productive Cycle of the Elements. So the 10 Heavenly Stems are really just the complete cycle of the Elements.

The relative luck of the Stems is related to their association with the trigrams. The unlucky Stems in this case (1 and 9) are associated with Ch'ien and K'un trigrams, which are unlucky because they are overwhelmingly yang or yin respectively with no admixture or balance.

Contrariwise, because Stems 3, 4, 7, and 8 have a suitable mixture of yin and yang, they are considered lucky.

Stems 2 and 10 are referred to as "yin emptiness": quite the reverse, but again an undesirable state, with no balance asserting itself. Orphan-emptiness literally means "unlucky" in Chinese.

Stems 3 and 7 are referred to as "yang prosperity." Again a lucky blend. "Prosperity-assistance" is the Chinese compound word for "lucky."

Stems 5 and 6 stand for the center and do not partake of any particular direction. On the scale of numbers 1 to 10 they also stand at the middle. They are also allocated to no trigram, as there are only eight trigrams to go around ten Stems. These two are referred to as the "Tortoise-shell." In other words, if they cannot be the trigrams or numbers seen by Emperor Yu on the tortoise shell, then they must be the shell itself.

Stems 5 and 6 are considered negative, rather than unlucky, in that they may be used to control the dispersal of *sha* (noxious vapors) by imposing the rule of the tortoise on the sha to dispatch it to its proper place. They are almost impartial guardians against sha because they have no specific ch'i attributed to them with which to become involved.

12 EARTHLY BRANCHES

We now come to another set of symbols, which tie together direction and time. Western science has talked about the space-time continuum for less than a hundred years.

Chinese science has been aware of the connection between time and space for over a thousand years!

The 12 Earthly Branches are most commonly remembered as the 12 so-called "animal zodiacal signs" of popular Chinese astrology. Branch I is associated with the Rat, Branch II with the Ox, and so on.

⊛ The Branches also correlate with the seasons (4 seasons x 3 months each = 12 Branches) and the 12 double-hours of the day.

Most important for our purposes is the attribution of each of the 12 Earthly Branches to the compass directions. The most important Branches marking out the four cardinal points are highlighted in table 2.3. From this you can see that the Branches tie time and years to directions.

So as not to confuse the numbering of the Stems and the Branches, it is traditional to number Branches with Roman numerals (I–XII) and the Stems with Arabic numbers (1–10).

....

Table 2.3: *The 12 Earthly Branches, or Ti Chih*

Branch		Direction		Years		Season	Month	Hour
Branch Number	Earthly Branch Name	Compass Direction in Degrees	"Animal Sign"	Example Corresponding Years			Solar Month Number	Double Hour
I	tzu	352.5–7.5 **(N)**	Rat	1996, 2008		mid winter	11	11pm–1am
II	ch'ou	22.5–37.5	Ox	1997, 2009		late winter	12	1am–3am
III	yin	52.5–67.5	Tiger	1998, 2010		early spring	1	3am–5am
IV	mao	82.5–97.5 **(E)**	Rabbit	1999, 2011		mid spring	2	5am–7am
V	ch'en	112.5–127.5	Dragon	2000, 2012		late spring	3	7am–9am
VI	ssu	142.5–157.5	Snake	1989, 2001		early summer	4	9am–11am
VII	wu	172.5–187.5 **(S)**	Horse	1990, 2002		mid summer	5	11am–1pm
VIII	wei	202.5–217.5	Sheep	1991, 2003		late summer	6	1pm–3pm
IX	shen	232.5–247.5	Monkey	1992, 2004		early autumn	7	3pm–5pm
X	yu	262.5–277.5 **(W)**	Rooster	1993, 2005		mid autumn	8	5pm–7pm
XI	hsu	292.5–307.5	Dog	1994, 2006		late autumn	9	7pm–9pm
XII	hai	322.5–337.5	Pig	1995, 2007		early winter	10	9pm–11pm

The 12 Earthly Branches integrate directions with various time periods. For example, the Branch *tzu* correlates with the sign of the Rat, the North, mid-winter, and midnight.

Separately, the Stems and the Branches don't mean very much, but when combined they are used for all sorts of counting. Taken together they are referred to as the *kan* (Stems) *shih* (Branches) system. *Kan shih* is sometimes spelled *ganzhi*. These look quite different until you say both out loud, then you can hear that they are simply two different ways of spelling the same thing. Let us now look at how the Branches interact with the Stems.

60 SEXAGENARY COMBINATIONS OF HEAVENLY STEMS AND EARTHLY BRANCHES

The kan shih are made up of two Chinese characters, are used for time counting (years or days), and feature heavily in many Rings of the lo p'an compass. If there are 10 Heavenly Stems and 12 Earthly Branches, how many combinations can you have—120? Wrong: just 60 combinations. The reason is that essentially the 10 Stems are made up of two sets, the yin and yang versions of the 5 Elements. Therefore when it comes to combining them with the 12 Earthly Branches, the rule is that only yin Stems can go with yin Branches (and only yang Stems can go with yang Branches), resulting in just 5 x 12 = 60 combinations.

In the older textbooks on feng shui and Chinese horoscopes, these 60 combinations are called the Sexagenary characters, or combinations, which simply means the 60-fold pairs of character combinations made of one Branch combined with one Stem. You will sometimes find the 60 Sexagenary combinations called Binomials, literally the "two numbers." The first Sexagenary combination for example is *chia tzu* (i.e. the Heavenly Stem number 1 *chia* plus the Earthly Branch I tzu). The Chinese name for these 60 combinations is chia tzu.

Let us look at the complete set of combinations:

Read table 2.4 by selecting combinations of one Stem and one Branch. Where they intersect is the number of the Sexagenary combination. You can see clearly why there are only 60 and not 120 combinations. Half the combinations are disallowed because they mix yin and yang. Again, only yin Branches mate with yin Stems, and only yang Branches mate with yang Stems. For example, read down the column headed by the Stem chia, and across the line of the Branch tzu. From this you can see that the combination chia tzu is Sexagenary combination number 1. It is a yang combination made up of Stem 1 and Branch I.

Let's try something more complicated. Find Sexagenary combination 52. Yes, it's Branch IV and Stem number 2, or *i mao*.

What about the combination *ping ch'ou*? The square is blank . . . it is not there because *ping* is yang, but *ch'ou* is yin; therefore the combination can *never* exist. The combinations are either all yin or all yang, one sex or the other!

Now let us look at the other information on the table. Look for example at the 53rd Sexagenary combination. It is *ping ch'en*. What are its qualities? It is a yang Fire (*ping*) Dragon (*ch'en*). Ah, a yang Fire Dragon. Suddenly these otherwise inscrutable pairs of Chinese words have meaningful qualities. Look at another one, take chia shen. Its qualities are yang Wood Monkey.

Now let us use these 60 Sexagenary combinations for a practical purpose: the counting of years. We will find later that this counting method is important for determining the "luck" of a house built in that year, and also the luck of its occupants.

THE 60-YEAR CYCLES

The Chinese count the reigns of their Emperors and even their own age in terms of time Cycles of 60 years' length. Guess what? It's the Sexagenary combinations that are used to label each of these years. Particular years have a character derived from the Stem and Branch used to label it. At the popular Chinese astrology level, people talk about a Dragon year (2000 for example) or a Snake year (2001). Look again at table 2.4 to find out what animal sign applies to this year. What they should really be saying is that the

Table 2.4: *The 60 Sexagenary Combinations of Heavenly Stems and Earthly Branches*

				Stem (across) Stem yin/yang Stem Element									
Branch (downwards)	Branch Animal Sign	Branch yin/ yang	Branch Element	1 chia yang Wood	2 I/yi yin Wood	3 ping yang Fire	4 ting yin Fire	5 wu* yang Earth	6 chi yin Earth	7 keng yang Metal	8 hsin yin Metal	9 jen yang Water	10 kuei yin Water
I	tzu	Rat	yang	Water	1		13		25		37		49	
II	ch'ou	Ox	yin	Earth		2		14		26		38		50
III	yin	Tiger	yang	Wood	51		3		15		27		39	
IV	mao	Rabbit	yin	Wood		52		4		16		28		40
V	ch'en	Dragon	yang	Earth	41		53		5		17		29	
VI	ssu	Snake	yin	Fire		42		54		6		18		30
VII	wu*	Horse	yang	Fire	31		43		55		7		19	
VIII	wei	Sheep	yin	Earth		32		44		56		8		20
IX	shen	Monkey	yang	Metal	21		33		45		57		9	
X	yu	Rooster	yin	Metal		22		34		46		58		10
XI	hsu	Dog	yang	Earth	11		23		35		47		59	
XII	hai	Pig	yin	Water		12		24		36		48		60

Read the table by selecting combinations of one Stem and one Branch. Where they intersect is the number of the Sexagenary combination. You can see clearly why there are only 60 and not 120 combinations. Half the combinations are disallowed because they mix yin and yang. Only yin Branches mate with yin Stems, and only yang Branches mate with yang Stems. NB: Sexagenary just means "60-fold"
* don't confuse the Stem wu with the Branch wu: they are totally different words in Chinese

year 2000 is governed by the Branch ch'en, while the year 2001 is governed by the Branch *ssu*. Ssu just happens to sound like a snake hiss! Obviously the Elements also play a part— 2000 was the year of the Metal Dragon, and 2001 that of the Metal Snake.

We know the Sexagenary combination measure years. The first Sexagenary combination, or chia tzu, corresponds to 1984, the year of the yang Wood Rat. (Check the first line of the table). This combination is therefore the beginning of every cycle of 60 years, which is why we will learn later that 1984 was an important cycle change year. The combination will repeat in 1984 + 60 years = 2044. This is how the Sexagenary combinations measure the cycles of 60 years.

As a matter of interest, these Cycles of 60 years are not arbitrary but correspond to the cycle and return to the same position of the planets Jupiter and Saturn, which come to rest in the same place relative to each other roughly every 60 years. Sexagenary combinations are also used to measure months and days.

This may sound complicated, but suddenly the calendar and the measurement of time become so much richer. Not all days are equally good. This is a notion that we instinctively understand, but which the mechanical nature of the Western calendar, where each day is just a number, prevents us from appreciating. You can tell, by checking the Sexagenary combination, what exactly are the qualities of any particular day. This has important implications for:

- buildings (ask when they were built)
- humans (ask when they were born), and
- feng shui (ask what ch'i tide is running now, and when will it change)

Ch'i tides also change their quality according to the time of day, month, or year. Anyone who has watched the sunrise across the ocean on a clear day will know what I mean when I say that the ch'i tide running at that time of day is fundamentally different from that running at sundown or midnight. You can use the Sexagenary combinations to learn the qualities of buildings or humans from the combination that prevailed at the time of their birth.

These tides are used in Flying Star feng shui to determine the best tide or time to do something, from getting married or signing an important contract to placing a feng shui cure in a specific room or digging a new fish pond in the back yard.

The qualities of their time of birth are imprinted on people or buildings and continue to influence them all their lives. Put very simply, checking the Sexagenary combinations of a person against those of a building will help indicate if the building is going to be good for him or her to live or work in. A yang Metal building, for example, would not be good for a yin Wood person, as Metal destroys Wood.

The Sexagenary combinations define the type of ch'i flowing in that particular year, month, day, and hour. The year flow is the strongest of these three. A person born at a particular moment will "inhale" a particular type of ch'i, which will define their personality and the broad outline of their fate during the course of their life. This is the basis of 4 Pillar astrology, where everyone's destiny can be read by a skilled (Chinese) astrologer from the Sexagenary combination for the hour, day, month, and year of their birth.

These tides have a very real effect on people, and an analysis of the time of birth can really tell you statistically important things about a person.

YOUR 4 PILLARS OF DESTINY

Much has been written about the 4 Pillars of Destiny. In a nutshell, they are simply the four Sexagenary combinations for the year, month, day, and hour of your birth.

Westerners primarily see Chinese astrology as connected with the animal zodiacal sign, one for each year. A whole industry is based on books written about this apparently simple system and the "character" of each of these signs. This is an oversimplification of Chinese astrology. In fact these are not zodiacal signs in the strict sense, because they change yearly, not monthly. They do however correspond to the 12 Earthly Branches.

As we have seen, these 12 Earthly Branches cycle every 12 years. The Branches are important, and no serious astrology book in Chinese deals with the so-called "animal sign" except to mention it in passing in connection with the Branches. The animal signs therefore are just the popularization of a very small piece of just *one* of several forms of Chinese astrology.

Look a bit closer at 4 Pillar astrology. There are two characters for the year, two for the month, two for the day, and two for the hour of birth. They are usually stacked on the page to form four "pillars": one pillar for the year, one for the month, one for the day, and one for the hour. The Chinese name for this form of astrology is *pa tzu*—literally "eight characters," or 4 Pillar astrology.

As you may have guessed, each Pillar is a Sexagenary combination and has one Branch character and one Stem character. The popular animal sign is only *one* of these eight characters of the horoscope (in fact, the Branch character of the year). So "animal sign" astrology gives you less than one eighth of a full reading. I say *less* than one eighth because much of the reading also depends upon the interaction between these eight characters.

As we have seen, each Stem and each Branch belongs to one of the 5 Elements and has a yin/yang reading assigned to it. It is this balance of Elements that is used to judge the basic character and destiny of the person being "read."

For example, if you had an Element balance of three Fire, two Wood, one Earth, and two Metal, it should be obvious that you have an excess of Fire in your nature. This is in fact aggravated by the two Woods that will contribute to producing more Fire (according to the Production Cycle of the Elements). In addition, there is no Water that might have acted as a control on the Fire.

Now because this book is about feng shui and not astrology, I am not going further into the complex process of calculating the complete 4 Pillar horoscope or its many uses. But it is necessary to show how the Sexagenary combinations are an integral part of this form of Chinese astrology.

Lastly, our friends the Sexagenary combinations are key to feng shui as they occupy many of the rings of the feng shui lo p'an compass and are an integral part of "advanced" feng shui.

THE 180-YEAR GREAT CYCLE

In America, many homes have been built within the current 60-year cycle, but to look at older properties, or houses that were built centuries ago, we need to widen our horizons a little.

Utilizing the 60 Sexagenary combinations, we establish a number of cycles important to the practice of feng shui. The 60 Sexagenary combinations mark out 60 years. Three of these periods make a Great Cycle of 180 years, during which various different types or qualities of ch'i circulate, before eventually returning again to the same type of ch'i which started the Cycle.

The 180-year Great Cycles are divided into three Eras, or yuan, of 60 years. Each Era is then divided into three Periods, or yun, of 20 years each. (See appendix 6 for an alternative way of dividing up the Eras.) That means there is a total of nine 20-year Periods in each Great Cycle. The current 180-year Great Cycle is shown in table 2.5. To calculate dates before 1864, keep subtracting 20-year Periods. To go forward beyond 2024, keep adding 20-year Periods.

I have listed the current Yuan or Periods below. You will need to keep referring to this table whenever you do the time element of a Flying Star analysis.

Table 2.5: *Flying Star Time Periods*

Era or *Yuan*	Yun	Starting Year 4/5 February of	Starts with Sexagenary Combination
Upper Era	Period 1	1864	chia tzu
	Period 2	1884	chia shen
	Period 3	1904	chia chen
Middle Era	Period 4	1924	chia tzu
	Period 5	1944	chia shen
	Period 6	1964	chia chen
Lower Era	Period 7	1984	chia tzu
	Period 8	2004	chia shen
	Period 9	2024	chia chen

Each Period is 20 years long. Each Era runs through the full 60 Sexagenary characters. The Great Cycle of 180 years uses these characters three times over.

The system of dividing time into the three Eras of 60 years each may have arisen in the early Ming dynasty (1368–1644) when it was called the *San Yuan* (or "three-cycle") system, because a 20-year Period is called a Yuan.

It was secretly supposed to be able to predict the rise and fall of dynasties, quite a dangerous thing to do in any era. There is in fact a type of symmetry in the length and commencement dates of many of the major Chinese dynasties, which might easily encourage such speculation. Certainly it was common to allocate one of the 5 Elements to successive dynasties, usually in the order of the Cycle of Destruction (see figure 1.3 in chapter 1) on the very reasonable assumption that each dynasty arose from the destruction of its predecessor. Indeed, many dynasties actually adopted the color of the expected corresponding Element as part of its livery. Table 2.6 lists the more obvious examples.

Table 2.6: *Elemental Attributes of Some Chinese Dynasties*

Emperor	Dynasty	Element	Color
Huang Ti (the Yellow Emperor)		Earth	Yellow
Yu		Wood	Green
King T'ang	Shang	Metal	White
King Wen	Chou	Fire	Red
	Ch'in	Water	Black
	Han	Earth	Yellow

(Taken from the *Spring and Autumn Annals* (circa 239 BC) with an extrapolation by Derek Walters). Note that Earth is destroyed by Wood which is destroyed by Metal, which is destroyed by Fire, and so on.

Just as the 5 Elements fit in with some dynasties, if we use the 180 year Great Cycles, we come rather close to the reign dates of many of the major Chinese dynasties, as table 2.7 shows. Although the fit is not perfect, it is easy to see how the theory arose that these Great Cycles were somehow linked to major events in the Chinese world. See appendix 8 for fuller details of the main Chinese dynasties.

The start date of the current Great Cycle, February 4, 1864, is of no special significance either dynastically or in terms of the Christian/Western calendar. It will finish in February 2044. However, in the context of the Chinese calendar it is the end of the 25th Grand Cycle (of 180 years) since Chinese cyclical dating began in 2637 BC. As you can see, the Chinese have had accurate calendars a lot longer than the West.

With each 20-year Period change, the ruling Star changes.

Inside each Great Cycle there are three Eras, or yuans, (of 60-years) and nine 20-year Periods or Yuns. In each case the beginning of each Yuan is on February 4/5.

Table 2.7: *Great Cycles Compared with the Rise and Fall of Some Major Chinese Dynasties*

Nearest Great Cycle Dates	Elapsed Period	Dynasty	Actual Reign Dates
1555–1015 BC	3 Great Cycles	Shang	1557–1027 BC
1015–235 BC	4 Great Cycles+1 Era	Chou	1027–221 BC*
475–235 BC	1 Great Cycle+1 Era	Warring States	476–221 BC*
AD 244–424	1 Era	Chin	AD 265–420
424–604	1 Great Cycle	Southern & Northern	420–589
964–1144	1 Great Cycle	Sung	960–1127
1324–1684	2 Great Cycles	Ming	1368–1644

* = date is correct despite apparent overlap

Later we will see how the change from one Yuan to another on February 4, 2004, will have a significant impact on Flying Star feng shui.

HISTORIC CYCLES

There are even bigger cycles, all based on the 60-year cycle. These do not have much relevance to our everyday life but have been used to chart the rise and fall of dynasties:

1 Great Year	= 12 years (or one revolution of Jupiter round the Sun)		
1 Yun	= 20 years		
1 Cycle (or Era)	= 60 year	= 3 Yun	= 5 Great Years
1 Great Cycle	= 180 years	= 9 Yun	= 15 Great Years	= 3 Cycles (or Yuan)
1 Epoch	= 3,600 years	= 180 Yun	= 300 Great Years	= 60 Cycles (or Yuan)

Talk about long-range planning! Therefore, more than 4,637 years after the origin point of the Chinese calendar, we are in the 78th cycle of 60 years. If I wanted to use Chinese dating, I could say that I am writing this book in the year of the Metal Snake, in the 18th cycle of the 2nd Epoch (or in short 2001). In practice most Chinese dates were written in the form, "the Xth year of the reign of Emperor Y, of the Z dynasty."

In this chapter, we have looked at the mechanics of time as conceived by the Chinese. The least you need to know is:

- The Chinese use a lunar calendar for festivals and popular astrology but a solar calendar tied to the seasons for agriculture and feng shui, which begins on February 4 or 5.
- The solar calendar is divided into 24 mini-seasons and correlates with the solstices, equinoxes, and 5 Elements.

- The 5 Elements are "doubled" by considering their yang/yin natures to form the 10 Heavenly Stems.
- The 12 Earthly Branches relate time (years, months, hours) to direction.
- The 10 Heavenly Stems multiplied by the 12 Earthly Branches form the kan shih (ganzhi) or Sexagenary combinations.
- The kan shih are used to mark out 60-year Cycles, which are the time basis of Flying Star feng shui.
- There are three 60-year Cycles in a Great Cycle. The current Great Cycle started in 1864 and will end in 2044.
- 4 Pillar astrology uses 8 kan shih or the 4 Pillars of year, month, day, and hour to judge the birth date of a person or building.

Chapter 3

Space Dimension

The Chinese compass, or lo p'an, is much more complicated than a maritime compass. In fact the lo p'an was the predecessor of the maritime compass. Alternative spellings include *luo pan*. The first Chinese compass dates back to the 4th century BC , some 1,500 years before the adoption of the compass for navigation in Europe in around AD 1190. Even in China the use of the compass for navigation was probably delayed until AD 850. Before that it was only used for land navigation and feng shui. Wang Chih (who lived during the Northern Sung dynasty 960–1127) established the lo p'an in its modern form, with about 17 Rings, at least one of which had on it the main ring of the 24 Directions.

THE PHYSICAL LO P'AN

By this time the compass came in two distinct parts, a square wooden base into which snugly fits a wooden saucer-shaped disk, averaging six to ten inches (15 to 25 cm) across. This disk, or "Heaven Plate," revolved freely in the square "Earth Plate" base. Across the compass from side to side were two sighting lines, like the cross hairs of a rifle sight, made of red thread (or nowadays nylon). In the center is a glassed-over "well" containing the needle, which is magnetized and finely suspended and used to align the lo p'an correctly. This needle aligns North-South, but the Chinese always thought of it as pointing South. Western compasses simply look at the same instrument as pointing to magnetic North.

On the disk there are a series of concentric rings that contain a huge amount of feng shui information in Chinese characters, although partial English versions* of the lo p'an are becoming increasingly available.

---

* At the time of writing, perhaps the most useful lo p'an with an English guidebook is that produced by Raymond Lo and Ricky Tan and sold through Thompson House in Hong Kong.

THE 39 RINGS OF THE LO P'AN

All lo p'ans have rings around the central needle well. These are called *tseng* (which means "layers"), and there may be anywhere between 7 and 39 such rings, or *tseng* (see figure 3.1). They may exist, but I have not personally seen a usable compass with more or less rings than this range. In size lo p'ans range from 2.5 inches (6 cm) to more than 3 feet (1 meter) across. Very small ones tend not to be accurate, and the larger ones require the assistance of staff to use. There are certain key rings that are common to all compasses. In addition to these rings there are special rings specific to particular Schools of feng shui, or even to a particular feng shui Master.

The rings are carved, painted, or etched on the surface of the disk, and each ring is divided into between eight and 720 divisions or sectors . Each division is labeled in black or red or gold Chinese characters. One of the brilliant things about Chinese characters is that, on the whole, they fit into a more compact space than the equivalent English words, thus enabling an enormous amount of information to be inscribed on one lo p'an. Even the underside of the disk often bears a quick look-up San He table.

The lo p'an is considerably more complex than the Western maritime or trekking compass. Fortunately, we only need to use the one ring in order to practice basic Flying Star feng shui.

An important concept to remember is that Western compasses measure points, but Chinese compasses measure sectors, or "pie wedges" if you like. For example, South on

Fig. 3.1 *A Complete Lo P'an from the Ch'ing Dynasty*

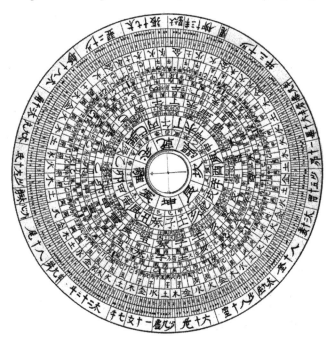

a Western compass is located at exactly 180 degrees. On a Chinese compass South is the *range* 157.5 degrees to 202.5, in other words a 45-degree span centered on 180 degrees. Remember there are 8 directions x 45 degrees = 360 degrees. More precisely, mid-South (or the direction wu) is 172.5 to 187.5 degrees.

Before you think that is too complicated, consider the following: On Western compasses when you need to pinpoint precise directions, you finish up saying something complex like "steer a course North-nor-nor-West by North," or some similar contortions. How many non-mariners could say exactly how many degrees that is!

The Chinese compass has only 24 Directions (8 directions x 3 subdivisions = 24). These are adequate to identify any compass bearing you might like to name. For example North-nor-nor-West (348.75 degrees) is a point that falls in the Chinese sector *Jen*. So "steer for Jen" becomes the instruction. In practice the Western compass can be more complicated than the Chinese compass.

To recap, Western compasses measure points, but Chinese compasses measure sectors. In feng shui, although you occasionally measure down to within one degree accuracy, what you usually have to determine is into which of just 24 Directions (or sectors) a particular house, water, or hill alignment falls.

In this chapter, we analyze which symbols compose just one ring, perhaps the most important of the lo p'an. This ring contains the 24 Directions. Using only this ring, we look at how the lo p'an is practically used in taking the compass direction readings of a front door, for example.

HOW IT ALL FITS TOGETHER

A Chinese lo p'an is a sort of round Lo Shu. You can start with the Lo Shu, and from it evolve the 24 Direction Ring. You remember from chapter 1 that the Lo Shu is a 9-cell figure related to the 8 directions. If we put in the directions, it looks like figure 3.2 (I have also put in four of the trigrams).

If this is represented in a circular fashion you get something like figure 3.3.

Each of the 8 directions is again divided into three subsections, making a total of 8 x 3 = 24 Directions, as shown in figure 3.4.

You can see how our discussion of feng shui principles has evolved from the 9-squared Lo Shu into one main compass ring. Too many books on feng shui talk as if the *pa kua (bagua)*, the Lo Shu, and the compass are completely different and unconnected. In fact the pa kua (bagua) and the Lo Shu are the building blocks of this ring of the lo p'an compass. Now, let's take a closer look at this ring, examine its makeup, and find out how to use it.

Fig. 3.2 *The Lo Shu with the Directions and 4 of the Trigrams*

SE ☴ Hsun	S	SW ☷ K'un
E	CENTER	W
NE ☶ Ken	N	NW ☰ Ch'ien

Fig. 3.3 *The Lo Shu Expressed in a Circular Fashion*

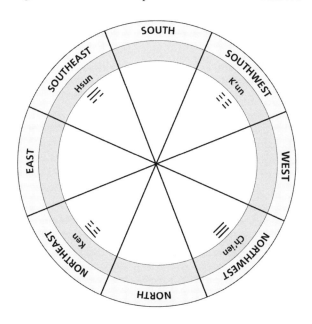

Fig. 3.4 *The Lo Shu with Each Direction Divided into 3 Subsections*

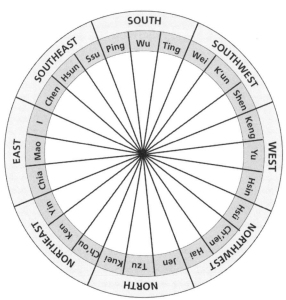

The 24 Directions or Mountains

This ring has 24 segments, which are usually called (slightly confusingly) the 24 Directions, or in Chinese, the 24 shan (literally, Mountains). We can talk of the 24 Mountains, using the word in the technical sense rather than that of a physical mountain. In fact this ring is so important, that it is repeated no less than three times on *San He* lo p'ans. (San He is one of the major Schools of feng shui).

Each of the 24 Directions or Mountains consists of 15 degrees. Why 15 degrees? The whole circle has 360 degrees. If we take just one twenty-fourth of the circle (360/24), we get 15 degrees.

What is on this ring? Initially confusing, this ring is made up of three different sets of symbols that we have already encountered: the trigrams, the Earthly Branches, and the Heavenly Stems. You might ask, "How can 8 trigrams, 12 Branches, and 10 Stems add up to 24 Directions?" Let me explain using figure 3.5:

4 Kua / Trigrams

First, as we have seen above, the so-called "corner points" of SW, NW, NE, and SE are marked by four of the 8 trigrams. These important trigrams are respectively K'un, Ch'ien, Ken, and Hsun. These are the trigrams for Earth, Heaven, Mountain, and Wind.

12 Earthly Branches

Next, we take the 12 Earthly Branches. We put one Branch on each of the cardinal points, N, S, E, W. Then we put one Branch on either side of each of the 4 trigrams,

Fig. 3.5 *The Full 24 Mountains*

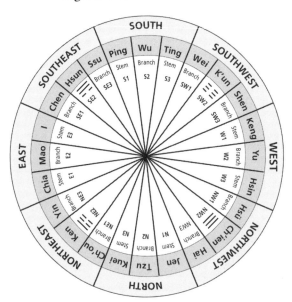

Table 3.1: *The 24 Mountains, Their Compass Readings, Origin, and Chinese Names*

Direction	Compass Degrees	Chinese Mountain		Stem/Branch/ Trigram	Cardinal Point
S1	157.5–172.5	*ping*	丙	Stem	
S2	172.5–187.5	**wu**	午	Branch	South
S3	187.5–202.5	*ting*	丁	Stem	
SW1	202.5–217.5	*wei*	未	Branch	
SW2	217.5–232.5	*k'un*	坤	Trigram	
SW3	232.5–247.5	*shen*	申	Branch	
W1	247.5–262.5	*keng*	庚	Stem	
W2	262.5–277.5	**yu**	酉	Branch	West
W3	277.5–292.5	hsin	辛	Stem	
NW1	292.5–307.5	*hsu*	戌	Branch	
NW2	307.5–322.5	*ch'ien*	乾	Trigram	
NW3	322.5–337.5	*hai*	亥	Branch	
N1	337.5–352.5	*jen*	壬	Stem	
N2	352.5–7.5	**tzu**	子	Branch	North
N3	7.5–22.5	*kuei*	癸	Stem	
NE1	22.5–37.5	*ch'ou*	丑	Branch	
NE2	37.5–52.5	*ken*	艮	Trigram	
NE3	52.5–67.5	*yin*	寅	Branch	
E1	67.5–82.5	*chia*	甲	Stem	
E2	82.5–97.5	**mao**	卯	Branch	East
E3	97.5–112.5	*I*	乙	Stem	
SE1	112.5–127.5	*chen*	辰	Branch	
SE2	127.5–142.5	*hsun*	巽	Trigram	
SE3	142.5–157.5	*ssu*	巳	Branch	

(The cardinal points are shown in bold.)

using up all 12 Branches. As the lo p'an measures Earth energies, you would expect the Branches to be fully represented on it.

8 Heavenly Stems

Finally, we take just eight of the 10 Heavenly Stems and fill the remaining vacant places on the ring. Symbolically this is Heaven penetrating Earth. The two remaining Stems are attributed to Earth and therefore go in the Center. They have no place among the 24 Directions.

What we are left with is the full Ring of 24 Directions as shown in figure 3.5.

Note that the 12 Branches take every second position, and that the trigrams take the corner positions. The Stems are placed so that they fall in the appropriate Elemental direction and alternate between yang (+) and yin (-).

For ease of reference, I have also put this into tabular form. You will need to refer to table 3.1 time and time again.

So that is the all-important 24-Directions or Mountains ring. It is usually found a few rings out from the center on most compasses. If you have a lo p'an, look now to see if you can identify it. If you don't have a lo p'an, don't worry, we can adapt an ordinary compass. On San He compasses this ring occurs three times—but Flying Star feng shui always uses the innermost (Earth) ring of 24 Mountains, so you can safely ignore the other 2 occurrences.

FINDING A LO P'AN

There are four ways you can go about securing a usable instrument:

1. In most large cities there will be an area usually referred to as Chinatown. Here you will usually find a range of Chinese shops. Try asking at the Chinese supermarkets or Chinese religious supplies stores. But remember, because Chinese has so many dialects, even the most helpful assistant may not recognize your pronunciation of "feng shui" or "lo p'an," so take along an instantly recognizable picture of a lo p'an instead.

2. If you do not live near such shops, then your next best choice is to use the Web for ordering, by checking out Websites such as www.dragon-gate.com, or www.fengshui-centre.com.hk, or www.fengshui.net. A good lo p'an costs at least $200, and the more precision instruments sell for more than twice that amount.

3. If you feel that you are not ready to invest in a professional lo p'an until you have more experience of feng shui, then I suggest that you make a homemade lo p'an first. To do this, first photocopy figure 3.6.

   Mount the photocopy on a piece of cardstock. If you want to make it last, then encapsulate it in plastic (but that is not a necessary step). Then carefully cut out around the outer circle. Take a simple compass (like those made by Silva) and glue it

Fig. 3.6 *Cut-out Card Adapted to Make a Home Made Lo P'an*

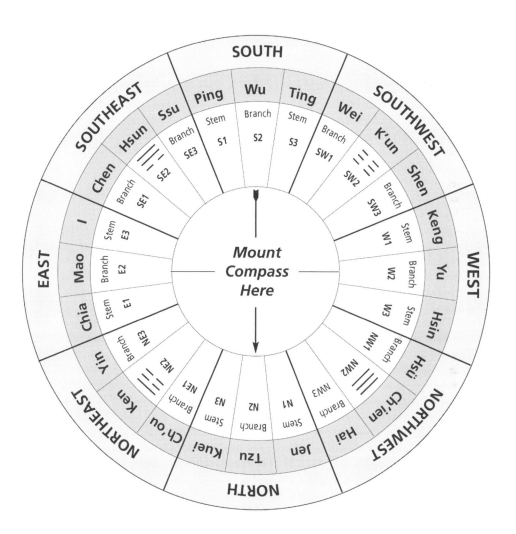

into the center of the card, so that the zero degrees, the arrow at tzu, and its North-pointing line (not the turning needle) all line up. Instant simple lo p'an.

When using this homemade lo p'an, place it so that the rotating needle's arrow head always lines up with N2, tzu. Then read the direction off the card that most closely approximates with the alignment you are checking.

4. If you haven't got a lo p'an and don't want to go to the trouble of making one, then try to lay your hands on a trekking, hiking, or military compass. Point and sight the compass and then simply read off the degrees, which will be some number between 0 and 360 degrees. You will then need to use table 3.1 (or appendix 2) to convert the number of degrees to their lo p'an or Chinese equivalent. For example, a reading of 94 degrees will convert to mao, or E2, using the table. A reading of 363 will convert to tzu, or N2, and so on. The major drawback to using a hiking compass however is that it does not have a large flat edge to align with doors or walls, so the chance of making a sighting error is greater.

How to Read the Proper Lo P'an Compass

You now need to know how to use a lo p'an to take the basic readings used by Flying Star feng shui. Regardless of whether you have been lucky enough to have acquired a good lo p'an, made one yourself, or have a hiking compass, it is important that you get familiar with it. The following description applies to using a proper lo p'an. If you are using a homemade lo p'an or a trekking compass, skim down until you find those instructions instead.

How to Read a Traditional Lo P'an

How do we find out, for example, which direction the front door of our house faces? First stand outside, in front of the front door, and hold the lo p'an level with both hands. Place one edge of the square outer plate of the compass firmly against the door. Using your thumbs, turn the disk slowly till the needle lines up with the line on the bottom of the well. Look closely at figure 3.7. Make sure that the end of the needle with the bulge lines up between the two dots on the bottom of the well (see figure).

If you find this all a bit wobbly, then place the compass on a wooden support at waist level. Resist the temptation to use a tripod that is made of magnetic metal, as this will severely distort the accuracy of your reading.

Check again to see that you are holding the whole compass level: more sophisticated lo p'ans from Taiwan often incorporate spirit levels so that you can be sure that they are perfectly level. Now look at the crosshairs. One points at right angles out from the door. Where it crosses the ring containing the 24 Directions furthest from the door is called the Facing direction. When you have found this particular direction, you have just done your first real feng shui lo p'an reading.

Look along the same crosshair to the part *closest* to the door. Where it crosses the ring of 24 Directions closest to the building is the Sitting direction. The Sitting direction is *always* exactly opposite the Facing direction.

Fig. 3.7 *The Needle "Well"*

South

North

How to Read a Homemade Lo P'an

If instead of a traditional lo p'an compass you are using a cut-out cardboard and mounted compass homemade lo p'an then proceed as follows. Stand in front of the door facing the door. Hold the homemade lo p'an compass flat at waist level. Turn it till the moving needle points to the tzu N2 sector. Then, holding it steady, look to see which sector is furthest away from the door (not so easy to do without the proper lo p'an's crossed threads). This will be the Facing direction. Then look to see which sector is closest to the door: this will be the Sitting direction.

In both cases we are assuming that the house is a straightforward rectangular shape with the front door is squarely in the middle of the front side of the house. We will later look at what to do with more complicated houses.

How to Read a Trekking Compass

Stand with your back to the door. Hold the compass level and steady.

- If it is a simple compass, turn it till the needle head points to north. Read the number of degrees at the point furthest away from the door. This is the Facing bearing.

- If it is a sophisticated military compass with a sight, look out from the door at a point directly in front of the door. Read off the number of degrees. This is the Facing bearing.

Take the Facing bearing and look it up in 3.1 table or in appendix 2. Read off the Facing direction. For example a Facing bearing of 94 degrees would yield a Facing direction of mao, or E2.

The Sitting direction is found by adding 180 degrees to the answer. If that makes a number more than 360, instead subtract 180 degrees from your Facing bearing. This will give you a Sitting direction, in this example 94 + 180 = 274 degrees. Upon looking it up you can see that the Sitting direction is *yu*, or W2. As a quick mental check on your calculations, we can see that mid East (E2) is directly opposite to mid West (W2), so the calculation is correct.

Choose whichever of the three instruments you own and practice the method, taking the Facing direction of your own front door, your gate, and perhaps a neighbor's door on the opposite side of your street. When you are confident that you can find a Facing direction easily, move on to the next section that considers some of the difficulties that you may encounter.

SPECIAL LO P'AN READING CONSIDERATIONS

There are five things you should be aware of when taking a reading:
1. Magnetic interference. This is often indicated by the needle swinging backward and forward a lot before settling down. It is usually caused by the presence of metal or electrical equipment. A good needle away from magnetic interference should settle down after two or three swings. Try to avoid magnetic interference.

   Because in this modern world there is a lot of electrical equipment, like computers and mobile phones, the needle of even the most stable compass can be deflected. This is a problem that was not encountered by the old feng shui Masters. The simple solution is to take at least three readings: back away from the object being measured and take one reading on the door, one 3 feet (1 meter) from the door, and one 12 feet (4 meters) out. Make sure you are measuring the same thing by tying a (red) thread to the door and to a stake at right angles to the door, to make sure that the readings are taken along the same alignment. Then average these three readings (add them together and divide by 3).

   The complex solution (as used for example by Master Tan in Singapore) is to use a theodolite (a stable table on tripod legs containing a telescope sight used by surveyors) which can be set up with the lo p'an some distance from the thing being measured, well away from potential electrical interference. Traditional Chinese Masters go to great lengths to get scientifically accurate readings, and you should also be as careful as you can. With my background as a geography lecturer, I find the theodolite a most appealing feng shui adjunct.

   Sometimes you will have to pull away from a door because of its metal hardware.

   Incidentally, it helps to get rid of any potentially magnetic or chunky jewelry, watches, or belt buckles before using the lo p'an.

Please check your work, and do not try to substitute intuition for accurate measurement.

If the local magnetic declination has been altered by the presence of naturally occurring magnetic rocks, don't worry; this should not be corrected for, as it also affects the ch'i in the same way.

2. The determination of Sitting and Facing directions is not as simple as just checking the front door, and further consideration will be discussed in detail later in this chapter.

3. The third and rather basic problem is that most lo p'ans are inscribed in Chinese. One solution is to buy one which has been produced with English inscriptions. On this the 24 Directions are written as "ping, ting . . ." or as N1, N2, N3, NE1 . . . rather than entirely in Chinese. Alternatively, when you get more familiar with the lo p'an, you might decide to learn the 24 basic directions in Chinese, just so you can recognize them on any lo p'an—but that does require a bit of dedication!

   The third solution is the easiest. The outermost ring of most modern lo p'ans should also be instantly recognizable, as it shows the 360 degrees of the compass. You can, if you want to "cheat" just a bit (and avoid Chinese characters altogether) just use this ring, plus the key table 3.1 or appendix 2 to translate basic degree readings into the 24 Mountains. This way you don't have to recognize the Chinese characters for the 24 Mountains. Your work should be just as accurate. You will soon discover that a real lo p'an is much easier to align, even if it takes a few minutes longer to decipher the characters.

4. On San He lo p'ans there are three rings containing the 24 Directions. The inner ring is the "Earth Plate" ring, and this is the one we will use for the rest of this book. The second similar 24-Direction ring (moving outwards from the center) is the "Man Plate" ring, and it is turned 7.5 degrees west of north. The outer ring of 24 Directions is the "Heaven Plate" ring, and it is turned 7.5 degrees east of north. For the purposes of this book you will only need to use the *inner* ring of 24 Directions. For those of you who want to know a bit more, you might notice that the 3 rings all carry the same characters, in the same order, but the two outer rings are turned 7.5 degrees to the left or right of the innermost ring. Despite what it says in several well-respected books on feng shui, these differences do *not* reflect changes in the position of the magnetic pole over the centuries. Each of these rings differs by exactly one half of one segment, and this reflects the fact that they are each used for 3 distinctly different purposes.

5. The last thing to be aware of only relates to using a trekking compass. A lot of feng shui books recommend you use an ordinary trekking or military compass instead of a lo p'an. There is nothing wrong with this if all you really want is a rough idea of which of the 24 Directions the house, office, or building faces. However there is one big drawback: most Western compasses are round. (The exception is a map compass, which is set into a clear plastic rule that is quite useful for feng shui). Remember, you

cannot easily align a *round* compass parallel to a *straight* wall or a door, for the very good reason that round compasses don't have a flat side!

As we have already seen, you have to stand in a doorway and simultaneously squint at the compass and at some imaginary point in the middle of the path leading from the door (assuming it is straight). Using this tactic you are lucky to be able to take a reading within 10 degrees of accurate. (Of course if there are any military types or geometricians out there, I'm sure you could devise some system to determine a sighting point, but for the rest of us it simply would not work.)

The beauty of the lo p'an is that we can simply place the flat outer edge against a wall or door, and turn the inner circular plate at leisure. I know it is a bit more complicated than this, but you get the general idea that a circular trekking compass can only do so much.

FACING AND SITTING DIRECTIONS

For Flying Star feng shui our lo p'an reading is designed to determine which way a building faces. If you imagine a building as a squat figure sitting cross-legged and staring out at the view, then you will have a feeling for which is the Sitting and which the Facing directions of the building.

Fig. 3.8 *Look at the House As If It Were a Sitting Person*

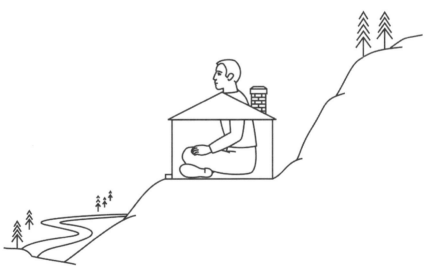

These two directions are conceived of as the directions from which come two very different "luck Stars." This use of the word "Star" has no immediate connection with the stars of astronomy, as we will see in chapter 4. I have capitalized the word "Star" to distinguish it from the stars in the night sky.

These two Stars are referred to in different books in different ways. I will call them the Facing Star and Sitting Star, but they are also correctly called the Water Star and the Mountain Star.

- The Facing Star refers to the front of the analyzed building. In Chinese it is the hsiang hsing (sometimes spelled siang sin), pronounced "she-ang shing."

- The Sitting or Mountain Star refers to the back of the analyzed building. The Chinese term is simply the Chinese character for mountain, shan hsing or tsuo hsing (sometimes spelled chor sin).

To summarize, the different ways of referring to these two stars are as follows:

What do Facing and Sitting really mean? Well at the simplest level the front door is (in most cases) on the Facing side of the building, and the Sitting side is the opposite side. But to do these two terms justice, you have to "feel" your way into a building. Treat the building for a few seconds as a living thing, and ask yourself "which way is it looking?" and "where is it sitting?" Most buildings are obvious, and often have big windows and big doors (like eyes) on the Facing side. Perhaps with a smaller, lesser-used back entrance on the Sitting side.

Table 3.2: *The Different Names for the Facing and Sitting Stars*

	Facing Star	Sitting Star
Name	Water Star	Mountain Star
Significance	Wealth	Health and family
Chinese names (Wade-Giles)	hsiang hsing	tsuo hsing
	siang sin	chor sin
Where placed in a Lo Shu Square	top right	top left

Don't confuse the front door position (which is important to other styles of feng shui) with the Facing Direction of Flying Star feng shui. Mostly they will be on the same side of the building, but not always.

Most buildings face the street. If building on a hillside, most architects will face the building to the view downhill, with its Sitting side nestled into the higher ground behind. But it isn't always so. Some buildings have had their mouth or main door stopped up, and a new door opened. So what are the tests? You have to balance the factors listed in table 3.3 to arrive at the most likely Facing and Sitting direction.

But remember Facing and Sitting will *always* be directly opposite each other.

Table 3.3: *Tests to Determine Sitting and Facing Directions*

Facing Direction	Sitting Direction
Front door	back door
Big door	smaller door(s)
Big windows	small windows
Side with most impressive view	less interesting view
Main road	service lane
Most heavily used door	hardly used door
Near gate or main access path	near back fence
Side of most social activity	least activity
Side facing a body of water	away from water
Downhill	uphill
Sunniest side	shadiest side

If in doubt, score points for each of the above criteria, to see which side comes out strongest.

These two Stars relate to two of the main aspects of your life. The Sitting Star (Mountain Star) relates to your family, relationships, health, and fertility. The Facing Star (Water Star) focuses on your wealth, finance, and career.

This chapter has examined the space dimension starting with a description of the lo p'an and how it may be evolved from the Lo Shu. The most important Ring, the 24 Mountain Ring, was then explained. It is made up of 4 trigrams, 12 Earthly Branches, and 8 of the Heavenly Stems. We then looked at how to make and use a homemade lo p'an and how to use the traditional lo p'an. Finally, we looked at how to determine the Sitting and Facing directions of a building, which are essential for Flying Star feng shui. Let us now look at the Flying Stars themselves.

Chapter 4

Flying Stars

We have looked at the basic arithmetic and alphabet of feng shui in chapter 1. In chapter 2 we looked at the time framework of feng shui, while chapter 3 introduced the lo p'an compass, a tool we can use to measure direction and hence space. In this chapter we will actually meet the Flying Stars themselves.

THE NORTHERN LADLE OR *PEI TOU*

The nine Flying Stars are an earthly energy reflection of the seven real astronomical stars of the Northern Ladle (or Big Dipper or Plough asterism), which is a part of the Great Bear (Ursa Major) constellation, plus two other "stars" which are not visible.

This group of stars appears to point to and circle around the Pole Star as shown in figure 4.1. For the Chinese, the Pole star (or Polaris) was the fixed point, very close to the North Celestial Pole, the center of the stars, and hence seen as the center of the universe. Hsuan T'ien Shang Ti (or Chen Wu) is the Lord of the Black Heaven of the North and God of Winter. His throne is the North Pole Star in the Dark Palace. He is also called the Dark Warrior, and he wears a dark purple robe and is portrayed with long, flowing, jet-black hair. He has two assistants, the Snake (symbol of fertility) and the Turtle (symbol of longevity), which when curled together in an embrace form the Celestial Animal attributed to the North (not just the turtle by itself). It is also this precise symbology that definitively assigns black as the color of the Element Water, rather than the modernized attribution of blue. In fact, physical water is neither blue nor black but clear. The Chinese Element Water is, however, black.

The Northern Ladle appears to make a full rotation around the Pole Star every day. For city dwellers, unaccustomed to watching the night sky, it should be pointed out that it is the rotation of the Earth every 24 hours that makes the stars *appear* to rotate in the sky. The Northern Ladle also makes an annual rotation, moving one (Chinese) degree forward from its previous day starting position every day. Please note, these observations

Table 4.1: *The 7 Stars of the Northern Ladle, with Their Secret Taoist Names*

Star Astronomical	Arabic Name	Longitude in 2000˙	Chinese Star Name
1 alpha Ursa Major	Dubhe	15 Leo 12'	Celestial Pivot
2 beta Ursa Major	Merak	19 Leo 26'	Celestial Template
3 gamma Ursa Major	Phecda	0 Virgo 29'	Celestial Armillary
4 delta Ursa Major	Megrez	1 Virgo 4'	Celestial Balance
5 epsilon Ursa Major	Alioth	8 Virgo 56'	Jade Sighting Tube
6 zeta Ursa Major	Mizar	15 Virgo 42'	Opener of heat/yang
7 eta Ursa Major	Alkaid	26 Virgo 56'	Twinkling Brilliance
8 no corresponding physical star			Grotto Luminosity
9 no corresponding physical star			Hidden Prime

˙ This is a modern day indication of their position. The longitude would have been quite different when the Northern Ladle was first observed by the ancient Chinese.

only apply to the Northern Hemisphere. To determine which season you are in, you should face North and observe the direction of the pointer of the Northern Ladle at midnight. The "handle" will appear to point upwards at midnight at mid-summer (circa June 21), to the left (or West) at the autumn equinox (circa September 21), downwards at midwinter (circa December 21), and to the right (or East) at the spring equinox (circa March 21) every year. In this way it both marks off the seasons of the year, the days, and also the hours of the day. In figure 4.1 it is shown at 6 p.m.

The Northern Ladle was venerated as a deity (or the throne of a deity) as early as the late Shang dynasty (13th–11th century BC), which shows the deep roots of these associations. In the Han dynasty (206 BC–AD 220), the Northern Ladle was seen as the conduit of ch'i energy, which comes from *Tai yi* (the Supreme Unity), who dwelt at the Pole itself. So the Northern Ladle became a sort of "sprinkler" of different types of ch'i into the world. Its hands acted as a celestial clock, and each of its constituent Stars spread upon the world one of the 9 different types of ch'i energy that are symbolized by the 9 Flying Stars. It is now easy to understand why Flying Star feng shui measures the changing patterns of ch'i in the seasons and in a specific building over time and why it is connected with this particular constellation.

Modern astronomers only number seven stars in the Northern Ladle, but the ancient Chinese included two additional invisible "assistant" stars. There are at least three ways of interpreting these 2 Assistant Stars:

1. These are often shown in ancient Chinese texts as attached to the 6th Star. It is only erroneous modern texts which show them attached to the 7th Star. This 6th star is

Star Name	Taoist Star Name	Taoist Secret Name	Taoist Name
T'ien shu	T'ien feng/p'eng	Tzu-ch'in	Yang luminosity
T'ien hsuan	T'ien ping/jui	Tzu-hsu	Yin embryo
T'ien ch'i	T'ien ch'ung	Tzu-ch'iao	Perfected person
T'ien ch'uan	T'ien fu	Tzu-hsiang	Occult tenebrity
Yu heng	T'ien ch'in	Tzu-ch'in	Cinnabar prime
K'ai yang	T'ien-hsin	Tzu-hsiang	Northern extremity
Yao kuang	T'ien chu	Tzu-chung	Heaven's bar
—	T'ien jen	Tzu-ch'ang	Sustainer
—	T'ien-ying	Tzu-ch'eng	Straightener

Fig. 4.1 *The Northern Ladle As a Celestial Clock Pointing Always to the North Pole Star at the 4 Seasons*

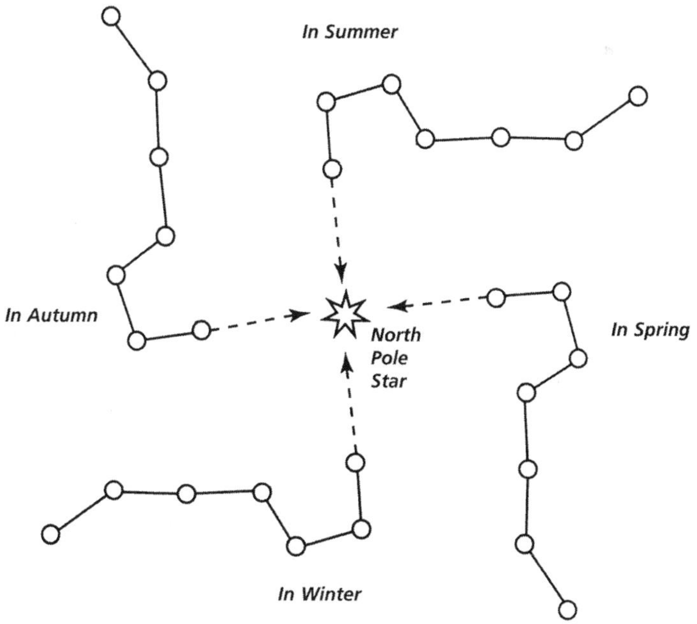

referred to as "*zeta* Ursa Major," or Mizar ("The Girdle"), by Arabic and modern astronomers. This is quite interesting because astronomically the 6th star is not in fact a single star but the most famous multiple star in the sky. Under very good conditions you can just see one of its two "assistant" stars, but the observation that there are two "assistant" stars is a remarkable deduction to make thousands of years ago without the use of a telescope.

2. Alternatively, the Left and Right Assistants might be mapped onto the two stars in the constellation of Draconis, which also were used to locate the Pole Star: these were called in Chinese the Pivot of the Left and the Pivot of the Right.

3. Another similar tradition suggests that the Assistants are the two stars called Violet Tenuity and Celestial August by the ancient Chinese, who spoke of these stars as the elder siblings of the seven stars of the Northern Ladle. There is a very interesting side temple devoted to the worship of the mother of both these stars and the Northern Ladle stars, which I have seen in the White Cloud Monastery in Beijing, and which suggests that all these stars belong to the same family.

THE NORTHERN LADLE AS THE UNIVERSAL CLOCK

The stars of the Northern Ladle are often depicted as the Emperor's carriage, rotating around the center of the sky, and hence the center of the universe. The great Chinese historian Ssu Ma Ch'ien (145–87 BC) described the Northern Ladle as follows:

> *Pei tou* (the Northern Ladle) serves as the chariot of the Emperor and effectuates his control over the four cardinal points by revolving around the center; it separates the yin and the yang and regulates the four seasons; it maintains balance between the five Elements; it regulates the moving of the celestial objects; it determines the timing and periods of the calendar.

It was seen as a giant clock that regulated the fluctuations of the seasons, the Elements, and the waxing and waning of yin and yang. Therefore it is only a small jump of the imagination to see that the microcosmic changes in the ch'i tides in a building may also be regulated by the Northern Ladle. To refer to these tides as "Stars" flying from one part of the building to another with the change of season is just one small poeticization of and extension of the basic idea. The blurring of the line between real stars and Flying Stars is so complete that to make the distinction I will sometimes use the term "Fate Stars" to separate them from astronomical stars.

The visible Stars are numbered and named as shown in figure 4.3.

The power of the Northern Ladle is such that it is also used talismanically, showing the stars as circles joined by lines. One of the most powerful Taoist protections is the sword, and not just any sword but a sword linked with the Northern Ladle. These swords are engraved on one or both sides of the blade with a series of 7 circles connected by a jointed line, as much in the shape of the Northern Ladle as possible. Another form of "sword" used in feng shui to deflect evil forces is the coin sword, made up of antique Chinese coins (circular outside with a square hole in the middle) tied together in the shape of a sword. Such things were and are still considered powerful protections.

The sword is meant to be hung horizontally on a wall or over a window in a bad sector or as a protection against a sha ch'i line visible through the window. Antique coin

Fig. 4.3 *The Nine Stars of the Northern Ladle*

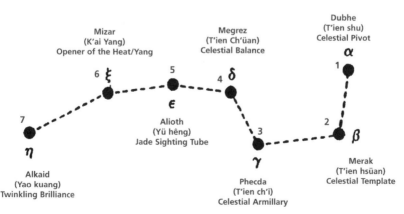

Fig. 4.4 *A Taoist Magical Sword, Drawing Its Power from the Northern Ladle*

swords are collector's items and can be quite expensive, but modern ones are more reasonably priced.

THE FATE STARS IN THE CHINESE ALMANAC

This section is a more detailed look at other Fate Stars, and if you like you can skip it and go directly to the next section without missing anything critical. But for those of you who wish to understand the nature of the Flying Stars as part of the larger system of Fate Stars, and how these fit into Chinese culture generally, this section should be fascinating.

The annual Chinese Almanac or *T'ung Shu* (or *T'ung Sing*) is the place to look to find out the strength and disposition of the various Fate Stars for each new year. This reference book is bought every year by more than 3.5 million Chinese and is found in many Chinese homes. It is used to check the disposition not just of the 9 Flying Stars with which we are here concerned but also of hundreds of other Fate Stars who arrive and leave from different quarters as the months and years roll by.

You will be pleased to know that a working knowledge of Chinese is not required to consult the *T'ung Shu*, as there are several (partial) English versions (see bibliography). To find out the annual location of the 9 Flying Stars, you can simply look up appendix 4 of this book. However here we will briefly look at some of the other Fate Stars to be found in the *T'ung Shu*, to widen your perspective on the whole subject, before concentrating specifically on the 9 Flying Stars.

Fate Stars are sometimes seen as minor officials in the complex bureaucracy of the so-called Ministry of Time, which is presided over by *T'ai Sui*, otherwise known as Counter-Jupiter, the planet whose revolution round the sun marks out an almost exact 12-year period (11.86 years to be exact). T'ai Sui itself is one of the most important Fate Stars. Although T'ai Sui is often referred to as Jupiter, in fact it is "Counter-Jupiter," a hypothetical planet that is described by the Chinese to be traveling in a fashion that is the mirror image of the path of the physical planet Jupiter (called *Sui Hsing*). It still traces out the approximately 12-year path around the sun that makes Jupiter an ideal clock, but does so backwards. This cycle of 12 years (or one Great Year) mirrors the cycle of 12 solar months in a year, and the 12 (Chinese) hours in the day, all of which are counted using the 12 Earthly Branches. Interestingly, if you multiply this all important number 12 by the number of Elements, 5, you get 60, which is the other important time cycle counter number.

These Fate Stars all have a name and a function, which might be desirable or undesirable. There are at least 254 such Fate Stars, of which 88 are usually considered good, 162 of them bad, and 4 neutral.

The good Stars rejoice in such names as Heaven Virtue, Moon Virtue, Five Harmonies, Five Riches, Holy Heart, Heaven's Messenger, Yin Virtue, and Six Rights. They are shown each year on what is effectively the first page of the *T'ung Shu* in an octagonal chart that looks superficially like a Chinese horoscope. In fact it is not the horoscope of any person, but what could be described as the horoscope for the whole year ahead. It is in effect a miniature lo p'an just for the year of publication showing the direction of the main Fate Stars (see figure 4.6).

The diagram in figure 4.6 consists of an octagon surrounded by 4 octagonal bands or rings. In the top right is the Sexagenary combination that identifies the year (one of the 60 combinations of Earthly Branch and Heavenly Stem that are used to count out cycles

Fig. 4.5 (left) *The Spring Cow Page of the* T'ung Shu *for 2002*
Fig. 4.6 (right) *The Flying Stars and Other Fate Stars Shown in the 2002 Chinese Almanac*

of 60 years). For example, in the 2002 issue of the *T'ung Shu* shown in figure 4.6, the Sexagenary combination is marked as *jen wu*. This means the characteristics for that year are derived from the nineteenth Sexagenary combination made up of the Heavenly Stem *jen* (9 - yang Water) and the Earthly Branch *wu* (VII - yang Fire).

0. In the innermost octagon are the four cardinal directions, N, S, E, and W, in Chinese, with of course North at the bottom.

1. In the first ring out from the center are the Chinese names for the 8 trigrams, or pa kua, showing, for example, Tui to the right.

2. The second ring is of most interest to us, as it shows in Chinese the names of the 9 Flying Stars, which are more important than the other Fate Stars. Each is marked with two characters, simply the Star's number and its color, like 1-white or 5-yellow. (S=2-black, SW=4-green, W=9-purple, NW=8-white, N=3-green, NE=1-white, E=5-yellow, SE=6-white, and of course 7-red is by implication in the center.)

3. The third ring carries the names of the 24 Mountains (see chapter 3) that form the most important ring on any lo p'an.

4. The fourth double ring carries the names of other, perhaps less well known Fate Stars. These outer Fate Stars are an intriguing mixture of astrological and astronomical terms, theoretical mirror planets like Venus, T'ai Sui, star deities, moon nodes, and so on. Out of the 254 possibilities, there can only be 24 on this diagram, one for each of the 24 Mountains. The calculations as to which ones have flown into prominence in any particular year are quite complex, and these are why many people buy the *T'ung Shu*. On these detailed points not every edition of the *T'ung Shu* will agree, although they are always unanimous about the 9 Flying Stars.

5. At the four inter-cardinal points beyond the last ring are 4 curious Fate Stars that are regarded as the Guardians of the 4 Celestial Gates. The 4 Gates are always:

> Gate for Ghosts – NE
> Gate for Men – SW
> Heaven's Gate – NW
> Earth's Gate – SE

These Gates have a relevance in feng shui because the directions of the 4 inter-cardinal points are often used to determine special placing rules. For example one feng shui maxim is that you should not place "Fire at Heaven's Gate." By being aware that Heaven's Gate is in the NW, you can ascertain that placing the kitchen stove (physical fire) in that sector or facing that direction, might not be a good idea. Interestingly these "Gates" are the only directions among the 24 Mountains that are designated by trigrams. Circulating from Gate to Gate every 3 years are their 4 Guardians:

Ts'an Shih or House of Silkworms – present in the NE corner in 2002

Po Shih or the Scholar – present in the NW corner in 2002

Li Shih or the Warrior – present in the SW corner in 2002

Tsou Shu or Report to the Emperor –(effectively a star god reporting to Heaven on the conduct of every person in the household) – present in the SE corner in 2002.

6. In two columns on either side and below are further lists pertaining to the 24 Mountains and their various influences in that year. In the list of unfortunate Stars, the Three Curses (*San Sha*) has pride of place, followed by the troublesome 5-yellow Star (one of the 9 Flying Stars).

In the year 2000 edition of the *T'ung Shu* the Fate Stars were listed as in table 4.2 (don't worry too much about the third column):

Table 4.2: *Flying Stars and Other Fate Stars Shown in the 2000 T'ung Shu, or Chinese Almanac. (There are 3 Fate Stars for each direction, to correspond with the 24 Directions in all.)*

Direction	Flying Star	Fate Stars for the Year
E	7-red	*Ta li, yin tui, ta li*
SE	8-white	*T'ai sui* (counter-Jupiter), *hsiao li, chieh sha*
S	4-green	*Tzuo sha, tzai sha, tzuo sha*
SW	6-white	*Sui sha, ta li, ti fu*
W	2-black	*Ta li, yin fu, ta li*
NW	1-white	*Sui p'o, yi fu, t'ien fu*
N	5-yellow	*Hsiang sha, wu huang, hsiang sha*
NE	3-green	*Hsiao li, nian ke, wu ti*

You will be pleased to know that the above description of the opening page of the *T'ung Shu* is primarily to set the background and is not essential to the understanding of the Flying Stars or the rest of this book. Only one specific set of Fate Stars, the 9 Flying Stars, are the subject of this book, along with just a few key Fate Stars such as T'ai Sui (Counter-Jupiter) and the San Sha, or Three Curses/Killings. It is important to realize that the knowledge, location, and qualities of the 9 Flying Stars and Fate Stars are an integral part of Chinese culture. This knowledge is common knowledge and not restricted to ancient esoteric Chinese texts, as it is also present every year on the shelves of more than 3.5 million ordinary Chinese homes in Hong Kong and elsewhere. This means that it is read by perhaps three or four times that number of people, many of whom will know where, for example, 5-yellow is in the current year.

THE 9 FLYING STARS

We will look first at how the Flying Stars are related to the trigrams, then to their correspondence with the numbers of the Lo Shu, and then the meanings of their strange names. Finally we will look at which are lucky and which are considered unlucky.

So what are Flying Stars? The Chinese words *fei hsing* (sometimes spelled *fei sin*) are usually translated as "Flying Stars." They are pronounced "fay shing." The Chinese character *fei* is connected to birds and flying. Although the Chinese word for Element and star are both transliterated as "*hsing,*" they are totally different characters, and there is no apparent linguistic connection between them. Here, *hsing* definitely means a star, but these energies are not stars in the astronomical sense, nor do they fly. The full name of the system in Chinese is "Purple-White Flying Star" because of the colors of the first and ninth stars.

These stars are in fact types of energy that move from one section of a building to another as the tides of ch'i energy change. The stars measure the waxing and waning of ch'i inside and outside a building. These fluctuations of ch'i are conceived of as stars moving from one section of a building to another as the tides of ch'i change. One recent and excellent book decided to call them "Floating Stars." They do, however, correspond with the seven real astronomical stars of the Northern Ladle, plus two Assistant Stars, unlike most Fate Stars.

The 9 Flying Stars are also closely associated with the 8 trigrams that we touched upon in chapter 1. In fact there is a sequence by which one trigram is generated from another, which at the same time puts the Flying Stars in correct sequential order. To do this you must start with the basic female generative trigram K'un, which is made up of three yin lines:

— —
— —
— —

Using a system colloquially referred to as the Flipping Trigram, each successive trigram is generated by changing only one line at a time to its opposite, a yin line to a yang line or vice versa. The first transformation is achieved by changing the top line, while the other two lines stay the same:

— —	changes to	———
— —		— —
— —		— —
K'un		Ken
		Forming Star 1 – *t'an lang*

So trigram K'un changes into trigram Ken and generates the first Star, whose strange name is *t'an lang*, or the Covetous Wolf star.

In turn the Ken trigram changes its middle line to generate the trigram Hsun, and the second Star *chu men*, or Great Door star thus:

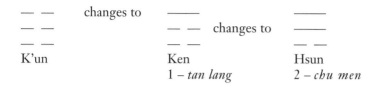

You can guess that now it is the turn of the bottom line to change to produce the trigram Ch'ien, and the third star *lu ts'un*, or Rank (or Salary) Preserved star:

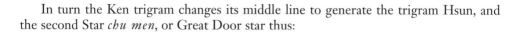

The process of successive transmutation continues rhythmically, with the middle line changing, then the top line, then the middle line, then the bottom line, then the middle line, and finally the top line. This is best visualized as a sort of sine wave, with each trigram evolving from its predecessor, showing the whole cycle of all possible combinations of yin and yang in the trigrams as shown in figure 4.7.

Chinese philosophers, particularly the Taoists, saw the universe in terms of unceasing change and transmutation, rather than the static view typical of Western philosophy. Those of you familiar with the *I Ching* will recognize that this process also occurs with the hexagrams, which mutate from one to another via individual lines changing from yin to yang or vice versa. What we observe here with the trigrams is a graphical representation of the basic mechanics of change. It is only by correctly observing these cycles of change that the future can be predicted with tolerable accuracy. This is a view that is incidentally also held by technical (but not fundamentalist) stock traders, who see chart pattern changes in terms of repeating cycles.

Let us look at the complete cycle generating 8 of the Flying Stars from the 8 trigrams in figure 4.7. In each case the "o" indicates the line that is about to change.

Fig. 4.7 *The Generation of the Trigrams One from Another with Their Corresponding Flying Stars*

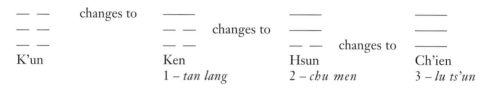

Trigram									
Trigram	K'un	Ken	Hsun	Ch'ien	Li	Chen	Tui	K'an	K'un
Star	1	2	3	4	5	6	7	8	9
Name	t'an lang	chu men	lu ts'un	wen ch'u	lien chen	wu ch'u	p'o chun	chu men	tso fu & yu pi

Incidentally, each of the 9 Flying Stars can be linked with any of the 8 trigrams: in fact as the 9 Stars cycle through the house or the Lo Shu diagram they arrive in turn at each of the Palaces of the 8 trigrams. The arrangement of trigrams and Stars that is most commonly shown, is not the generative one as shown in figure 4.7, but is simply to use the numbers of the Lo Shu in turn to correspond directly with the Star numbers as in table 4.3 below. Note that this leaves Star 5 without a corresponding trigram.

Leaving behind the "Flipping Trigram" origins of the 9 Flying Stars, let us list the Stars out by themselves, with the English meaning of their names.

Table 4.3: *The 9 Flying Stars, with the Literal Meaning of Their Name and Trigram*

Star Number	Chinese Name	Character	Meaning	Trigram
1	*t'an lang*	貪 狼	Covetous Wolf	K'an
2	*chu men*	巨 門	Great Door or Great Gate	K'un
3	*lu ts'un*	祿 存	Rank (or Salary) Preserved	Chen
4	*wen ch'u*	文 曲	Civil or Literary Career (literally "windings")	Hsun
5	*lien chen*	廉 真	Honesty, Purity, and Uprightness	Center
6	*wu ch'u*	武 曲	Military Career (literally "windings")	Ch'ien
7	*p'o chun*	破 軍	Broken Army	Tui
8	*tso fu*	左 輔	Left Celestial Assistant*	Ken
9	*yu pi*	右 弼	Right Celestial Assistant*	Li

* These two Assistant Stars are slightly different from the other 7, and if these are taken separately, you get 9 Stars in all. You should also note that the so-called "hidden stars" the Left and Right Assistant are often treated as one star, so that the system easily fits in with the 8 directions and the 8 trigrams. In one sense Star 9 is the shadow side of Star 8. They are often taken together and called *fu pi* rather than *tso fu* and *yu pi*.

MEANINGS OF THE STAR NAMES

The Star names don't immediately look internally consistent. The literal meaning of their names is confusing, and on the face of it, not a good guide to their nature. However we have to dig a little deeper into the original Chinese meaning of their names, which have never before appeared in English, to understand the real nature of the Stars.

1. The first Star, the Covetous Wolf, is, despite its name, a lucky Star. It is difficult to see how anything called the "Covetous Wolf" could be a beneficial or auspicious Star. The name in Chinese is T'an lang. *T'an* means avaricious, covetous, or greedy

for something precious, not a good start till you examine the radical (root) of the character, which means "precious." *Lang* means "wolf," which is made of two parts, the first of which means "dog," often thought of as man's closest domesticated friend. The second phonetic part (*liang*), which means "good or wise," has undergone many changes but the primary meaning was "the nature of man, a gift from heaven," is good.

Therefore deeply hidden in the roots of these characters may be the meaning "a precious gift from heaven." Such buried meanings (or puns) are common in old feng shui manuals, even if its linguistic extraction would not always be scholastically acceptable today. One of this Star's other names is *sheng ch'i*, or Generating ch'i, which also shows its beneficial qualities. You can now begin to see how the Covetous Wolf is a good Star.

2. Star 2, or Great Door, is an appropriate name as it is associated with the dark Mother of the K'un trigram. From the "door" of the Mother all things are born. Because of its association with fertility and abundance, it is traditionally thought of as a lucky Star (even if its modern meaning is the reverse of this). Some readers will find it very strange to see the 2-black Star listed as an auspicious Star. This is because its basic essence is that of the K'un trigram, symbolizing fertility, which is in essence auspicious. Its Element of Earth, however, has meant that it has become closely associated with the troublesome 5-yellow Star, which is also Earth. In addition, this Star is deeply Untimely, and has not therefore been directly auspicious since 1903, so most modern Masters simply ignore its basic meaning and treat it as inauspicious. This is how I will also treat its qualities in the rest of this book, but I have placed it in table 4.5 in its traditional position as an auspicious star. Its other names include "Heavenly Wealth" and "Heavenly Doctor." From the latter you can see why (only when it is in negative mode) it is associated with disease. *Chu*, the Chinese character for "great," also has the meaning of the instrument or square that "was the guide when building or laying out a plot of ground," almost certainly a feng shui reference.

3. Star 3, Rank (or Salary) Preserved, is the first of the inauspicious Stars and was associated with career in the sense that it ensured the preservation of minor rank. The character lu in its name lu ts'un is in fact the same character as Lu, the God of Wealth, one of the three gods you see in almost every traditional Chinese home: Lu, Fu, and Shou. One of its other names, *Huo hai*, literally means calamity, misfortune, and "to injure."

4. Star 4, Civil/Literary Career (or "Windings"), is unlucky. Stars 4 and 6 are associated with the two major career choices of an ambitious young Chinese of imperial times: the civil service or the military service. The Chinese word *ch'u* can also mean "twisted strokes or lines" or "windings" but makes more sense if read as "activities." One of its alternate names, *Liu sha*, means "six curses." In imperial times, admission to the civil service required the passing of a set of rigorous examinations that included a knowledge of classical Chinese literary works, hence the association of a

civil career with literary activities. Passing such rigorous exams led to well-paid jobs and considerable social standing. It allowed bright students to cross social barriers and join the Mandarin class. (Although much can be said for and against the imperial Chinese system of civil service recruitment, it at least ensured that candidates for government posts had a reasonable level of intelligence, culture, and ability, which is probably not a bad thing, even these days.)

5. Star 5, *Lien chen*, literally means "honesty, purity, and uprightness." These are strange meanings for a Star that is traditionally considered to be the most inauspicious of all. On the face of it, Star 5 seems to be concerned with morals, but is nevertheless a very unlucky Star. One of its alternate names is *Wu kuei*, or "five ghosts/demons."

6. Star 6, Military Career (or "Windings"), is the second career choice of Chinese imperial times, that of military service. Star 6 is considered lucky, as the military were seen as those who stopped potentially hostile incursions into the Middle Kingdom, thus preserving peace. Other names for this Star include "Golden Water" and "Lengthened Years," indicating wealth and longevity.

7. Star 7, or Broken Army, obviously indicates an unfortunate defeat or bad outcome, and is indeed an unlucky Star. (From 1986 to February 2004 it is a current Period Star and therefore considered lucky for that Period, but for every other period it is unlucky.) One of its alternate names is "Severed Fate," which is a dire prediction indeed.

8, 9. The two Stars 8 and 9 are a pair, being both Celestial Assistants. Both are lucky, but Star 9 takes on the luck quality of any other Star it is associated with. Later you will see that these two also represent the Sun and the Moon, in a real sense Celestial Assistants to Heaven. The fact that the Moon reflects the light of other bodies is an indication of the adaptive and "ghostly" nature of Star 9, which is in a sense the obverse or reflection of Star 8.

THE 4 LUCKY AND 4 UNLUCKY STARS

There is much more meaning behind the names and attributes of the Stars than first appears. We can now divide the 9 Stars into 4 broadly lucky and 4 broadly unlucky Stars. The Left and Right Assistants are here grouped together as one Star. The traditional effect of each of these Stars on occupants of the part of the building or room they are located in is shown in the fifth column of table 4.4. Of course, these broad-brush delineations are over-simplified and have to be modified when two or more Stars interact at the same location.

You can see that the 9 Flying Stars have just as strange names as the other Fate Stars. Some of you will notice that the 9 Flying Stars are also 9 of the hundreds of stars used in Chinese Purple Star (*Tzu wei tou shu*) astrology, which I don't intend to go into here.

Table 4.4: *The 9 Flying Stars Divided into 4 Auspicious and 4 Inauspicious Stars (Theoretical division)*

No.	Four Lucky Stars	Also known as	Traveling Star name	The general influence of this Star results in:
1	Covetous Wolf (*T'an lang*)	Purple Breath *Tzu ch'i*	Generating Breath *Sheng ch'i*	Occupants will be intelligent. Their children will be intelligent and filial (behave well toward their parents).
2	Chief Gate/Door (*Chu men*)	Heavenly Wealth *T'ien tsai*	Heavenly Doctor *T'ien yi*	Occupants are honest and sincere and will be blessed with long life. They will also have wealth akin to that of an (imperial government) official. The modern interpretation of this Star is an inauspicious one.
6	Military Career (literally "Windings") (*Wu ch'u*)	Golden Water *Chin shui*	Lengthened Years *Yan nien*	Occupants will be both wealthy and prosperous and will be blessed with robust health and longevity.
8&9	Left and Right Assistants of the Celestial Emperor (*Tso fu* and *Yu pi*). *Fu pi* means both Assistants	Sun [the great yang] and Moon [the great yin] *Tai yang* and *Tai yin*	The Hidden Position *Fu wei*	Occupants will be wealthy and will be blessed with kind children. They will also be blessed with officialdom, i.e., government office.

(continued)

Table 4.4 (cont.): *The 9 Flying Stars Divided into 4 Auspicious and 4 Inauspicious Stars (Theoretical division)*

No.	Four Unlucky Stars	Also known as	Traveling Star name	The general influence of this Star results in:
3	Rank (or Salary) Preserved *(Lu ts'un)*	Illuminated Orphan or Solitary Sunlight *Ku yao*	Accident and Mishap *Huo hai*	The occupants will be dull-witted and foolish.
4	Civil or Literary Career (or "Windings") *(Wen ch'u)*	Sweep Away *Sao t'ang*	Six Curses *Liu sha*	The occupants will be cursed with bad gambling habits. Couples will be unfaithful to each other (and sexually promiscuous). Hypocrisy will be common among occupants.
5	Honesty, Purity, and Uprightness *(Lien Chen)*	Agitated Fire or Moving Fire *Tsao huo*	Five Ghosts *Wu kuei*	Occupants will meet with severe problems like road accidents that may result in death in the worst case. Their children will be rebellious and unreasonable.
7	Broken Army *(P'o chun)*	Heavenly Dipper constellation *T'ien kang*	Severed Fate *Chueh ming*	The occupants will either be thieves, or they themselves will be robbed. Occupants will also be confronted with many legal matters directly concerning them. "Severed fate" also implies death.

Others may recognize the alternate names of the 9 Flying Stars. These have appeared in English language feng shui books as the names of the 4 auspicious and 4 inauspicious directions or locations, determined by the calculation of a person's annual "kua number" but are more correctly referred to as Traveling Stars. These names (sheng ch'i, t'ien yi, etc.) are usually tabulated without explaining that they are in fact an integral part of the 9 Flying Stars system. This will be explained in more detail in chapter 12.

In the simplified East House/West House system of feng shui, all of the directions, such as the sheng ch'i direction, change according to your year of birth. The reason for this is that this "direction" is actually determined by one of the Flying Stars that moves from one Palace or direction to another, every year, as well as every twenty years. Once you know that sheng ch'i (or Generating Breath) is just another description for the location of t'an lang, the beneficial Star 1, then it makes much more sense. In chapter 12 you will learn how to calculate the Annual movements of the Stars, which explains the roots of the East House/West House system.

This chapter has examined the whole idea of Fate Stars and how these are part of everyday Chinese life, being set out each year in the Chinese Almanac. We related 7 of the 9 Flying Stars to stars in the Ursa Major constellation and discovered that the two Assistant Stars (although invisible to the naked eye) are connected with the 6th Star. It is important to remember that the 9 Flying Stars act as traditional markers of the hour and season and point to the Pole Star, the apparent pivot of the Northern Hemisphere sky, from which they control fluctuating patterns of ch'i on the Earth. We looked at how they relate to the 8 trigrams, their meanings, and how they divide in to 4 Auspicious and 4 Inauspicious Stars.

Chapter 5

Star-by-Star

Flying Star feng shui assumes there is a very real link between the present time, the orientation of a building, the time it was built or occupied, and the luck of its occupants. We have so far looked at the Chinese system of measuring time (chapter 2), the use of the lo p'an to determine the orientation of the building (chapter 3), and the origin and idea of Fate Stars (chapter 4). Now we look at the Stars themselves and their qualities.

The essence of Flying Star feng shui diagnosis is to make sure that important functions like sleeping, eating, and studying are done in rooms or parts of the building that contain favorable Flying Star configurations. Rooms where you sleep, eat, study, or make money should be rooms where the Flying Star combinations are good. On the other hand, rooms like the "wet rooms," bathroom, toilet room, washroom, and even kitchen, may be located where the Flying Star combinations are *not* good, where they will have their energy drained by the draining water.

Where a potentially bad Flying Star combination falls into an important room, then a knowledge of the cycles of the Elements (see chapter 1) should be used to modify, reduce, or defeat these effects (see chapter 15). Conversely, beneficial Flying Star combinations can be intensified by appropriate Element placement. The effects of such feng shui work can often be impressive and very rapid. This is the essence of Flying Star feng shui. To put this knowledge to use we need to understand the correspondences of each Star. First we will consider their colors, then how they relate to the 5 Elements. Finally, we will consider their timeliness and how this affects their natures.

THE STAR COLORS

In the last chapter we looked at the strange proper names of the 9 Flying Stars. Nowadays individual Stars are usually spoken about as if their names were made up just of their number and their color. So you might refer to the first Star, in conversation, not as t'an lang, the "Covetous Wolf," but as the "1-white" Star. Likewise the Right Assistant Star would be referred to as the "9-purple" Star. Their other names are kept semi-secret and are seldom used when speaking about them, perhaps for fear of waking them up. In order to call them by their number-colors we must look at the colors associated with each Star.

Each Star has a color associated with it. At first sight these colors make little sense. That is because the origin of the colors is a bit complex. These colors initially came from the custom (dating from the second century BC or earlier) of distinguishing all stars in Chinese star catalogs (not just those of the Northern Ladle) by three colors: red, black, and white. These colors corresponded to star groups catalogued by three different early Chinese astronomers. This accounts for the colors of Stars 1, 6, 8 (white), 2 (black), and 7 (red).

The other colors come from the Element associations of the Stars, so that 5 is yellow (because it is Earth) and 3 and 4 are green (as they are Wood). That just leaves the Right Assistant star (number 9), which is purple because of its association with the Pole Star (symbolic of the emperor, whose color is imperial purple).

The colors are also a partial indicator of the nature of the Star. For example, as we saw in the previous chapter, the basic nature of the three white Stars (1, 6, 8) is favorable.

The green and red Stars 3, 4, and 7 are basically unfavorable (except where they are the current Period Star, as 7 is for example from 1984 till February 2004).

The yellow Star 5 and black Star 2 are both Earth Stars, and unfavorable.

The purple Star 9 is basically favorable, but modifies its nature to whatever star it is with. With a favorable Star, it is favorable; with an unfavorable Star, it is unfavorable. It is, if you like, a modifiable Star that accentuates its companion Stars.

Table 5.1: *The 9 Flying Stars, Their Colors, and Basic Nature*

Star Number	Star Color	Basic Nature
1	**white**	**favorable**
2	black	unfavorable**
3	jade green*	unfavorable
4	dark green	unfavorable
5	yellow	very unfavorable
6	**white**	**favorable**
7	red	unfavorable
8	**white**	**favorable**
9	**purple**	**modifiable**

* The Chinese word for this color is pi, which is often translated turquoise, which is perhaps closer to its real meaning than the usual "green" or "jade green."

** The 2-black Star is currently unfavorable.

Even more important than the colors of each Star is the Element of each Star. When we get to the practical work of making feng shui alterations in response to discovered Flying Star patterns, we will be mostly using cures that depend upon the 5 Elements. It is therefore essential that you understand these.

The Flying Stars and the 5 Elements

Having looked at how the Stars derive their colors in part from the 5 Elements, we now look to see how the 5 Elements relate to the Stars. There are at least two ways of relating the 5 Elements to the 9 Stars, according to the two traditional differing arrangements of the pa kua (8 trigrams) that we briefly looked at in chapter 1. The most common arrangement is the Heaven or "internal" arrangement, which depends on the Later Heaven Sequence correlation between the Star numbers and the trigrams. There is, however, a second Earth or "external" arrangement, which is used for Form School correlation of real mountain and river shapes associated with the 9 Stars. The external arrangement also correlates the Planets with the 5 Elements.

I have shown both arrangements in table 5.2 below, but when deciding internal Flying Star chart Elements and their remedies, use the internal arrangement. When you correlate the 9 Flying Stars with the external landforms, use the external arrangement. I have added in the full names of the Stars here as they are more often used when talking about the external landform features.

The most important column in the table 5.2 is the 5th. I cannot stress enough how important it is to have the Element correspondences of the Stars at your fingertips. In fact it is worth rereading them in a more simplified form:

Star	Element
1-white	Water
2-black	Earth
3-jade	Wood
4-green	Wood
5-yellow	Earth
6-white	Metal
7-red	Metal
8-white	Earth
9-purple	Fire

It is not a bad idea to write this out on a note card and keep it with you when working on Flying Star feng shui.

Table 5.2: *The Elements and the 9 Stars (showing both Heaven and Earth arrangements)*

Star	Name	Meaning	Later Heaven Sequence Heaven/**Internal**		Early Heaven Sequence Earth/**External**	
			Trigram	Element	Element	Planet
1-white	*T'an lang*	Covetous Wolf	K'an	Water	Wood	Jupiter
2-black	*Chu men*	Great Door/ Gate	K'un	Earth	Wood	Jupiter
3-green	*Lu ts'un*	Rank Preserved	Chen	Wood	Earth	Saturn
4-green	*Wen ch'u*	Civil Career	Hsun	Wood	Water	Mercury
5-yellow	*Lien chien*	Honesty, Purity	Center	Earth	Fire	Mars
6-white	*Wu ch'u*	Military Career	Ch'ien	Metal	Metal	Venus
7-red	*P'o chun*	Broken Army	Tui	Metal	Metal	Venus
8-white	*Tso fu*	Left Assistant	Ken	Earth	Earth	Saturn (+ the Sun)
9-purple	*Yu pi*	Right Assistant	Li	Fire	Water	Mercury (+the Moon)

Now we can start to use our knowledge of time and Period cycles. You'll start seeing the time element of Flying Star feng shui at work. More importantly we'll be able to start predicting things about houses, and the people living within them.

THE TIMELINESS OF THE STARS

However, nothing is as simple as that. As time passes, each Period number comes to prominence in its turn. This cycle is simple to remember, as long as you remember that the present 180-year Great Cycle began with number 1 in 1864. After that just keep adding blocks of 20 years. Here it is in a table form:

Table 5.3: *The 9 Current 20-Year Periods*
(For an alternative arrangement of these Periods see appendix 6.)

Period Number	20-year Periods Begin 4/5 February	"Home" Star
1	1864	Star 1-white
2	1884	Star 2-black
3	1904	Star 3-green
4	1924	Star 4-green
5	1944	Star 5-yellow
6	1964	Star 6-white
7	1984	Star 7-red
8	2004	Star 8-white
9	2024	Star 9-purple

after which the cycle repeats again

Much of this book was written at the tail end of Period 7 (in 2001), where the influences of Star 8-white in Period 8 (2004–2023) were already being felt. You may in fact be reading this book in Period 7 or maybe Period 8, so throughout this book, we will look especially at those two Periods.

Just as there is a good time and a bad time to see someone, so there is a good time and a bad time to come into contact with specific Flying Stars. What do I mean by that? Well it's a concept called "Timeliness." The Star of the present Period is always considered "Timely." The Stars of Periods in the immediate future are considered Timely. But, the Stars of the past Periods are "Untimely."

This means that Star 7 is timely throughout the Period from 1984 to February 2004. Stars 1–6, as they are before 1984, are all untimely. Star Periods 8 and 9 are in the future and so are "future timely."

THE VIGOROUSNESS OF CH'I OVER TIME

As ch'i tides wax and wane, so ch'i moves from being invigorating (and hence beneficial) to stagnant (and hence destructive or inauspicious).

There is another way of looking at the ch'i quality brought to the house by particular Stars, which is really an amplification of the concept of Timeliness. Ch'i quality is seen as a cycle of growth and decay over time. There are, of course, 5 phases or stages to this growth.

When a Star is the current Period Star, just as Star 7-red is during 1884–2004, it is in its "king ch'i," or ruling ch'i, phase, or in Chinese, *wang ch'i*: at this point it is strong and vigorous. After Stars begin to wane, they loose this initial energy, and go through the stages in table 5.4:

....

Table 5.4: *The 5 Phases, or Stages, of Ch'i*

Phase or Stage of Ch'i	Nature	Occurs When the Star Number Is...
Prosperous	*Wang* (related to the character for Emperor)	Same number as current Period
Growing	*Sheng* (strong energy; sheng is the same term as used in East House/West House feng shui)	Same number as next Period, or one after that
Retreating/ declining	*Tui* (not the same word as the trigram) or *shuai* ch'i	Same number as the previous Period
Dead	*Si* or *ssu* ch'i (the opposite of sheng ch'i)	A Star is considered si ch'i if it is Star 3, 4, or 5 in Period 7; or 2 or 6 in Period 8.
Destructive or killing	*Sha* (the familiar destructive or killing sha ch'i)	A Star is considered *sha* ch'i if it is Star 2 or 3 in Period 7; or 3, 4, or 5 in Period 8.

Obviously, the energy of Stars in their wang or sheng stage is much stronger than if they are *si*, or dead. A Star which is either si or sha cannot be relied upon to provide its positive qualities to any place in which it is found.

PROMINENT STAR

As the strength of ch'i is such an important consideration, specific labels are used for important Stars.

Of all the Stars in a chart, those numerically equivalent to the current Period are among the most important. Some Masters refer to the Period Star, when it appears as the Mountain or as the Water Star, as the Prominent Star (meaning the Star of this Period). This is an important term, which we will use again, so let us define it again: The Prominent Mountain or Water star is the Star with the same number as the current Period. Such Stars plus the Mountain and Water Star of the coming Period (soon to be Prominent) are among the most important Stars in the whole chart.

LUCKY NUMBERS

These Period and Star numbers generate "lucky numbers" in popular culture. Flying Star "lucky numbers" have become a part of daily life for a lot of Chinese and increasingly in the West, where "888" telephone numbers and car license plate numbers are the "in" thing. Currently when it comes to lucky license plates or telephone numbers, "8" is chosen in preference to "7," as Period 7 is on the way out. Combinations of 8 and 9 are also held in high esteem, 9 being future luck. You can see that this popular practice in fact derives directly from Timeliness and Prominent Star theory.

When we reach Period 8, after February 2004, the picture changes. Star 8 becomes Timely, and Star 7 and before become Untimely. Star 9 remains Timely, as it is in the future. In time, after 2024, the fashionable number plates will be combinations of 9 and 1, the future wealth Star for the period that arrives in 2044. So now you know which car number plates you should be buying up now!

Let's lay this out in table 5.5:

Table 5.5: *The Timeliness of the 9 Stars in Period 7 and in Period 8*

Star	20-year Period	Star Nature during Period 7 (1984–2003)	Star Nature during Period 8 (2004–2024)
1-white	1864–1883	Untimely	Distant Future Timely
2-black	1884–1903	Untimely	Untimely
3-jade green	1904–1923	Untimely	Untimely
4-dark green	1924–1943	Untimely	Untimely
5-yellow	1944–1963	Untimely	Untimely
6-white	1964–1983	Untimely	Untimely
7-red	1984–2003	**Timely**	Untimely*
8-white	2004–2023	Future Timely	**Timely***
9-purple	2024–2043	Distant Future Timely	Future Timely
1-white	2044–2063	Untimely	Distant Future Timely

* Star 7 reverts to its basic (unfavorable) nature after we move from Period 7 to Period 8.

See how it all "slips down a notch" as we move from the Period 7 column to the Period 8 column in 2004. You can see how February 4, 2004 is a key date for rechecking your feng shui. Many Flying Star feng shui practitioners are going to have to work very hard over that period!

How does that affect me? We know the basic nature of the Star. So let us put that into the context of timeliness. Let's first map it out exactly, so we can see how the basic nature of each of the Stars changes from one 20-year Period to the next. This brings together all of the above information, so if you got a bit lost back there, don't worry, just use the summary in table 5.6:

Table 5.6: *The Basic Nature of the 9 Flying Stars, and How This Nature Is Modified by Their Timeliness during the 2 Current Periods (1984–2023)*

Star	Basic Nature	Nature during Period 7 (1984–2003)	Result in Period 7	Nature during Period 8 (2004–2023)	Result in Period 8
1-white	Favorable	Untimely	B	Distant Future Timely	G
2-black	Unfavorable	Untimely	B	Untimely	B
3-green	Unfavorable	Untimely	B	Untimely	B
4-green	Unfavorable	Untimely	B	Untimely	B
5-yellow	Unfavorable	Untimely	Very B	Untimely	Very B
6-white	Favorable	Untimely	B	Untimely	B
7-red	Unfavorable	Timely	G	Untimely	B
8-white	Favorable	Future Timely	G	Timely	G
9-purple	Favorable	Distant Future Timely	G	Future Timely	G

Note especially how 1-white and 7-red change their resultant nature from Period 7 to Period 8.

B = bad   G = good

Now let us look at the effects of each Star.

THE BASIC NATURE OF THE 9 INDIVIDUAL STARS

Most of the Stars are marked B (bad) and only a few as G (good), in terms of Timeliness. This is a bit of an oversimplification, and you will find later how it is often the interaction between the Stars that *really* counts. Meanwhile, you should be aware of the type of luck that each of these Stars potentially brings, as laid out in table 5.7. You will also note how they behave a lot better when they are Timely, than when they are out of favor.

Table 5.7: *The Qualities or Potential Effects of the 9 Flying Stars (according to whether they are Timely or not)*

Star	Element*	Basic Nature	Qualities When Timely	Qualities When Untimely
1-white	Water	Favorable	Wealth, fame, fortune	Divorce, death, isolation
2-black	Earth	Unfavorable	Fertility, leadership	Illness, especially miscarriage or digestive difficulties, loneliness
3-green	Wood	Unfavorable	Prosperity	Misfortune, lawsuits, arguments, slander
4-green	Wood	Unfavorable	Academic/exam success, creativity	Divorce, extramarital affairs, romance
5-yellow	Earth	Unfavorable	Sudden unexpected wealth & prosperity	Catastrophe, severe illness, lawsuits: the most negative Star
6-white	Metal	Favorable	Wealth, achievement, leadership	Loneliness, isolation, sadness
7-red	Metal	Unfavorable	Wealth, fertility, pregnancy	Robbery, disputes, fire, injury, isolation, even imprisonment
8-white	Earth	Favorable	Happiness, wealth, fame	Children may be injured
9-purple	Fire	Favorable	Achievement, growth, success	Illness, especially eye problems, miscarriage, mental problems, employment problems**

*You will notice that the Star colors do not match the Elements in quite the way you might expect.

**Star 9-purple energizes any accompanying Star, favorably or otherwise, depending upon that Star's nature: It makes the bad worse, and the good better.

Don't worry, although this sounds like a real disaster catalog, whether or not these things begin to happen depends upon a number of things. These include the configuration of your home and the interaction of specific locations in your home, the activities that take place there, the surrounding landforms, and interaction between the Stars. Also, even the worst Stars are ineffective if you do not stir them up.

Growth and Decay of the Period Star

The Period (or Earth Base) Star is related to significant events within a building, such as its construction date. This has an effect on the energy levels within a building.

Because nothing endures forever, and everything (according to the Chinese) is cyclical, so there are times when the Stars are Prosperous, and there are times when the Stars are subject to decay. For a Star to be effective it has to be in its prosperous or Growth stage.

We have seen that each Star is at its strongest (and best behaved) when in its own birth Period; for example Star 7-red is strongest during its own Period 7 (1984–2004). After this the Star's strength "decays." When the 8th Period rolls around, the strength of this Period Star will begin to wane.

Let's look at this specifically in relation to the Period in which a house is built, its so-called Period Star. Some Period Stars have a better staying power than others, as you can see from table 5.8.

....

Table 5.8: *The Growth and Decay of the Earth Base (or Period Star) Energy over Time*

Period House Built in (birth)		Condition of Earth Base (or building) energy over the 9 Periods								
		1	2	3	4	5	6	7	8	9
1	1864 -	H	F	R	G	G	G	G	G	G
2	1884 -	R	H	F	D	D	D	N	R	D
3	1904 -	N	R	H	F	K	D	F	R	D
4	1924 -	G	G	R	H	F	R	N	G	G
5	1944 -	D	D	D	R	H	F	D	D	D
6	1964 -	G	G	G	G	R	H	F	G	G
7	1984 -	D	N	R	D	D	R	H	F	D
8	2004 -	G	G	G	G	G	G	R	H	F
9	2024 -	F	D	D	N	D	D	N	R	H

Key:
H = highest or birth energy   N = energy neutral
G = good energy   D = energy is dead
R = energy rising   K = energy is killing or destructive
F = energy falling

What does this mean from a practical point of view? First, do not confuse this table with Timeliness, which affects the quality and action of the Water and Mountain Stars (which we will come to later). Here we are solely considering the Period Star, or the Period when the house was built: we are talking about the main large Star number in the center of each square. It is common sense to say that old houses get tired and don't have the same vitality in their ch'i as brand new houses: something we all instinctively know. What is not quite so obvious is that their Period comes round again if you wait long enough. When it does, you often see whole streets being renovated at the same time or a suburb with same-age houses enjoying a "rebirth." This can provide an interesting clue to selecting a house in an up-and-coming neighborhood.

Some practitioners subscribe to the theory that the arrival of new occupants automatically resets the Period number to the current Period, so that because of the high turnover of modern house ownership and occupancy, many houses are reset already to the current or immediately past Period. Traditionally a house retains the Period number of its birth (or building) year, until its roof is replaced. A full renovation involving opening/lifting the roof will rejuvenate the house by updating its Period number to the current Period.

You can see that houses "born" or reset in the 7th Period will have falling energy in the 8th Period, and their energy will be "dead" in the 9th Period, but will return to rising energy in the 3rd Period and again in the 6th Period, a long way in the future.

Don't worry too much about this, because the key issues are still the interaction between the Mountain and the Water Stars. However, there are other lessons to be drawn from this. For example, after February 2004 you can see by casting your eye down the second to last column of table 5.8 for the period 2004–2024 which houses will have the strongest Earth Base energy. These are in descending order those houses "born" in:

Highest	Period 8	2024–2044
Good	Period 6	1964–1984
Good	Period 4	1924–1944
Good	Period 1	1864–1884
Rising	Period 3	1904–1924
Rising	Period 2	1884–1904

In fact during this period, most houses will have good or rising energy. Only houses built in 1944–1964 will have dead energy, even houses "born" in Period 7 (1984–2004) will only have failing energy (which is still much better than "dead").

It is interesting that houses built between 1944 and 1964 have a longer period of dead energy than any other period. The reason from a Flying Star perspective is that they are Earth houses and therefore don't flourish in any other period except their own and the period immediately on each side of the 5th Period.

From a historical point of view (especially in Europe) these houses were built between 1944 and 1964, during and immediately after World War II, and are therefore most likely to suffer from material shortages and defects, and work by underskilled artisans. The immediate postwar period in Europe also saw the rise of huge and horrible, unimaginative council blocks and state-owned housing, much of which has come in for subsequent structural and aesthetic condemnation. Indeed a fitting monument to Period 5 building!

In total contrast, those houses that will be built between 2004 and 2024 are destined to retain good levels of energy over their entire life span, with no energetically "dead" periods. The same energetic quality only applies to Period 1 and Period 6 houses. Of course what we are seeing here is the trinity of the white Stars 1-6-8!

We have now come to know the Flying Stars in terms of their color and Element and how they react when they are timely or untimely, energetic or stagnant. You should remember that as Flying Stars represent different ch'i energies, the quality of this energy is of paramount importance. Having looked at the relationship between energy quality and time of building, it is time for us to look more deeply at the Flying Star in relation to the actual physical house and its landform surroundings. It is time to apply the theory to the real world in the next chapter.

Chapter 6

Analyzing the Floor Plan

It is all very well to calculate the disposition of the 9 Flying Stars and their positioning in the Lo Shu, but this is no help if you can't relate the Flying Stars chart to the house or building that you are diagnosing. This is a very important subject. To express it more technically, the problem is how we divide a building into its Palaces. "Palace" is the technical term for each of the 9 cells, and each Palace corresponds to one of the 8 trigrams (plus the central Palace). There are two basic ways to do this, and several minor variations.

When mapping the Stars onto the physical house, the first question that usually arises is, do you include the garage or the patio or other side structures in the analysis? There is also the problem of what to do with extensions and recently added-on rooms. The view of most feng shui Masters is that if the structure is temporary or open to the wind and rain, such as a patio, then it should be excluded from the analysis. In the case of a garage, if it is built into the house and is accessible through the house, then it should be included.

There is one school of thought that says that the analysis should only take into account the original structure, and that any new extensions should be ignored unless there was a corresponding re-siting of the front door at the time of the building of the extension. I don't buy this argument, because if the occupants occupy the extended space, then the ch'i of the house flows into the new rooms, hence these rooms must be part of the ch'i analysis of the house. Also there are many instances of the quality of the feng shui being radically altered by the addition of an extra room or two. In fact sometimes such additions can be an extreme way of improving the feng shui of a house.

Let us next dispose of the perennial question of the irregularly shaped house. Most buildings are in fact rectangular, and these present no problem. But what happens when you have an L-shaped house? What about "missing bits" when the house is not a perfect rectangle? The answer is simple, but necessitates us looking at traditional Chinese architecture.

TRADITIONAL CHINESE HOUSES

The basic unit of traditional buildings is a *chian*, structurally, a single room. In traditional China, houses were often built initially as three bays or rooms (called a three-chian structure). Each chian incidentally has very specific rules in terms of depth-to-width ratios. This is the nucleus of the habitation, which may remain this size or may grow over time.

As the family grew, it was the custom for sons to bring their new wives to the family home, rather than necessarily set up home elsewhere. This would necessitate adding a new room or a new wing at one side, forming an L shape. The original 3 chian is a yang number (being odd not even), and the family would try to add at least two chian at a time to continue to maintain a yang number. It is very unusual in China to see, for example, a 4 bay or chian house (4 being a particularly unlucky number). A feng shui analysis done at that point would take the whole rectangle, incorporating a "missing bit" of open space. That was considered quite natural, and the ch'i attributes of the missing bits were no longer available (at this stage) to the occupants of the house.

Do not be tempted (as some modern books have suggested) to put a Lo Shu over the two wings separately. The house is an organic whole and should always be treated as such from an energy and feng shui point of view. It is only in rare extreme cases where, for example, the connection between the two parts is a covered walkway that two Lo Shus should be superimposed on the building. With very complex shapes, go for complete coverage.

In the example above of a traditional Chinese dwelling, the missing bit would be balanced as soon as practicable by adding a wing at the other side of the original structure, as balance is so important to feng shui. At this point, a feng shui analysis of the now U-shaped structure would include the open piece, leaving probably two of the nine sectors of the lo shu as open space. Mao Tse Tung's original house reflects a variation on this U-shaped structure, and its feng shui analysis was done in this way.

Finally, following our example, the two wings of the house might be joined, completely enclosing a courtyard, perhaps when the third son got married. The house is then "complete," especially as now it looks like the traditional Lo Shu shape with the center (Earth area) being a courtyard open to the sky.

This is the reason why Earth is attributed in the Basic Lo Shu to the central rectangle, because in a traditional house (before it is paved over) this central area will indeed be earth floored. Feng shui analysis of such a structure would naturally cover the whole house.

So you see, the Lo Shu is designed to grow with the house. Bear in mind that what appear to be problems in a feng shui analysis often melt away into the realm of common sense when they are considered from a Chinese architectural and cultural perspective; after all, these things are commonplace to a traditionally educated Chinese practitioner. To devise outlandish, multiple Lo Shu analyses as an "intuitive" solution to the perceived problem is a waste of time and will only produce erroneous analyses.

If the family continues to grow, then typically another inner courtyard will be built at the back. The more public courtyard is then typically referred to as the interior *ming tang*, or "bright hall," a term which also applies to the pool in front of a gravesite. This term has also come to mean the cleared land in front of the property in more modern texts. In contradistinction, the more secluded back courtyard was sometimes called the "dark hall," as it was away from the prying eyes of the general public.

Fig. 6.1 *Growth of a Typical Chinese House, showing the fit of the Lo Shu at each stage of development*

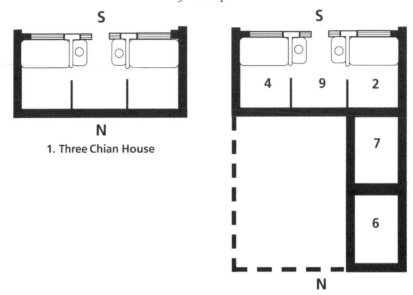

1. Three Chian House

2. L-shaped Extension Added to House

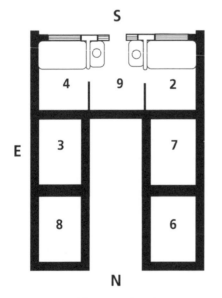

3. Double Extension Creates U-shaped House

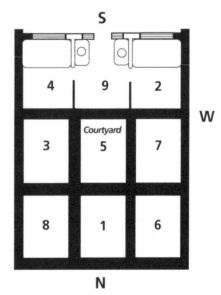

4. Complete Lo Shu Form House with Enclosed Courtyard

An interesting sidelight on this is that it is the main bays (or chian) that were considered from a feng shui point of view, rather than the subsidiary rooms, which were often created within them by non-load-bearing partition walls. This is a useful clue for later on when we look at individual rooms and have to decide what Palace of the Lo Shu they fall into.

Having established what part of the building is covered by the Lo Shu, the next problem is the precise placing of the Lo Shu over the included area. There are two main methods, the pie slice, or 8-sector pie wedge, method and the 9-cell grid or Palace method. Both have their plus points. In a nutshell, the division arose because a number of more modern practitioners decided that if you are using a circular lo p'an compass, then it makes more sense to regard the whole building as radiating out compasslike from a central point. Traditionalists retained the slightly less elegant rectangular Lo Shu–shaped division, which appears to sometimes compromise the exact readings.

You should use both systems on your first few analyses so that you get the hang of both, and then you can see for yourself what the pros and cons are of each system. Let me explain.

THE 8-SECTOR PIE WEDGE METHOD

This method is currently very popular in Hong Kong. It has the advantage of being very precise and apparently scientific and is used by many Masters. It relies upon taking very precise readings with the lo p'an. The procedure is as follows:

1. Ensure that you have an accurate reading and a drawn-to-scale floor plan of the building that you are dealing with. It is no use having a quick sketch on the back of an envelope. In fact proper architect-drawn plans are quite useful for feng shui analysis. If the building shape is awkward (that is, not a regular rectangle), then it is especially important to have plans drawn up precisely.

2. Find the exact center. This is best thought of as the center of gravity of the building. With a rectangular shape this is simple: just draw in the diagonals as dotted lines, and where they cross is the exact center. If there is a missing corner, simple extend the outline to enclose this and then draw the diagonals as usual.

   If the shape is irregular, one technique often used is to paste the plan onto a piece of cardboard. Then cut out the shape. Then suspend the cardboard shape in turn from each of its corners. Using a thread with a weight tied at the end, mark where the thread crosses the center of the cutout. With a number of these lines marked on, it will soon become obvious that the center is where they intersect. Mark the center.

3. Align the paper (or cardboard cutout) so that the north point of the building's plan precisely faces magnetic north. Place the compass at the center, and align it so that the tip of the needle with a bulge points precisely to magnetic north. Because lo p'ans are often bigger than the plan you are working with, it is usually more practical to use a clear plastic circular protractor marked with degrees from 0 to 360. In fact special feng shui protractors are available in Hong Kong, made for this very purpose.

Fig. 6.2 *Ways of Determining the True Center of Gravity of Any Building*

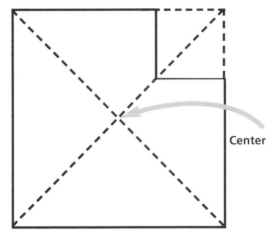

Rationalize the shape, and draw in diagonals.
Where the diagonals cross is the center.

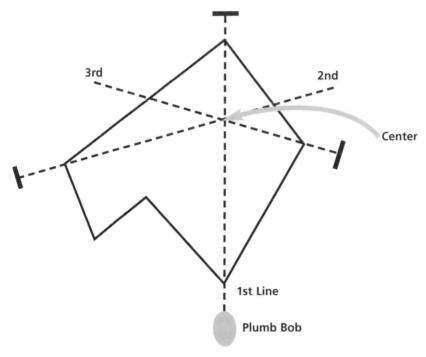

Use a plumb bob hung from each corner of an irregular shape.
The "center of gravity" is where these lines cross.

4. Mark off the 8 main sectors of the pie where the rim of the compass shows the following readings: 22.5, 67.5, 112.5, 157.5, 202.5, 247.5, 292.5, and 337.5 degrees.

   With a pencil connect these marks to the center and extend them beyond the outer walls of the building. You have created an 8-sector pie wedge division of the building. Mark each wedge in turn as follows:

337.5 to 22.5°	– N
22.5 to 67.5°	– NE
67.5 to 112.5°	– E
112.5 to 157.5°	– SE
157.5 to 202.5°	– S
202.5 to 247.5°	– SW
247.5 to 292.5°	– W
292.5 to 337.5°	– NW

   Congratulations. You have now drawn up a pie wedge feng shui division of the building in question.

5. Transfer the 3 Star numbers (which you will learn to calculate for each Palace in chapter 9) out of the conventional Lo Shu shape into each relevant pie wedge. Hence if the Stars in the North Palace of the Lo Shu are 5–3–2, then these numbers need now to be written in the pie wedge marked "N," and so on for all 8 outer sectors. The numbers in the central square of the Lo Shu should be written close to the central point.

6. Finally, you need to interpret the results of your work, which we will learn how to do in chapter 10. Now we are only concerned with the mechanics of transferring the Stars to the real world of house plans. Often, using this method, you will find that a single room is split between two, sometimes even three, of the pie wedges. Look to the predominant one when analyzing the Flying Stars of this room. However, when placing feng shui remedies in the room, remember to place them within the boundaries of this pie wedge.

Pros and Cons of the 8-sector Pie Wedge Method

Pros:
- Uses the actual orientation of the building
- Seems more realistic, and therefore more intellectually satisfying
- Marks out exact sectors
- Commonly practiced in Hong Kong

Cons:
- It is not traditional
- Does not work well with smaller properties; in fact it makes nonsense out of terrace houses or houses that are, for example, one room and a corridor wide

- Sometimes difficult to interpret
- Makes odd and often difficult shapes that sometimes divide a single room into a number of conflicting sectors
- May make analysis and placement of remedies more difficult
- Produces 8 cells rather than 9 cells, which then does not correspond exactly the 9 Flying Star Lo Shu

Fig. 6.3 *The "Pie Wedge" Technique of Dividing Up the Building*

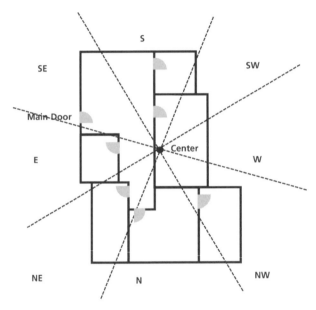

Note that although the left side of the house is the East side,
the main door falls in the SE section.

THE 9-PALACE LO SHU METHOD

This is a much more traditional, and incidentally, faster method of dividing the building in question up into 9 rectangular cells. Proceed as follows:

1. As with the previous method, you need to use a ground plan of the building drawn to scale. Use dotted lines to square up any missing corners. If there is a small protuberance such as a bay window, ignore it and use the main wall alignment.

2. Mark in the position of North (or South if you prefer), which you will have previously ascertained by using the lo p'an compass. Although it always pays to be accurate, you don't have to be quite as precise with this method as with the previous one.

Fig. 6.4 *Treatment of a House with Slightly Irregular Structure*

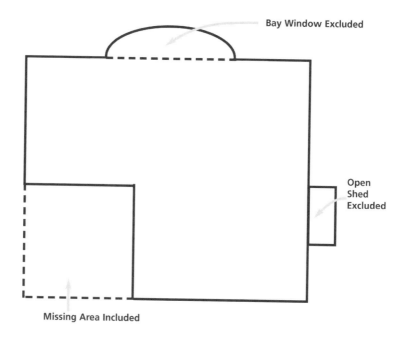

Bay Window Excluded

Open
Shed
Excluded

Missing Area Included

3. Divide the building into the by now familiar Lo Shu or tic-tac-toe format. The easiest way to do this is to divide each of the four sides of the rectangle into thirds (i.e.,
   measure the length and divide that number by three). Make two marks on each side.
   Join the opposite marks up, dividing the building neatly into 9 equally proportioned
   rectangular cells.

4. Decide if North falls in the middle of a side, or at the corner of the building. These
   are the *only* two possibilities. This is a key decision, so consider it carefully. The two
   possible formats you can have as a result of this are as shown in figure 6.5.

5. Having marked North, now mark South in the opposite cell. Add East and West. You
   will notice that in the first diagram the cardinal points correspond with the sides of the
   building; in the second the Cardinal points correspond with the corners. This is simply a reflection of the orientation of the house. Add the inter-cardinal points of NW,
   NE, SW, and SE between the relevant cardinal points as shown in figure 6.6.

6. Finally, carefully transfer the Star numbers calculated on the Lo Shu to the Lo Shu
   you have projected onto the building's floor plan. Be especially careful where the cardinal points correspond with the corners, as you will have to mentally wrench the
   directions around. It helps if you turn the floor plan so it corresponds with the Lo Shu

that you used to work out the Stars while you are making this transfer of data. Be most careful with this step.

7. Now do the analysis of each room in turn. Where one room shares two sectors, it is usual to take the Stars of the predominant sector.

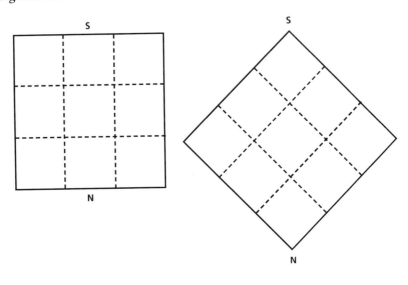

Fig. 6.5 *The 2 Possible Lo Shu Orientations in Relation to the House*

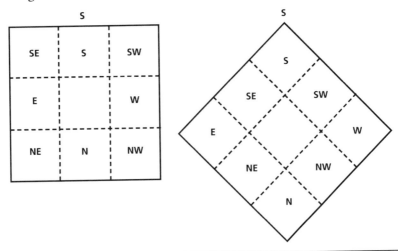

Fig. 6.6 *The Finished 9-Palace Division in Both These Cases*

Fig. 6.7 *The Finished 9-Palace Division with Period 7 Stars Inserted to Show Different Orientations*

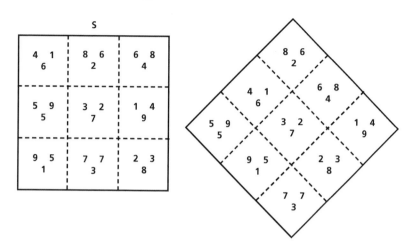

8. This procedure will usually do the trick, but there is a further refinement which I suggest you make. Where a room is 90 percent or more belonging to one cell, or where the Lo Shu division line almost coincides with a main structural wall, I suggest you move the division line *in that room only* so that it actually coincides with the wall. The room then becomes 100 percent belonging to that cell.

Don't go messing with *all* the rooms, just where it is very obvious. You will find that this will clarify your thinking and simplify your analysis enormously. The objective rationale behind this is that even if 10 percent of a room has allegiance to the adjoining cell and its Stars, the walls are more likely to condition the flow of ch'i than an arbitrary line, so that the predominant Stars should be allowed to predominate in the room in question.

9. Lastly, and rather controversially, some feng shui Masters actually modify the Lo Shu format even further in the case of smaller buildings. For example, in the case of a terrace house (or link house, as it is called in the East), there is often just one room width plus a corridor running the full length of the house. It seems more natural to divide this kind of structure into two rather than three lengthways. Consequently some feng shui Masters will divide this structure as if three of the central cells of the Lo Shu, when viewed lengthways, are missing as in figure 6.8. The objection of course is, what happens to the Stars so squeezed out? The answer is that such structures do not have as complex feng shui as a larger house.

Obviously the structure of the house must affect the real dynamics of the feng shui. We know that ch'i enters by doors and windows, and that it is blocked or guided by internal walls. It is a mistake to think that the theoretical lines we use to determine what type

Fig. 6.8 *An Abbreviated Lo Shu Applied to a Terrace or Link House*

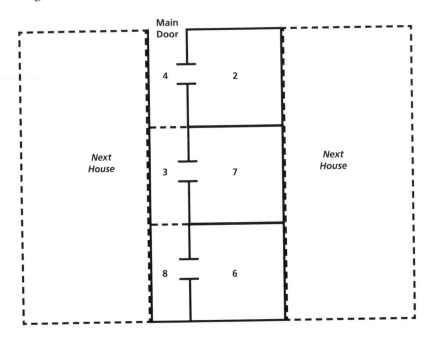

of ch'i is to be found in each room are stronger boundaries than the physical walls already present. Any practitioner will know not to make this mistake so common among armchair theorists.

Once you have identified the Stars present, take full notice of the walls and interior door opening directions, for these truly channel the ch'i. Start to analyze in the real world of the house, not just the rarefied atmosphere of paper calculations. Just because you cannot see or feel the ch'i (unless you are trained to do so) does not mean that ch'i will behave like Casper (the Friendly Ghost) and just pass through walls at will. Don't forget that in many ways ch'i is *much more concrete* than, for example, radio waves. Ch'i is guided and contained by walls and alignments.

PROS AND CONS OF THE 9-PALACE LO SHU METHOD

Pros:
- Traditional: has the weight of hundreds if not thousands of years practice behind it
- Easier and faster to do
- Makes room diagnosis easier
- Produces 9 cells rather than 8 cells, which then corresponds to the Lo Shu
- Commonly practiced in Southeast Asia and Taiwan.

Cons:

- Often the Palaces will not occupy the same extent (or volume) as they would if measured radially
- Appears to disregard precise orientation (after all, what is the use of using a compass accurate to one degree if you subsequently approximate to as much as 22.5 degrees?)

This issue is very important, as often the sector, or Palace, into which the main door falls (an important feng shui consideration) differs from one method to the other. Although we are looking primarily at Flying Star feng shui, the above considerations also apply to *pa chai*, or 8 Mansion, feng shui, where the second traditional method of division appears to work much better than a pie wedge division. Some rooms will fall into completely different Palaces, and so have completely different Stars. The only real way to test which method is "correct" is to do both analyses on the same property. Where they diverge, it will soon become obvious as to which one really reflects the current situation and problems of the occupants. I have found in practice that one method works more often than the other, but I suggest you taste and try both methods over a number of real-life examples, and I think that the correct method will become obvious by examining the case history of these buildings.

The experience of doing this little piece of detective work will be invaluable and sharpen your investigative attitude to feng shui generally. Feng shui can only benefit from such an attitude, which is the basis of all real scientific research, rather than dogma. An ounce of such real-life experience is worth a ton of theory.

This chapter has been the first truly practical chapter and has put you in touch with very real considerations dealt with on a day-to-day basis by feng shui practitioners. It is only when you have to break down a real house or an architectural plan that you begin to notice that the block drawings in many current books on feng shui do not relate at all to real-life situations. Western houses do not come conveniently divided up into nine equal squares without connecting corridors! We looked to traditional Chinese architecture to solve other apparent theoretical problems. Finally, we compared the two main methods of house division, the 8-sector pie wedge versus the traditional 9-Palace grid. I recommend that you use both these methods on at least six different houses before proceeding to the next chapter.

Chapter 7

Room-by-Room Analysis

Now that we have mastered the techniques for placing a grid over the floorplan, I want to consider in more detail the different sorts of structure. If we leave airports, bus stations, and public buildings to the experts, we are left with apartment blocks, apartments, houses, offices, and individual rooms to consider. Let us look first at individual rooms, analyzing them according to their function in the home. Here you will start to appreciate the very specific results generated by specific Star combinations.

It is useful to see what are the ideal Stars and the least desirable Stars in each room of a typical house. There may be some latitude for swapping room functions to make better use of the Stars. The following is a sort of checklist of rooms that may need analyzing.

1. ENTRANCE

This area is key to the feng shui of the whole house. The main entrance (often but not always on the Facing side of the house) is the mouth through which the house inhales its ch'i. Therefore the sort of ch'i entering the house is conditioned by the Stars at the doorway. Having good Stars at the entrance is a very good start. In fact if you had, for example, a 5-2 (bad) combination at the entrance but an 8-8 (good) or other similarly beneficial combination at another secondary entrance, it would be very beneficial to seal up the existing front entrance and use the other entrance as your new main entrance. This might be the most significant feng shui change you could make in this example.

Auspicious Period-Facing Star combinations include the three white Stars 1-white, 6-white, 8-white, and in some circumstances 4-green. Before February 2004 the Star 7-red is also good. The 9-purple Star will help enhance any of these, although some practitioners do not like to see the 9-purple at the entrance.

The worst combinations for this crucial area are of course 2-5 as well as 2-2, 5-5, and either of these activated by a 9-purple Star is a real no-no. Any of these 2-5 combinations definitely require the installation of a remedy. Even the presence of a white Star in 1-5-4 is not enough to counteract the strong and troublesome 5-yellow. If, however, the good

Earth Star 8-yellow were present, then 1-5-8 will work, even though it is heavily biased to Earth.

The 2-3 combination will provoke controversy, quarrels, and perhaps even litigation. Especially after February 2004, the 6-7 combination will attract thieves and burglars, not a good combination to have at your front door.

2. LIVING ROOM OR FAMILY ROOM AND DINING ROOM

The usual prohibition against the 5-yellow and the 2-black apply in the family room. The quarrelsome combination of 2-3 is also a no-no in the family room, for obvious reasons. The Stars 6-7 predispose toward robbery, not a good thing to have at the heart of the house in the living room.

In past times, when the threat of fire was ever present in cities of predominantly wooden houses, combinations like 9-7 or 2-7, especially with an added 9-purple Fire Star, were avoided. This is not so important now, but still a consideration, especially if you have an open hearth, which unfortunately many of us do not.

The best combinations are between the trustworthy 1-white, 6-white, 8-white, and if you have a literary bent, the 4-green, although the 4-green can also stimulate gambling and generally loose sexual behavior. A 4-8 is also said to be a good family room combination.

If we are considering a dining room, then all of the above considerations pertain. In addition the ingestion of food means that Stars to be especially excluded are the 2-black (illness) Star and its combination with the 3-jade Star, which will provoke arguments at mealtimes—not a good way to promote healthy digestion.

In these rooms, the Mountain Star should be particularly checked. When examining the micro feng shui of this room, use a smaller version of the Flying Star chart and (leaving it orientated in the same way as the macro chart over the whole house) check where furniture is placed within the room. Try to identify any good Mountain Stars with a real exterior mountain feature, or an area that has weighty furniture, or at the least an area that is peaceful and not overly aggravated by the television or stereo.

3. BEDROOMS

We spend a third of our lives in our bedrooms. The time we spend here asleep is when we are at our most vulnerable. Therefore the bedroom needs to be sited where there are good Star combinations and protected from other threats, like an adjacent and visible toilet or bathroom and other Form alignment considerations. Among the worst Star combinations to have here are the 2-black (illness) Star or the troublesome 5-yellow.

Positive combinations can include the three white stars, or the Star of the Period (7 till February 2004, thereafter the 8-white). The 9-purple is good here if accompanied by a good Star. In certain circumstances, a 4-green located in the bedroom might lead to regular sexual conquests, or unfaithfulness, whichever way you look at it. A 3-jade will not be threatening, but will tend to have a dulling effect on the sleeper. In the bedroom the Mountain Star is again the most important.

Where there are several available bedrooms, you should select the one with the best Stars as the master bedroom, not necessarily the largest.

4. KITCHEN

This is a critical room, in a sense almost as important as the entrance. Most of us living in the 21st century have forgotten the importance of the kitchen as a place to gather, a place to gossip, and a place to keep warm. In older times, the kitchen stove would often be the heat focus for the whole house. From a Chinese perspective, the preparation and eating of food is much more important to the family's nourishment and well-being than casual chomping on a Big Mac. The entrance provides the source of ch'i for the house, but the kitchen provides ch'i energy directly to the occupants in the form of food.

The Elements are at their strongest when they are real, not just symbolic. Why do you think that a fish tank is a stronger feng shui remedy than a photograph of a waterfall? Because it contains real water not just symbolic water. In the kitchen the Element of Fire is real and strongly manifested, very strongly in wood burning stoves, less so in gas stoves, and least of all in electric stoves or microwaves. However, any stove has a strong Fire energy, and with this energy you should be careful.

In the kitchen, the stove of course contributes a lot of the Element Fire, and so any kitchen combination should perhaps avoid the amplifying Fire Star 9-purple. Another bad choice for the kitchen is the sickness Star 2-black. Nobody wants to symbolically cook "sickness" into the food. In period 7, the 7-red Star should not be located in the kitchen as the Fire symbolically "melts" that Metal Star.

Those old enemies 2-black and 5-yellow should be kept out of the kitchen if possible, especially as the Fire of the stove will strengthen the Earth of both of these undesirable Stars (Fire produces Earth). A Star combination 2-3 is also not great, as it will add arguments and disharmony to the kitchen.

For the generation of strong ch'i in the kitchen, combinations including 1-white, 6-white, 8-white, and 4-green are effective. A 1-6-4 combination is very suitable for a kitchen. The combination 8-8-4 in the kitchen is by some thought to affect children badly, but I have not noticed that happening.

Symbolically, because the kitchen "puts food on the table," its Stars are also related to the career of the household breadwinner. Therefore the combinations 3-7 and 6-7 in the kitchen will tend to make it more difficult to earn a living, and hamper the career of the breadwinner.

As moving the kitchen is relatively expensive, you should look at countermeasures if the Stars in your kitchen happen not to be auspicious.

5. THE STUDY, HOME OFFICE, OR DEN

A Star that responds well to this type of environment is the 4-green star, which aids with written work or study. The other Stars suitable here depend upon how much time is spent in the study and how serious the work done there is. If you work from home and therefore earn your living from this room, then be careful to choose a room with good Stars. It is usually not a good idea to do this sort of work in the bedroom, where the functions of sleep and work are diametrically opposed to each other.

If the study is used by children for their homework, then it is important to have good Stars at work there to help improve their school grades. Academic prowess can be stimulated by Star 4-green or its good combinations 1-4, 6-4, 8-4, and 9-4. A 1-9-4 combination will also do very nicely. Less effective for academic work are 6-8 and 1-6.

The troublesome 5-yellow may encourage misdeeds at school and a shirking of homework. Argumentative combinations like 2-3 are also not suitable for the quiet concentration of study and are more than likely to provoke family rows about incomplete homework. In fact, this is a common phenomenon in children working at their homework in a 2-3 room.

If the study is used for business, then the 4 Star combinations will do nicely. If the study is in the NW sector of the house, this should also be auspicious, according to 8 Mansion feng shui. To activate this Earth sector with Earth Star 8-white will be very effective. You should not have the other Earth Stars, 2-black or 5-yellow, located here though.

Some practitioners suggest that 2-black Star is okay in a NW sector study if with the 8-white Earth Star, but not without its modifying influence. But be very careful of the 2-black as it can lead to illness, and illness of a business can lead to bankruptcy.

6. The Wet Rooms: Bathroom, Washroom, and Toilet Room

Strangely enough these are good places to have bad Stars. So think yourself lucky if the old 5-yellow or 2-black fly into one of these rooms. Why is that lucky? Well, all wet rooms involve the draining of water, which also drains the adverse ch'i of these Stars. Conversely, if you have good Stars in a wet room, then they are wasted.

7. Box-Rooms, Closets, Spare Bedroom, Utility Room, and Integral Garage

Although these rooms are usually not large, they are important in a negative way. If you have normally damaging combinations involving, say, the 5-yellow or 2-black Star, these are another good place to have them. Combinations of 5-9 and 2-9 are best suppressed with inactivity, so these are great rooms for such combinations. If the ch'i represented by these Stars is not disturbed often, then their malefic effect on your life will also not be stirred up.

The garage is a special case because although the room is not lived in, a bad Star here will be stirred up to make trouble by the regular arrival and departure of a motor vehicle. If however the garage is mostly used as a workroom, then it's okay for these bad Stars, but do watch out for the possibility of DIY accidents, especially with power tools, under such circumstances.

8. Hallways and Stairways

Hallways and stairways are conceptually the same from a feng shui point of view, as they both convey ch'i from the front door to the various rooms of the house. They are the ch'i conduits of any building. The only difference is that stairways have a gradient, and will therefore cause the ch'i to flow faster, and therefore more dangerously, as fast flowing ch'i easily changes to cutting ch'i.

Therefore perhaps the most important thing here is to check out what is at the bottom of such stairways, where the ch'i should ideally be slowed down with a windchime. It is desirable for these spaces to have good Stars, but as nobody actually lives in hallways or on stairways, the Star combinations in these spaces are not supercritical. It is a fallacy to think that the influence of Stars in the hallway will actively taint the ch'i of adjacent rooms.

That about sums up all of the typical rooms you will find in the average home. Obviously there are other priorities in an office or commercial building.

9. OFFICES

Key spaces in an office are the CEO's office and the boardroom where decisions crucial to the company are made. Inside both these rooms, the positioning particularly of the CEO's chair has to be carefully calculated. In both these areas plus the entrance areas there is an opportunity to position wealth-attracting aquariums. In fact, Bloomberg's offices in Finsbury Square, London, are a classic example of properly deployed aquariums.

To summarize this we see how best to utilize the locations into which the Stars fall.

1-white. This is a good Star for almost all activities. Its location is a good place to put bedrooms, living rooms, and kitchens.

2-black. This Star is not good for dining rooms, kitchens, or bedrooms (as it predisposes to sickness especially when it is Untimely).

3-jade. A bad location, tending to provoke arguments, and therefore not good in family or living rooms.

4-green. Try not to use the location of this Star for a dining room or family room. If well-aspected it can bring academic achievement and therefore can be used in a study or office.

5-yellow. This is undoubtedly the most troublesome Star. Try not to use this location for a bedroom, kitchen, or study. Heavy furniture that is not often used can beneficially "weight down" this area.

This area can have some interesting negative uses, for example if you can manage to put an adversary into this room position during discussions, or into an office afflicted by this Star, the negative effect of the Star may then be turned to your advantage.

6-white. A good Star, good for activity, bedrooms, dining areas, living rooms, workrooms. This Star is also supported by the Left and Right Assistants (Stars 8 and 9), with which it is (astronomically) linked.

7-red. This Star is inauspicious, except when it is timely (for example from 1984 till February 2004). Outside of this Period, try never to use its area for any important activity like a kitchen, dining room, master bedroom, or even a garage. Except when it is timely, try to use the area as a store room or closet.

8-white. As we have seen, the Left and Right Assistants are Stars that are not immediately physically identifiable in the Heavens. 8-white is generally considered good. It is therefore a beneficial location for all actively used rooms. Being Earth it helps with Earth-related tasks, such as real estate.

9-purple. This Star adapts to its company, be it bad or good. So it is okay wherever it is in good company, but not if it isn't.

MULTISTORY PROPERTIES AND APARTMENTS

In the case of a multistory building, you must use the Lo Shu on each floor in turn, regardless of which method of placement you use. Where the upper floors are of smaller extent than the ground floor, I suggest that you do not shrink the Lo Shu to fit, but just use that part of the ground floor Lo Shu that corresponds to the built portion of the upper floor. Multistory feng shui is quite complex and also relies on ascribing a different Element to each floor in sequence as you rise through the building.

Feng shui in many buildings in Southeast Asia is complicated by the frequent omission of floor number 4, and sometimes also of floors 14, 24, and so on. This is because, for Cantonese speakers, the word for "4" and for "death," *si*, sounds very similar. Consequently, floor 4 is even less rentable than, say, floor 13 in a U.S. or European complex.

Apartments are in a sense part of a multistory building. The question always arises, how do you treat facing direction or door direction for an apartment? To answer this you have to stand back and consider that what we are doing here is charting the flow and influence of ch'i circulating through a building. Whether the building is occupied by one family, an extended multigenerational family, or a number of different and totally unrelated families is irrelevant to the flow of ch'i. Ch'i will not stop to ask if a wall is a legal boundary between two unrelated families, or just a partition between a kitchen and a dining room within the same family apartment.

To quote Master Shen Chu Reng, "If a house is divided into rooms with private doors, then judge the (feng shui) luck from the doors. But if the house has through rooms, then judge it as one house (not two)." In other words, if the building has a common entrance and connecting halls, then the feng shui should be judged based on this main entrance. If however the structure is a terrace or link house ("with private doors"), then the feng shui is judged separately for each house, as they do not have a common main entrance.

Consequently the rule is that main door and facing direction of an apartment block affects every single apartment in that building. These are often the same in apartment blocks and are determined by the whole building's orientation, not that of the individual apartment. Certainly the facing of individual apartment doors within the block has a part to play in micro feng shui diagnosis, but the main orientation is that of the "mouth of ch'i" or the main block entrance way. The same rule applies to office blocks.

Having said that, there are macro and micro applications of feng shui rules. Always proceed from the largest and most powerful influence to the smallest and least significant influence. First look at the Lo Shu over the whole apartment building. Check the whole building Flying Stars to help choose the best apartment in the block.

Fig. 7.1 *The Use of the Lo Shu at the Macro Level (Apartment Building), Home Level (Apartment), and Micro Level (Room)*

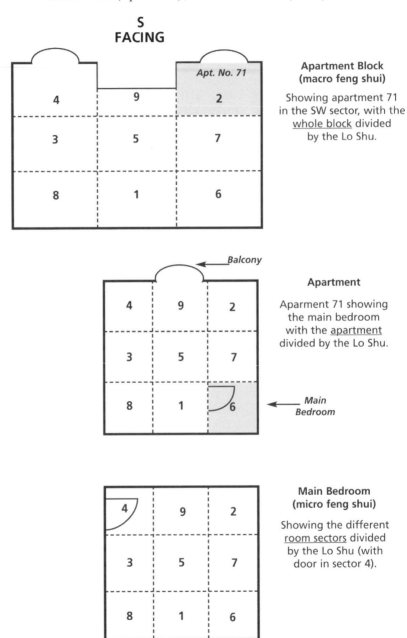

S
FACING

Apartment Block (macro feng shui)

Showing apartment 71 in the SW sector, with the whole block divided by the Lo Shu.

Apartment

Aparment 71 showing the main bedroom with the apartment divided by the Lo Shu.

Main Bedroom (micro feng shui)

Showing the different room sectors divided by the Lo Shu (with door in sector 4).

Take note of the building's orientation first, then look at the position of the apartment in the whole building, then do the Flying Stars for the individual apartment, then examine the micro feng shui of individual rooms, but in each case keep the Lo Shu orientation the same at each level of analysis.

There is a case for examining the flow of ch'i in relation to the individual door direction of each room, as BHS feng shui does, but it is not a strong one, and the results are much weaker than the macro feng shui analysis.

SMALL *T'AI CHI* OR MICRO FENG SHUI

Analyzing the Flying Star of the whole building or apartment by placing the Lo Shu over the building to determine the best rooms for particular functions is called working with the big *t'ai chi*. The same principles can also be applied to individual rooms. This process is sometimes called working with the small t'ai chi. When the Lo Shu is put over just one room, make sure you continue to orient it the same way. In other words, the South Palace must still point in the direction of actual South, and so on.

The purpose of placing the Lo Shu over an individual room is to check the positioning of the room's door and of individual pieces of furniture in that room.

POSITIONING OF THE ROOM DOOR

Still on a micro level, check the room's door. Examine the Flying Stars directly adjacent to the inside of the door. If these Flying Stars happen to be a particularly bad combination, such as 5-yellow and 2-black, and if you have the option, relocate the door. In most cases this will only be viable if you are working with an architect before a structure is built. The effect of bad Stars at the entrance of a room will be noticeable, but it is not as crucial as the macro feng shui of the building or apartment.

POSITIONING OF FURNITURE

The second micro feng shui consideration is the placement of furniture within the room. Here you have much more scope to move furniture from an inauspicious location to an auspicious one. The pieces of furniture whose location you should particularly check are:

1. the bed location in each bedroom, but particularly the bed in the master bedroom
2. the desk in the study or office
3. the stove in the kitchen.

Also important are the locations of the dining room table and its chairs and your favorite TV viewing chair.

All of these items are subject to Form School feng shui, and alignment rules apply that have been covered in a lot more detail in many other books on feng shui. After the best location has been determined in relation to doors, windows, and other alignments, briefly check the Flying Star feng shui by placing the micro Lo Shu over just the room.

Fig. 7.2 *Room with a Micro Lo Shu Placed over It*

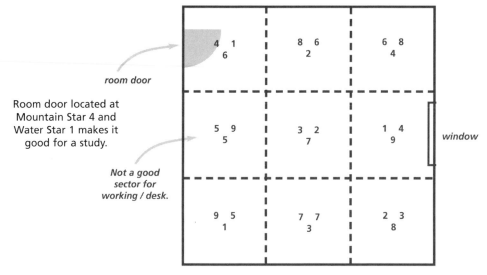

room door

Room door located at
Mountain Star 4 and
Water Star 1 makes it
good for a study.

*Not a good
sector for
working / desk.*

window

THE PLACEMENT OF THE BED WITHIN THE BEDROOM

The location of the bed within the room is a very important feng shui consideration. You should observe the following rules until you get as near as perfect a placement as you can. Although many of these rules are concerned with Form and alignment, not Flying Star, they are well worth repeating here so that you have a complete picture when trying to organize the placement of the bed.

The most important Form rules for bed alignment are:

- Do not locate the bed under an overhead beam (or a change of level in the ceiling) as this will cause an uncomfortable ch'i pressure on the sleepers during the night when they are at their most vulnerable, with the potential for illness.
- Don't position the bed so that its feet point out the door.
- Do place it where you can see all of the room when sitting in it.
- Don't position it so that you can see your reflection in a mirror while sitting in it.
- Don't position it so that you are aligned with the door opening into an en suite bathroom.
- Make sure that the bedhead is supported by a wall, and does not back onto a window.
- Don't put the bedhead under an overhanging built-in cupboard.

Once you have checked the Form rules for all of the above, there probably won't be many potential remaining locations. At this level Form takes precedence. With the locations that are left, check the micro Flying Star chart for the best Flying Star locations. Look especially at the Mountain Star (see next chapter) and try for a positive one, 1-

white, 6-white, 8-white, or 4-green are good, plus any timely Stars such as 7-red (till February 2004). Sometimes poor Stars at the entrance of the room can be cancelled out by good Stars at the bed location.

I think that the positioning of items like the bed and the stove inside a room illustrate more than anything that feng shui is the art of the compromise. Not that feng shui theory is a compromise, but that its practice entails getting the best out of a set of conflicting priorities, like anything in life.

Obviously you should try strenuously to avoid 5-2 combinations for bed locations, particularly if they are reinforced by a 9-purple Star. A 2-3 combination will make for lots of bedtime arguments. A 4-green might promote sexual activity.

The Placement of the Study Desk

In the study, the placement of the desk is very important. First, there are the usual alignment rules which must be observed. These include orientating the desk so that the person sitting at it has plenty of back support. This means that the student should not sit with her/his back to the door or a window, but with their back preferably supported by a solid wall. Also the desk seat position must be such as to be able to command the room and immediately see anyone entering it. Do not locate the desk under a beam or level change in the ceiling, as this will generate a ch'i pressure that is not conducive to concentration and may even provoke regular headaches. For 8 Mansion feng shui reasons, the desk will be well-positioned if it is in the NE sector of the room.

Having accommodated those rules, let us turn to Flying Star considerations. To do this you must again put a micro version of the house Flying Star chart over just this room (oriented in exactly the same way as for the whole house). The same stars as apply to the whole study also have relevance at the micro level. For example, combinations of 4-green, the study Star, with one of the three good white Stars will be an auspicious combination.

To illustrate this, I am at present writing this chapter in a 8-8-4 room, suggesting future wealth from intellectual effort. On a micro level, I am in the same Palace of the room as of the whole house (8-8-4 again), and incidentally facing in my sheng ch'i position. This is the sort of configuration to be aimed at. The Earth nature of the two 8-white Stars also help to materialize thoughts in an Earthly written form. The 8-4 combination might have also be expected to produce a few good real estate investment ideas!

The Placement of the Stove within the Kitchen

The placement of the stove is one of trickiest feng shui placement jobs and one of the most important. There are many rules governing the placement of facilities in the kitchen, particularly the placement of the stove, so that its "fire mouth" is pointed in a favorable direction.

Consider just the kitchen itself on a micro level. Place the micro Lo Shu grid over the kitchen (oriented in the same way as the grid covering the whole building). Using what you know about Stars that are desirable or undesirable for the kitchen as a whole (from the previous section), try and work out a suitable position for the stove. Sometimes this position will be impractical, if for example the doorway or a corner position is indicated, and so you might have to settle for second best.

Watch also that you don't "burn" the Prominent Stars of the period. By this I mean that if the Period is 4, then make sure that the stove is *not* located (on the micro Flying Star chart) under the Star 4. It is not acceptable to place the stove under the 5-yellow Star as the Fire will feed the Earth of this Star and cause even more trouble.

Having found a site for the stove in the kitchen, you are not yet finished. The next consideration is which way the "fire mouth" or "fire gate" faces. There is a lot of twaddle written about this. The "fire mouth" was originally the point where the wood was put into the stove and from which heat and flames escaped. There is a modern tendency to suggest that as the wood is considered as fuel, therefore in the case of an electric stove the fuel source must be the fire mouth. The result of this line of thinking is that some practitioners concern themselves about the direction from which the electrical "fuel" comes, in other words the direction in which the electric socket points. This is a misconception. The point of the stove is that it produces heat or Fire. Anyone who has slaved over a hot oven knows precisely where the fire mouth is: the oven door, not the innocuous (and cold) electric power socket.

The traditional rules that concern the fire mouth are as follows. The Fire mouth should preferably not point out the door of the kitchen. A stove *can* be built facing directions of sheng (birth/growth), wang (prosperity), *shuai* (decline), or ssu (dead) ch'i of the house. But ideally you should avoid sheng (birth/growth) and wang (prosperity) ch'i directions. The cooker/stove's Fire mouth (*huo men*), facing 1-white Star, which is Water, is okay. The Fire mouth can also face 3-green or 4-green (which are both Wood breeding Fire), and all these are auspicious cooking directions. The fire mouth facing 8-white has Fire breeding Earth; and this is only fairly auspicious. The Fire mouth facing 9-purple is also fairly auspicious—here, Fire is reinforcing fire, and this might be too strong. The main thing to note is that, with the 9-purple Flying Star, you must avoid too much Fire ch'i, which may lead to Fire disasters.

It is not suitable to have the Fire mouth facing the 6-white or 7-red Stars, because these are both Metal Stars and Fire ch'i damages Metal. The 2-black and 5-yellow Stars are even more unsuitable. This is because the 2-black Star is a symbol of illness and the 5-yellow also implies diseases.

THE KITCHEN GOD, TSAO CHUN

One of the most popular gods in late imperial China, and even today, is Tsao Chun (also spelled *Zao Jun*) the kitchen god. Although he has nothing directly to do with the Flying Stars, he symbolizes not just the kitchen but also the family and its deeds and misdeeds for the year. This in turn is supposed to affect the family's luck. His presence defines a nuclear family. The fastest way to determine how many separate traditional Chinese families live in a sprawling multiple-occupancy building is to count the number of Tsao Chuns pasted up.

At the end of each annual cycle Tsao Chun was supposed to report the family's deeds and misdeeds to Heaven. His image was taken down and burned at the end of the year (thus sending him on his way to Heaven) and a new one put up for the beginning of the new year: the positioning being subject to strict feng shui rules.

The point of introducing Tsao Chun is to point up the centrality of the kitchen for the traditional family, and thereby stress the feng shui importance of the kitchen. The fact that illustrations of Tsao Chun often show him with a Treasure Urn in front of him filled with gold ingots, pearls, jade, and silver confirms the feng shui identification of the kitchen as a place that also affects the wealth of the household. Tsao Chun is sometimes called the "Overseer of Destiny of the Eastern Hall." As an overseer of destiny he provides a direct link (an umbilical cord if you like) between the feng shui of Earth and the destiny of Heaven.

Other placement rules in the kitchen depend upon straightforward Element conflicts. It is often said that Water appliances should not confront or abut Fire appliances. If they do, then try to insert something Wood between them, as Water feeds Wood which in turn feeds Fire. Water can work with Fire, conceptually to produce steam, but at a simplistic level these two Elements should not directly confront each other.

Another placement rule that is important in the kitchen is that the center of this room or t'ai chi should not be occupied, so that the island preparation area so beloved of today's cooks is a definite no-no.

In this chapter we have acquired an understanding of how particular Flying Stars influence particular functions and rooms within the house. We also looked at how apartments relate to apartment blocks. Finally we looked at the micro-feng shui of individual rooms.

In chapter 9 we will "fly the Stars" and find out which Stars are actually present in the rooms of our own house. But before that, in Chapter 8, we need to look outward at the area surrounding the house, and come to terms with the concepts associated with Mountain and Water. Remember that however good we might become at doing these calculations on floorplans and on paper, the essence of feng shui is still how ch'i is channelled in the physical world. So let us first look at the very physical feng shui of the world outside the house.

Chapter 8

Landscape Effects

When you draw up Flying Star charts, each square of the Lo Shu is occupied by 3 Stars: a Period Star (derived from the Period in which the house was built), a Water Star, and a Mountain Star. In this chapter we look at what is meant by a Water Star and a Mountain Star, in terms of physical landscape.

Remember that feng shui originates from analyzing the energies inherent in the landscape, so it is important to see how the Flying Stars interact with the actual physical surroundings. In fact a lot of the rules and ideas that help relate the Flying Star chart to the external world come from the San He School of feng shui.

If you think symbolically for a moment, it is the stable Mountain of good health, good relationships, a loving and supportive family, from which flows the Water of wealth, just as physical rivers flow from the springs found high up in physical mountains. This saying encapsulates the reason why Mountain Stars equate with health, relationship, and family, while Water Stars equate with wealth.

However, this relationship is definitely more than just symbolic, as the pooling of water in the right place really does also concentrate the ch'i, which in turn contributes in a more than psychological way to the generation of wealth.

So how do you define Mountain and Water at a micro level in the building or home? The obvious example is that a room that opens on to a vista that includes a pond or lake might be characterized as a Water room. A room that looks out onto a mountain or indeed just a tall building may be characterized as a Mountain room. So do not just bury your head in charts and calculations. Go outside and look around, really look, and take notes of what you see, first in the foreground and then in the background. Feng shui is nothing if not an observational science. Just as perspective shows closer features as larger, so closer mountains or bodies of water are more powerful than distant ones.

It is also important to look *into* each room to see if it has the interior physical characteristics of either Water or Mountain. The most obvious examples of this is a room with a lower floor level than the rest of the house, or a room with a large fish tank, both of which should be seen as a Water room.

Using this external evaluation, check how Water and Mountain affect each other and the Stars of the room. A strong Water Star in a real Mountain type location is *not* beneficial, neither is a strong Mountain Star in a real Water area. Such a configuration is often referred in Chinese Flying Star manuals as "Mountain falls into Water," and is not a good configuration. The interpretation of a Water or a Mountain location does not have to be totally literal. A Mountain location in a room might simply be indicated by the presence of lots of heavy furniture, while a Water location might simply be a lower or open area.

EXTENDED MEANING OF MOUNTAIN AND WATER

The extended meanings of Mountain and Water (ranging from the macro environment to the micro) are as shown in table 8.1.

Table 8.1: *The Many Interpretations of Mountain and Water*

Mountain governing people	Water governing wealth
Country/real:	
Mountain chains	the sea
Mountains	rivers & lakes
Hills	streams
Raised earth mounds	pools
Urban/real:	
Buildings	roads and pathways
Walls	ponds
Rock gardens	swimming pools
Conceptual/Symbolic:	
Higher ground	lower ground
Quiet area	busy area
Yin area	yang area

Any of these structures in the first column of the table can and will activate the Mountain Stars. Any in the second column will activate Water Stars. The strongest activation will be derived from country or real Mountain/Water Structures. Significant but less of an activation will come from the urban structures, and the conceptual or symbolic structures will be less effective still. The most important Mountain Star to support in any chart is the Prominent Mountain Star, in other words the Mountain Star with the same number as the current Period.

Water structures will beneficially activate Water Stars and Mountain structures will beneficially activate Mountain Stars. However, if you cross match these so that Water Stars correspond to Mountain structures or so that Mountain Stars correspond to Water structures, not only will the Stars be neutralized but they may even manifest some of their opposite nature. This piece of information can be turned to your benefit: bad Stars can be muted by the placement of opposite real structures adjacent to them.

Ideally we want the auspicious Mountain Stars and the inauspicious Water Stars to be placed adjacent to a real mountain. We also want the auspicious Water Stars and inauspicious Mountain Stars to be placed ideally near real Water features.

One point that is often forgotten is that a beautiful Mountain/Water structure will be more effective and positive than one that is less so, so in changing the landscape gardening around a building, strive for elegance and beauty. Many students forget that these things are still important and wrongly think that delivering a pile of earth off the back of a dump truck is all they need to do to create a Mountain structure. Anyone who has whiled away hours in Classical Chinese gardens, such as those at Suchow, will know that this is far from an adequate response to the perceived pattern of Flying Stars. The new mountain needs to be coaxed into integrating with the landscape and becoming a true tributary of the right kind of ch'i to the adjacent building.

Throughout your studies of feng shui you should remember that basic Form School feng shui is more powerful than the Stars or other numerical formula. Feng shui, after all, is the study of ch'i flow through the physical environment (or Earth) conditioned by the influences of Heaven and of Man. You might also have noted from the above table 8.1, that Water features are yang (active and bright) while Mountain features are yin (cold and dark and still). Don't be led into the mistake of assuming that water is yin because it is yielding. Over time it is the mountains that yield to and are worn down by water.

Consequently large Earth features like lakes or mountains condition ch'i flow on a large scale, much more so than the shade of blue on the North wall of Mrs. Smith's bedroom, for example. Feng shui is about balance, and I might add, also a sense of proportion. The physical surroundings of any site are proportionately much larger and potentially more powerful than a window or mirror in a cottage.

But, you might say, it's the ch'i flow in that cottage that is most interesting to its occupant. This is true, and therefore we come to a very important rule of Flying Stars feng shui: *The conditions and luck settings determined by the Flying Stars are only confirmed or triggered by Form, or the support or lack of it, in a corresponding physical feature.*

For example, an 8 Water Star in the facing Palace is a good thing to have for wealth luck in Period 7 or 8. But an 8 Water Star in this Palace is only really effective if *outside* the facing Palace there is also a Water feature, particularly if it's real water. If it is blocked by a mountain, then it is ineffective.

In urban and suburban areas, neighboring buildings and walls adequately take the place of mountains, and roads and lower ground can take the place of water. Of course the real thing is always better!

THE MOUNTAIN FORMS OF THE 9 FLYING STARS

Each of the 9 Flying Stars has an associated mountain form whose shape links it with that particular Flying Star. There are four levels of support by a physical mountain of an auspicious Mountain Star:

1. Obviously, a Mountain Star is supported if there is a physical mountain in its sector.

2. However, it is much better if the shape of the physical mountain is of the same (or a supportive) Element.

3. If the physical mountain is in the shape of the particular Flying Star, then this very much increases the power of its influence.

4. Finally, if the physical mountain exactly corresponds visually to the Mountain Star in the chart, then its force is almost irresistible.

You need to be aware of the mountain shapes corresponding to each of the 9 Flying Star so that you will be able to recognize them in the field.

To correctly identify the mountains, observe them carefully. In many cases the mountain will not exactly conform with one of the archetypal shapes shown in table 8.2. If that is the case then you should look for other Element indicators. For example, in an ambiguous case, outcrops of rounded, metallic-looking rocks on the sides of the mountain might predispose you to classifying it as a Metal Mountain and therefore as supportive of the 6-white or 7-red Star (*Wu ch'u or P'o chun*).

Very knotted and winding hills might be seen as either Star 4-green (Wen ch'u) or Star 9-purple (Yu pi). If there are several rows of hills, one behind another, then it is more likely to be 9-purple (Yu pi). Structures like Ayres Rock in central Australia would qualify as a Metal Star 6-white (Wu ch'u) mountain, and mesa or butte-shaped plateaus would qualify as mountains of the Star 2-black (Chu men).

(See appendix 5 for more details on mountain forms and appendix 10 for a chart of water forms.)

The power of external landforms should not be underestimated in their ability to either trigger or cancel the Stars in the chart. This is one of the reasons why authentic feng shui can never be done just sitting at a desk with a plan. The feng shui Master must go on site, in just the same way that an architect must also check the lay of the land before setting pen to paper.

Now that we have considered what exactly a Mountain or a Water Star is, and how they are affected by the surrounding landscape, it is time to move on to drawing up Flying Star charts.

Table 8.2: *The 9 Flying Stars with Their Physical Mountain Shapes and Corresponding 5 Elements (Earthly or External Arrangement)*

Star	Chinese Name	Shape	Meaning	External Element	Planet	Description
1-white	貪 狼 *T'an-lang*		Covetous Wolf	Wood	Jupiter	Rounded with a knoll or prominence somewhere along its top. Lucky when symmetrically formed, but unlucky when lopsided.
2-black	巨 門 *Chu-men*		Great Door/ Gate	Wood	Jupiter	Steep-sided or plateau-like
3-green	祿 存 *Lu-ts'un*		Rank (Salary) Preserved	Earth	Saturn	Flatish topped hill with 3, 4, or 5 outcrops (called "toes"), but it some times takes other shapes. It allows men to reach low-ranking offices but it can be slightly malignant.
4-jade	文 曲 *Wen-ch'u*		Civil Career ("Windings")	Water	Mercury	Looking down from an aerial perspective, this mountain is irregularly formed with windings and twists.
5-yellow	廉 真 *Lien-chien*		Honesty, Purity, Uprightness	Fire	Mars	Sharp, jaged, with a single or multiple peaks
6-white	武 曲 *Wu-ch'u*		Military Career ("Windings")	Metal	Venus	Evenly domed or semi-circular without sharp peaks
7-red	破 平 *P'o-chun*		Broken Army	Metal	Venus	Multiple peaks (but more rounded than the 5-yellow Star mountain), with incursion by valleys
8-white	左 輔 *Tso-fu*		Left Assistant	Earth	Saturn (also the Sun)	Mountain with two rounded peaks
9-purple	右 弼 *Yu-pi*		Right Assistant	Water	Mercury (also the Moon)	Twisted mountains, often with several layers, divided by valleys

Chapter 9

Flying the Stars

Now we come to the interesting part, the core of this book. We looked at what the 9 Flying Stars are, their correspondences, and how they relate to different time periods. We also looked at the meaning of each Star and how it relates to the real world. Now we look at how these energies enter the home or office by the Facing and Sitting directions of the building, and how they then move around inside the home or office, according to a specific pattern.

We need to see how the Stars combine together in specific parts of the house to give very specific readings for these locations. Finally, in chapter 15, we consider what changes we need to make to the Elements to boost or diminish the effect of these Stars and so improve the luck of the people living there.

THE 9 PALACES

The location of the 9 Flying Stars is usually plotted in any building on the 9-cell Lo Shu diagram (see chapter 1). The normal, or base, Lo Shu has the number 5 in the middle. The Star occupying this central position changes every 20 years, and the other Stars move around to accommodate this. Each of the 9 cells of the Lo Shu is called a Palace. It is usual to refer to these cells, or Palaces, by the trigram that rules them, so you should speak, for example, of the K'un Palace or the Ch'ien Palace. To make things simpler we will in this book instead refer to the Palaces simply by their compass direction, as this is easier to grasp. In the case of the above examples, instead of referring to the Ch'ien Palace we call it the NW Palace. Instead of referring to the K'un Palace we will call it the SW Palace.

SE Hsun Palace 4	S Li Palace 9	SW K'un Palace 2
E Chen Palace 3	CENTER Central Palace 5	W Tui Palace 7
NE Ken Palace 8	N K'an Palace 1	NW Ch'ien Palace 6

THE PATHWAY OF THE STARS

Put simply, the nine Flying Stars are ch'i energy configurations that move from location to location inside a building, changing position over time in a complex dance. The dance actually has a pattern, a sort of step sequence chart, which we will come to when we "fly the Stars."

If you trace your fingers over the squares of this Lo Shu, starting with the Palace containing 1 and ending up at 9, you will have traced out the pathway of the Stars, the pattern of movement that is used in all Flying Star feng shui. This is the route that the Stars fly as they move from one Palace of the Lo Shu to another over time. These numbers fly from square to square as the 20-year Periods, the years, the months, and even the days, change.

This is the basis of time dimension feng shui, for luck changes as time passes, as we all know instinctively. Each month has a different Flying Star, each year has a different Flying Star, and most importantly each 20-year luck Period has its own Flying Star.

The yearly cycles are tied to the Chinese solar calendar, which commences on February 4/5 each year. It is not, as some writers suggest, the beginning of the Chinese lunar calendar, whose date fluctuates from year to year, between mid-January and mid-February. Incidentally, if you mistakenly use the Chinese lunar calendar, then you are stuck every few years with a 13-month lunar year, which completely throws out the monthly Flying Stars year-to-year sequence.

Fig. 9.2 *The Pathway of the Stars Superimposed on the Lo Shu*

4	9	2
3	5	7
8	1	6

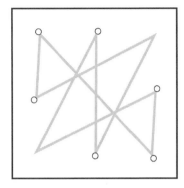

Remember that the change point for the next Period is February 4, 2004. At this point the ruling lucky Star changes from 7 to 8. You should therefore make sure that at the latest, you recalculate your 20-year Period Flying Star feng shui on or before this date. It will be a time of great activity for feng shui Masters, as they struggle to keep up with client demands for the new Period!

THE FLYING STARS IN THE LO SHU SQUARE

All Flying Star feng shui charts are worked out on the Lo Shu square. Added to the Lo Shu is the zigzag Pathway of the Stars that shows the sequence or the pathway on which the Stars fly.

Fig. 9.3 *Basic Lo Shu Diagram*

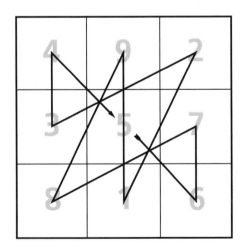

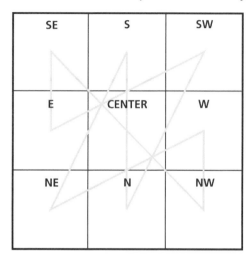

The Basic Lo Shu is the one we are familiar with. It is only one of nine different number arrangements, generated by moving around or flying these numbers from Palace to Palace (or if you like, cell to cell). Each arrangement is easily identified by the number located in its center Palace. The normal or base Lo Shu has 5 in its center Palace. Each arrangement belongs to a different time Period. With Flying Star feng shui we will work with all nine different arrangements.

Figure 9.4 shows the Basic Lo Shu.

We can also look at this square with just the 8 compass directions shown. It is the diagram shown in figure 9.4 that will be a useful template for all your Flying Star calculations.

We also must consider time, as we saw in chapter 2. The time Element is shown by the Period Star or Time Star, which is worked out using table 2.5. This table gives a Period number for every 20-year Period. This number is sometimes called the Earth Base number, because when the house is built it is thought that the act of building encapsulates the Earth energies of that Period or Time into the structure. The precise date is the time the ridgepole or roof is put on. At this point Heaven ch'i and Earth ch'i are locked together in a new environment for Human ch'i. After all, feng shui is about the way our Human ch'i is affected by our surrounding Heaven and Earth ch'i.

Of course, with Chinese traditional buildings it is a little different because after the basement and floor has been established, the main roof supports are put in place, and then the roof put on. At that point the walls (which are seldom load bearing) are filled in. If a building has been renovated subsequently (to the degree that the roof was replaced) then the Period number moves forward to the time of this replacement.

I recently did the feng shui on a château that had originally been built in 1720, but had lost part of its roof in the 1999 gales that swept through France. Because this damage was extensive, and the roof was partly replaced, I chose to re-base the Period date of this ancient château from Period 2 to Period 7 (1984–2004). However, renovations without at least partial roof replacement don't count.

To check the building date of a building, you might have to check the title deeds, the local council/municipal records, or even local history books if the building is old enough. You only need to get the right 20-year period, but be particularly careful if the building was built close to one of the period boundaries.

With ancient Chinese homes, quite often the same family would occupy the same building (albeit adding on new wings) for a number of generations, thus the original building Period number stays valid. The rapid buying and selling of houses that occurs now in the Western world is a relatively new phenomenon. There has therefore sprung up a variation on the traditional view, which is that the Period date should be based on the occupation date by the current family. The supporters of this theory point to the fact that although Heaven and Earth ch'i are locked together at the point the roof is put on, Human ch'i only comes into play when the house is occupied. Indeed you could go further and ask what is the relevance (if any) of the previous occupant's ch'i.

This is all very convenient, because given our frequency of moving these days, most people will have moved into their current house since 1984, or during Period 7. This has resulted in some authors *only* considering Period 7 and Period 8, which is of little use to those who wish to use the construction date as their Earth Base Period number, or to those of us who moved into our current property before 1984! In this book, I provide tables for every Period. I focus on the February 2004 changeover from Period 7 to Period 8, not in terms of construction Period number, but in terms of the change in the nature (and timeliness) of the contained Stars that will occur on that date.

That's enough background. Are we ready to start? Let's fly the Stars!

FLYING THE STARS

When you "fly the Stars" you insert them in order around the squares of the Lo Shu. This order always begins with the center square Star number. You fly the Stars in a positive direction by inserting Star numbers sequentially in the following order: Center, NW, W, NE, S, N, SW, E, SE. After you insert a 9, the next number will be 1, not 10. You fly the Stars in a negative direction by inserting Star numbers in the same order *but in a descending sequence*: 9, 8, 7, 6, 5, 4, 3, 2, 1.

FULL METHOD

For those of you who want to be able to calculate Flying Star charts without looking up the tables in appendix 1, I give the full method below. If, however, you are happy to use the shortcut method, then simply go to page 107. This is a little like modern books on the *I Ching* showing you how to select a hexagram by throwing 3 coins, when in fact the real ancient Chinese method of consulting the *I Ching* uses a bunch of yarrow stalks and takes considerably longer. Using the Flying Star tables is the equivalent of throwing the 3 coins. The equivalent of using the yarrow sticks is the following Full Method. It appears fiendishly complicated the first time around, but as you practice, it suddenly becomes clear.

The sequence of actions required to draw up a Flying Star chart using the Full Method is as follows:

1. Start with a blank Lo Shu showing just the 9 Palaces with the 8 compass directions marked in. (See figure 9.4)

Insert Period Star:
2. Determine the date of construction and hence the building's construction Period number from table 2.5. Put the Period number in the middle of the center square.

3. Fly the Period Star (always) in a positive direction, using the sequence Center, NW, W, NE, S, N, SW, E, SE. In other words, put in the remaining numbers (i.e., if 7 was the Period number at the center, put 8 in NW, then 9 in W, then 1 in NE, and so on).

Determine the Facing and Sitting directions:
4. Mark the Facing direction on the chart. Take the number in the box of the Facing direction. This is the Facing Star. Put this number in the Center square, above and to the *right* of the central Period Star.

5. Mark the Sitting direction on the chart. (It must be directly opposite the Facing direction.) Take the number in the box of the Sitting direction. This is the Sitting Star. Put this number in the Center square, above and to the *left* of the central Period Star.

Determine the Polarity (yin and yang direction):
6. Determine if the Sitting and Facing Stars fly in a yin (negative) or yang (positive) direction. Let's do this first with the Sitting Star:

7. If the number of the Sitting Star is odd (yang), then the flying directions are yang, yin, yin. If, however, this Star number is even (yin), then the flying directions are yin, yang, yang. (For example, 2 is even (yin). Therefore, its flying directions are yin, yang, yang.)
    Why are there 3 directions? Because the first is for a sub-sector 1 Star, the second is for a sub-sector 2 Star, and the third is for a sub-sector 3 Star.
    (For example, a 6 Sitting Star (yin) in W2 flies in a yin, yang, yang direction. As W2 is the *second* sub-sector it takes "yang" as its direction.)

8. There is, however, one exception, and that is the Flying Star 5-yellow; because it belongs to the center, it has no clearly discernable polarity. If you are examining a 5-yellow Star, then you must use a different rule:
    The rule is to use the Period Star number at the center of the chart instead (because, if you like, this is the Star that "usurped" the 5-yellow's position in the center). If the Period Star is odd, then the 5-Sitting Star flies yang, yin, yin; but if it's even, then the Sitting Star flies yin, yang, yang.

9. Mark the Sitting Star number in the center square with a minus "–" (yin) or a plus "+" (yang), according to its polarity.

10. Now repeat the same process (Steps 7 to 9) for the Facing Star, and mark it "+" or "–."

Flying the Sitting and Facing Stars:
11. Fly the Sitting Star. Start with the Center square left number. If it is marked with a "+," fly the Stars in a positive direction. If it has a "–," then fly the Stars in a negative direction. Place each Sitting Star in the left-hand upper corner of each square you come to.

12. Fly the Facing Star. Start with the Center square right number. If it is marked with a "+," fly the Stars in a positive direction. If it has a "–," then fly the Stars in a negative direction. Place each Facing Star in the right-hand upper corner of each square you come to.

Relating the Lo Shu to the real world:
13. Put the chart alongside the ground plan of your house, and align it so the facing direction of both points in the same direction. (In many examples, the Facing direction may correspond with the front door, but not always.)

That is your Flying Star chart.

It is not as complex as it looks. After a few tries you'll see that it works out quite naturally. Now let's look at the shortcut method, using the lookup tables in appendix 1 to speed up the process.

Shortcut Method

The sequence of actions required to draw up a Flying Star chart using the shortcut method is as follows:

1. Take a blank Lo Shu diagram just showing the 8 compass directions (or photocopy figure 9.4).

2. Determine the date of construction and hence the building's Construction Period number from table 2.5. This number is also called the Earth Base or Time Star.

3. Look in the Table for Generating Instant Flying Star Charts (appendix 1). Find the block in the table that applies to this Construction Period number (there are nine blocks in all). Copy out the numbers in the line at the top of the block into the *center* of each Palace of the Lo Shu, according to the compass directions indicated along the top row.

4. Use a compass to determine the Sitting (Mountain) sub-direction, as explained in chapter 3. Then look up this sub-direction in the *same block* in the same Table for Generating Instant Flying Star Charts in appendix 1.

5. Mark the Sitting (Mountain) direction on the Lo Shu with the Chinese character for shan or "mountain" (which is drawn a bit like an "E" on its back). Look down the table until you find this Sitting (Mountain) sub-direction. Copy the numbers in this row into each of the appropriate Palaces, writing the numbers into the top *left* of each square.

6. Directly opposite, mark the Facing direction on the Lo Shu chart with the Chinese character for "entrance," or an arrow. Read the next line downwards in the table. This gives the Facing sub-directions. Copy these numbers into the top *right* of each Palace.

That sounds pretty complicated, but it isn't. Let's do an example to get the hang of it.

EXAMPLES OF SETTING UP A FLYING STAR CHART

The following is an example of how you might apply Flying Star feng shui to a small squarish cottage built in 1989, facing 345 degrees (just west of magnetic North). This feng shui assessment was done in 2001.

Fig. 9.5 *Basic Chart Showing Period Star in Central Palace*

SE	S	SW
E	CENTER 7	W
NE	N	NW

Fig. 9.6 *Time Period Stars Placed in Each Palace (for Period 7)*

SE	S	SW
6	2	4
E	CENTER	W
5	7	9
NE	N	NW
1	3	8

Fig. 9.7 *Inserting the Mountain Stars*

Sitting Direction (S1)

山

	SE		S		SW
3		7		5	
	6		2		4
	E		CENTER		W
4			2 - Sitting	9	
	5		7		9
	NE		N		NW
8		6		1	
	1		3		8

向

Facing Direction (N1)

Fig. 9.8 *Example Flying Star Chart for a Cottage Built in 1989, Facing 345 Degrees Period number=7. Sitting direction=South-1. Facing direction=North-1.*

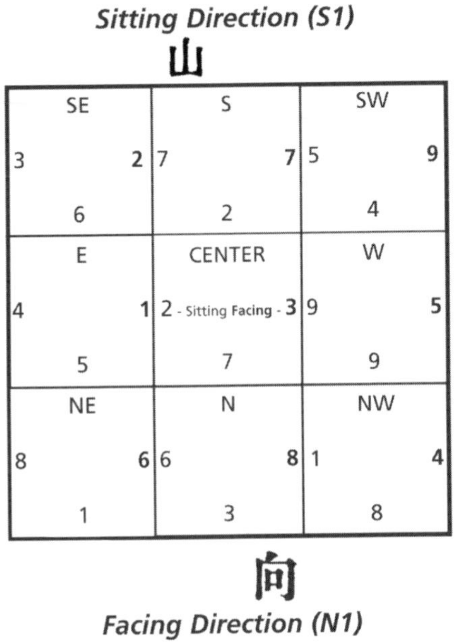

Sitting Direction (S1)

山

SE		S		SW	
3	2|7		7|5		9
6		2		4	
E		CENTER		W	
4	1|2 - Sitting Facing - 3|9				5
5		7		9	
NE		N		NW	
8	6|6		8|1		4
1		3		8	

向

Facing Direction (N1)

1. Start with a blank Lo Shu showing just the 8 directions drawn on a blank sheet of paper (or photocopy figure 9.4).

Insert Period Star:
2. Determine the date of construction and hence the building's Construction Period number from the Table of Flying Star Time Periods (appendix 3).

   You will see that for this house built in 1989, it is Period 7 (1984–2004). Therefore write "7" in the center of the Center Palace. See figure 9.5.

3. Use the first line of the Period 7 block of the Table for Generating Instant Flying Star Charts (appendix 1) to write in the numbers for the Construction Period in the order: Center, NW, W, NE, S, N, SW, E. As the Period number 7 is already placed in the Center, put 8 in NW, then 9 in W, then 1 in NE, and so on. See figure 9.6.

Remember, when counting Flying Stars, 1 comes after 9.

Fig. 9.9 *The Flying Star Chart in Relation to the Plan of the Cottage*

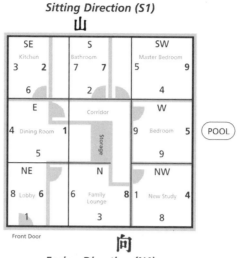

Sitting Direction (S1)

山

Facing Direction (N1)

Determine the Siting and Facing Directions:

4. In this case we know the cottage faces 345 degrees, so from appendix 2 we know that North-1, or N1 is its Facing direction. Its Sitting direction is therefore the opposite, or South-1.

5. Look down the Period 7 block of the table in appendix 1 till you find the S1 Mountain (Sitting) sub-direction. Use this line to put in the Mountain (Sitting) Stars into the top left corner of each Palace. See figure 9.7.

6. Read the Water (Facing) Star numbers on the next line down in the same table. Put these numbers in the top right corner of each Palace. See figure 9.8.

Take the architect's or a sketch plan of the cottage. Put the chart over the ground plan of your house. (See figure 9.9.) In this example the Facing direction and front door are on the same side, but do not correspond exactly, which is often the way. (If you feel that this is all still too labor intensive, then go to the Website www.fengshui-magazine.com. Here you can purchase *Software for Feng Shui*, a reliable Flying Star program that will take all the headache out of Flying Star calculation and give you a lot more besides.)

The number in the center of *each* Palace is the Period Star. Of the other two numbers in each Palace, the top right one is the Facing (Water) Star, while the top left one is the Sitting (Mountain) Star.

PRACTICE MAKES PERFECT

Now before you go any further, try a simple test. Work out which chart corresponds to your home. You will need to know when it was built, and you will need to use your compass to determine its Sitting direction. Use the blank chart diagram in figure 9.4 (or a copy of it) to draw it. Go for it!

Do a few different charts, maybe your friends' houses, till you feel comfortable working with them. But don't try feng shui diagnosis quite yet.

The table in appendix 1 gives you the Period, Mountain (Sitting), and Water (Facing) Stars for every possible combination of Period 1 through to 9, for every one of the possible 24 Sitting directions. The Full Method of calculation can be a bit confusing at first, and takes a lot longer to master than the shortcut tables, but the long method enables you to eventually work out the Flying Stars in your head.

If you look at any of these charts, you will note that the Period Star always flies in the following order: Center, NW, W, NE, S, N, SW. The Sitting Star and the Facing Star always fly in the same order, but sometimes in a positive (yang) order, sometimes in the reverse order (yin).

This chapter is the essence of the book, the drawing up of the Flying Star chart. In this chapter we established that the Stars move according to the zigzag called the Pathway of the Stars, inside the Lo Shu that represents the basic shape of the building. We looked at the Full Method and then the Shortcut Method, followed by an example. Before you turn the page, try to draw up a few sample charts so that you feel comfortable with the method.

You need to remember that:

- every Palace has 3 Stars: the Period Star, the Water Star, and the Mountain Star.
- the Stars follow the Pathway of the Stars, sometimes in a yang (positive) way, sometimes in a yin (negative) way.
- you should learn the Full Method of flying the Stars, but you may use the Shortcut Method to check your results or speed things up.

Having drawn up the chart we now need to interpret it.

Chapter 10

Interpreting the Stars

So the charts are drawn. How do we use them? There are many ways of extracting information from the Flying Star charts. It is easy to get confused, to let the eyes glaze over, and just to see a mass of numbers. Remember that these numbers represent various energies that can be quite concrete in their action: analyzing a chart is not like playing tic-tac-toe even if it sometimes looks like it.

The trick is to extract the most important pieces of information first, then work your way into the chart, bringing out more and more detail.

THE KEY PALACES

As you know, there are 9 Palaces in the Lo Shu. When placed over a building, it marks out the Palaces (or spheres of influence) of the various Stars in that building. Are all Palaces equally important? Definitely not. Let us look at the possible candidates for most important Palace.

Look at the basic chart generated in figure 9.8. Of the 9 Palaces, there are at least three which are a little special:

1. The first special Palace is obviously the Central Palace, that is also called the Heavenly Heart Palace. Why "Heavenly"? Because it is the Palace into which is put the Time or Period Star, which conditions the 20-year period in which the building was built or occupied. If the building was built (or occupied) over 20 years ago, this Period Star will not be the same Star as the current Period Star. This Palace generates the rest of the chart.

2. The second important Palace is the Sitting Palace. This is the Palace which is at the "back" of the building (and its Period Star becomes the Sitting Star in the Center

Palace). (This statement will only make sense to you, if you have worked thoroughly through the Full Method of setting up the chart in the previous chapter.)

3. The Facing Palace is perhaps the most important Palace. This is the Palace at the "front" of the building (containing the Period Star, which becomes the Facing Star in the Center Palace). It is this Palace which corresponds to the facing lo p'an reading. It is where the building receives most of its ch'i input. It will in many cases (but not always) also be the Palace that contains the front door.

4. If the Facing Palace doesn't happen to contain the main door, then the Palace that does is also important, because its Star combination will condition the ch'i that enters the house.

5. You will remember in chapter 8 that I emphasized that Stars often need an external landform stimulus to activate them. Because of this you should now check if there is any other Palace in the chart that is adjacent to, or opens on to, the view of a signifi-cant water or mountain feature: a river, a large rock, a building, a roadway, and so on. Any Palace that is activated by an external influence may also become a key Palace because it contains activated Stars.

So you can see that the significant Palaces might number anywhere from three to all nine, depending on the physical circumstances. This again stresses the fact that all feng shui is rooted in the external world, and the practitioner needs to get out and look closely at the building and site. It is not just a pen and paper parlor game. We can for the moment ignore the rest of the Palaces (they will later come into their own when we do a room by room analysis).

In practice, the first thing to discover is the overall type of chart. There are four basic types of chart, which we will consider in detail later in chapter 13 (page 149).

Then we should look at the key Palaces. Here are five basic ways to interpret each Palace. Remember to keep it simple; work out one Palace at a time, preferably writing down your conclusions into your practice book as you go. Look in turn at each Palace and consider the following points:

1. The basic meaning of each of the three Stars, the Mountain Star, Period Star, and the Water Star in that Palace (see table 5.1).

2. The timeliness of each of these three Stars (see tables 5.5 and 5.6).

3. The physical location of the Palace in the building and the type of use this room is put to.

4. The Element associated with each Star and how these Elements relate to each other (see table 5.2).

5. The external, real-world landform features and their effect on the Star combinations.

6. The detailed relationships between the Stars in each Palace (see chapter 11).

Let's take the cottage example from the previous chapter (figure 9.9) and consider it one criterion at a time. The chart happens to be a Double Sitting chart (a type we will meet in chapter 13), which is good for family, health, and relationships, but not for wealth.

What are the obvious key Palaces? These are the Center Palace, the Sitting Palace (in the South), and the Facing Palace (in the North). Notice how the front door does not fall into the Facing Palace, so its Palace, the NE Palace, also becomes important. If we discovered that there was a visible pool adjacent to the West Palace, then this Palace gets added to our list of key Palaces. Key Palaces are shaded in figure 10.1.

Look at each of the key Palaces and consider the three Stars within each in the following way:

1. The Meaning of Each Star

For the basic meaning of each Star you need to look at table 5.7. Here you will see that basically the white Stars, 1, 6, and 8 are beneficial, while 9 amplifies the character of the Stars in the same Palace (i.e., it makes the good better, but the bad worse). The green

Fig. 10.1 *Key Palaces in a Chart for a Cottage Built in 1989 Facing N1*

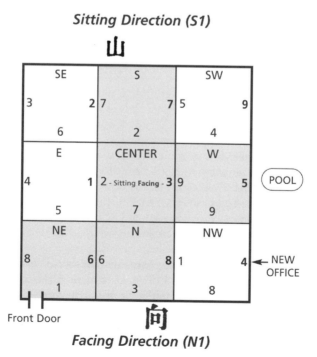

and red Stars are unfavorable, unless being Timely redeems them. Finally, the yellow and black Stars are unfavorable.

In our example, all three auspicious white Stars, 8, 1, and 6, fall in the NE Palace in figure 10.1, which means that the cottage inhales very beneficial ch'i through its front door.

2. The Timeliness of Each Star

Refer to table 5.6, where you can observe the basic nature of the Stars modified by their Timeliness. One of the best examples of this is 7-red, which is normally an unfavorable Star but becomes favorable during its own Period, the 7th Period (1984–2004). After February 2004 it becomes unfavorable again. It is rather like the change of mood brought about in an unruly child allowed to be "king for a day."

In our example (figure 10.1), the Sitting Palace (South) has a double 7, which is very auspicious, particularly for family, health, and relationships. But this will only be true until February 2004, when the double 7 Stars become Untimely and hence destructive rather than constructive.

Usable Stars

In addition to the Timely Stars, there are two other Stars in each Period that are considered "usable." Although they are not Timely, they are considered safe even if they are Untimely. This widens the range of acceptable Stars a bit. The usable Stars are as follows:

Table 10.1: *Timely and Additional Usable Stars*

Period	Period Begins	Timely & Future Timely Stars	Usable Stars
1	1864	1, 2, 3	2, 7
2	1884	2, 3, 4	1, 4
3	1904	3, 4, 5	8, 9
4	1924	4, 5, 6	2, 7
5	1944	5, 6, 7	2, 8
6	1964	6, 7, 8	8, 9
7	1984	7, 8, 9	1, 4
8	2004	8, 9, 1	3, 6
9	2024	9, 1, 2	3, 6

This means that during Period 7, the Stars that are beneficent are 7, 8, 9, 1, and 4. After February 2004 this changes to 8, 9, 1, 3, and 6. Although many practitioners remember that the 7-red Period Star hands the baton to the 8-white Star in February 2004, not all remember that the usability of Stars 1 and 4 is replaced by Stars 3 and 6. As Stars 1 and 6 are intrinsically auspicious Stars anyway, all you have to remember is that where 4-green was tolerable or indeed beneficial in Period 7, it will be replaced by 3-green as a usable Star at this changeover point.

In our example, during Period 7, the Stars 1 and 4 are both usable in the NW Palace. This is not a key Palace but this configuration makes a very good site for a study room (4-green is good for academic achievement while it is either timely or usable).

3. The Location of the Stars in the Building

The location of the Stars in the house under scrutiny is important. Having a great Star combination in a Palace that corresponds to the bathroom is a waste of opportunity, as these good Stars will simply be drained away and rendered worthless. The key is to find good Stars that correspond to key function rooms like the master bedroom, dining room, study, and so on.

Classical texts recommend that you change the function of the room to fit the Stars. Indeed in past times, before the advent of built-in wardrobes and plumbing, you could easily move the furniture around so that a dining room becomes a bedroom and so on. Kitchens and bathrooms, with all their special water and gas plumbing, are even more difficult to rearrange. I guess this is the price we pay for modern convenience.

The reverse of this also holds true. If you have a really diabolical Star combination located in the bathroom, or even a room like a storeroom that is used infrequently, you can relax. The draining effect of the bathroom (or the lack of stimulation) will weaken the Star to the point where it has little bad effect.

Think about it: feng shui is the relationship between the environment, the building, and its occupants. So with Flying Star the important thing is to arrange your activities to take advantage of the Stars. For example, if a great configuration is to be found in the spare bedroom, but a really lousy one is located in your master bedroom, then the time has come to swap the use of these rooms, even if the spare bedroom is smaller.

If you can't easily do this, then there are remedies—we will get to these in chapter 15.

In our example, the NW Palace is preferable to the East Palace as a study (despite the fact that they both have a 4-green combination) because the NW Palace has an 8-white Star which will add to the auspiciousness (particularly in the next Period) while the East Palace has a 5 Period Star (which will have a definite negative effect). Therefore we have derived a diagnosis that suggests an office swap in favor of the NW Palace would be in order.

4. The Element Associated with Each Star

The Elements are the major method of controlling or improving specific feng shui situations. Therefore it is important to check the Element of each of the three Stars in the Palace you are analyzing (using table 5.2). Then look at the relationships between the Elements discovered.

Remember the Productive, Reductive, and Destructive Cycles introduced in chapter 1? Ask yourself, do these Elements support each other (like Water supports Wood) or destroy each other (like Metal destroys Wood)? If one Star's Element is productive of another in the same Palace, then this is an advantage for the second Star (but drains or uses up the first Star). Thinking more subtly, sometimes an unfavorable Star can be destroyed by sharing a Palace with the Element it produces. (There, I told you the early theory stuff was going to come in handy!)

In our example, in the NW Palace, the Element of the 1-white Star is Water, which supports the Element of the 4-green Star, which is Wood. You see how it works. In addition, you know that the supported Star comes out strongest, in this case the 4-green, emphasizing that wealth will flow from this study.

5. THE EXTERNAL, REAL-WORLD LANDFORM FEATURES AND THEIR EFFECT ON THE STAR COMBINATIONS

Stars are just potentials if they are not stirred up. This is why it is commonly said that the best remedy for the troublesome 5-yellow Star is inactivity—just lock up the room it happens to be in (not however always practical advice). The reverse is true, that if there is a lot of activity in a room, or there is a prominent landform feature outside that particular Palace, then ch'i will be generated. If the Stars are auspicious, then well and good; but if not, then potential trouble becomes actual trouble.

In our example, the West Palace has a 9-9-5 combination. We know that 5-yellow is trouble, but here it is greatly amplified by the presence of not one but two 9-purple Stars, a very bad combination. But worse is to follow, as immediately outside the Palace is a pool that will contribute energizing ch'i to this Palace, making it much more powerful. A remedy is called for immediately, and we will consider this in chapter 15.

6. THE RELATIONSHIPS BETWEEN THE STARS IN EACH PALACE

Each of the 81 combinations of Stars (that is, 9 x 9) has a specific indication. Many of these indications can be reasoned out from a knowledge of the basic nature of each Star, its Elements, Timeliness, and so on. But it is also useful to be able to look up a table of combinations. We will look at this in detail in the next chapter.

In our example, if we look at the Facing Palace we see a combination of 6-white and 8-white. If we look up this combination in the table in the next chapter, we read "Two good Stars for wealth (particularly through real estate), good for career, fame, and reputation." Located in the Facing Palace, which is all about wealth, we can see that this is a very good combination.

I have chosen to look at just six ways of eliciting information from this chart, and you can see that there is a lot of concrete information and some clear and very specific advice arising from the diagnosis. As it turned out, the couple moved their study from the East Palace to the NW Palace and instituted a remedy for the 5-yellow Star in the West Palace (and also in the SW Palace), which immediately reversed a long run of bad money luck that they had been experiencing. This kind of improvement is essentially what Flying Star is all about.

Chapter 11

Combinations of Stars

Let us now look at various combinations of the Stars that can fall into each Palace.

It is usual to list Stars in the order Mountain-Period-Water (MPW) or Mountain-Time-Water (MTW). Using this convention, you can therefore tell that in the combination 8-6-1, the 8 is the Mountain Star (affecting family, health, and relationships), the 6 is the Period Star (related to the construction date), while the 1 is the Water Star (primarily concerned with wealth).

The order of the Stars is not so important when getting a general impression of the effects of the Stars, and the 6-1-8 combination will be as basically favorable as a 8-6-1 combination. However when deciding exactly what effects flow from a particular combination, it is important to know if the combination favors the Mountain Star (health, family, and relationship) or the Water Star (wealth).

In any Palace:

1. Water Star can react with the Mountain Star
2. Mountain Star can react with the Water Star
3. Water Star can react with the Period Star
4. Mountain Star can react with the Period Star

Triggers for these reactions can be:

5. Annual Star reacting with the Period Star
6. Annual Star reacting with the Monthly Star

We will look at Annual and Monthly Stars in the next chapter.

Of these, the most important effects are derived from the interaction of the Mountain and Water Stars. Some practitioners do not even consider the interaction between these two and the Period Star. (Some practitioners also look at the interaction of the Stars and the trigram of the Palace, but we will not go into this.)

SIMPLE COMBINATIONS

Let us look at a few *simple* combinations to get the general feel. Try to understand and then memorize these simple examples so that when you browse through the more comprehensive table 11.2, you will feel more at home with the complex combinations.

BASIC INAUSPICIOUS COMBINATIONS

2-5

Let's look at the *bad* combinations first. In general the worst combinations are 2-2, 2-5, and 5-5 which are the two unfavorable Earth Stars getting together and reinforcing each other. The 2-2 combination may bring chronic illness for anyone who regularly works, eats, or sleeps in a room under this influence. The combination 5-5 will bring other problems as well as serious illness. In all of these Earth-related cases do not stimulate Earth, but attempt to reduce its power with Metal (as Metal reduces Earth).

2-9-5

Remember that the 9 is also a Star that reinforces the good or bad qualities of its companion, so as you would expect, 2-9 and 5-9 are also bad combinations, and 2-9-5 is a real disaster. The Fire of 9 also "feeds" the Earth of both 2 and 5.

2-3

When Star 2 is paired with the quarrelsome Star 3 you can expect bickering, quarrels, and even lawsuits, so watch out for 2-3 and of course 3-2. Try to quiet down such a Palace: avoid stimulating it with the sound system or the television.

2-7

When the 2 is paired with 7 there is an increased threat of fire, which may manifest as a fever or as a real fire. The Element Water helps cool down this combination.

2-8

Fortunately 2-8 sees the bad qualities of the 2 modified by the good qualities of the 8, and this works well because they are both Earth Stars.

6-7

The combination of 6-7 (especially after February 2004) is double Metal, sometimes symbolized by crossed swords and often associated with robbery. Robbery seems to have been a major concern to the writers of early feng shui texts, who lived before the advent of almost universal insurance. Use the Fire Element to combat this combination, as Fire destroys Metal. The 3-7 (Wood and Metal) combination has a similar but less strident outcome. More will be said about detailed remedies for that in chapter 15.

BASIC AUSPICIOUS COMBINATIONS

Now let us look at some good strengthening combinations.

1-6-8

The 3 white Stars 1-6-8 in the same Palace is a great combination, as each of these is a favorable Star in its own right. This works as either 1-6, 1-8, or 6-8. Double 6, double 8, or double 1 are also good.

7-7

Star 7 is a bit more mixed. During the 7th Period, when 7 is timely, 7-7 is a very strong combination, but after February 2004 it becomes a very destructive combination. The 7-7 is particularly important if found in the Facing Palace or at the front door position.(Don't worry too much about the concept of Timeliness. I have written this book with the assumption that its readers are going to be living through Periods 7 and 8. Obviously houses have been built and occupied in other earlier periods [and these are amply catered for in the chart construction procedure] but in terms of timeliness *changes*, only Period 7 and 8 are currently significantly changing their Timeliness.)

8-8

It is very good when you get an 8-8 combination, as the 8 reinforces itself. Eight is a fortunate Star, but from February 4, 2004 through the following 20 years, it is even more fortunate, as it is then the Prominent Star (the number of the Period) as well.

When you are comfortable with the thinking behind the above simple combinations, you can go on to browse the list of the most important results of the 81 paired combinations that follows. These rules apply to any Stars within the same Palace including the Period Star, but they are particularly important to the Mountain/Water combination.

When evaluating these combinations, look at the relative Element strength of the Mountain and Water Star to see which side benefits most. To understand this, see the use of the Guest and Host principle later in this chapter. If, for example, there is a combination between a Metal Star and a Wood Star, at the simplest level, the Metal Star will benefit most, because Metal destroys Wood.

The health implications attributed to each combination are not meant to imply that anyone living in the room corresponding to the Palace under consideration will necessarily have those health problems. They are rather an indication that special care should be taken in those areas. For example, a couple wishing to have children should not consciously use a 1-9 room as a bedroom, because even though 1 is a beneficial Star, the combination 1-9 is associated with fertility problems.

Another way to use the health indications positively is to (discreetly) check if the indicated health condition is present in the occupant(s) of the room concerned. If so, then you effectively have an objective confirmation that the Flying Star chart has been correctly drawn up. If the health condition does not exist it does *not* mean that your Flying Star chart is wrong—but it might suggest to you to check your calculations. A table of the various diseases associated with each Star when it is badly aspected follows. The disease relates to the Element of the Star, and this can be used to diagnose other disease producing combinations.

Table 11.1: *Disease Most Often Associated with the Stars and Their Element (particularly when the Mountain Star is badly aspected)*

Star	Affected Body Part or Condition	Due to Element
1	spleen, kidneys, ear, blood	Water
2	abdomen, stomach, spleen, digestive system	Earth
3	liver, hands, legs, lungs, bladder, hysteria	Wood
4	liver, hands, legs, lungs, bladder, flu, colds	Wood
5	abdomen, stomach, spleen, digestive system	Earth
6	lungs, bones, headaches, pulmonary system	Metal
7	lungs, bones, mouth, tongue, head	Metal
8	hands, fingers, back	Earth
9	heart, eyes	Fire

Remember to pay attention to the positive qualities when the Star is Timely and the negative qualities when it is Untimely. This advice especially concerns Star 7, which passes from Timely to Untimely on 4 February 2004, and which is why this date occurs again and again in these tables.

Star interpretations will differ according to whether the Star is a Mountain or a Water Star. In the case of the 1-white Star, which has as its Element Water, it will obviously be more beneficial as a Water Star (in the right hand top corner of each Palace). It will not be so good as a Mountain Star. Conversely the good Earth Star 8-white will add extra luster to the combination if it is a Mountain Star (in the left hand top corner of each Palace), but will not be so good as a Water Star.

More succinctly, a Water Star is accentuated by the Water Element, and a Mountain Star is accentuated by an Earth Element, for good or ill.

Don't expect to memorize all of the following, but use the table as a reference. The interpretation of these combinations has been derived from the observations of many feng shui practitioners over a long period of time. You will often be surprised at how literally true many are. Indeed, as you work with the system you will notice cases where particular results can be attributed consistently to specific combinations, and will be able to add these to the commonly accepted combinations. If you find that very few combinations make sense, then go back and reread the section on simple combinations earlier in this chapter, and maybe even revise the nature of each Star as explained in chapter 5. There is no point in going on until you feel comfortable with the interpretation of a fair percentage of these combinations.

....

Table 11.2: *All of the 81 Flying Star Combinations*

Combination	Significance and Potential Outcome
1	Generally beneficial. As Water it represents wealth, but because of its Untimeliness it can represent long gone prosperity, at least until February 2004, when it will become future Timely again.
1-1	Wealth. A good combination, particularly if in the North (which is the home Palace to Water). Because of the watery nature of the Star, affairs of the heart, sometimes extramarital, are indicated. Is reputed to cause good luck for 60 years, but this goes against the idea of luck cycles changing after 20 years. On the health front, watch out for the health of organs that process water, including the kidney and bladder. This may be a good bedroom for someone with a Wood kua number of 3 or 4 (as Water produces Wood).
1-2	Marital problems. It may indicate a dominant female in the relationship, a henpecked male, and a reduction in sexual activity. Possibility of loss in business. Possible auto accidents and health problems involving abdominal pain, stomach, gynecological and digestive system (therefore not a good combination for a bedroom or garage).
1-3	A good combination yielding wealth and fame, with an emphasis on travel in Period 8. However watch out for fraud, arguments, and lawsuits. Health problems relate to the liver if 3 is the Mountain Star. This can also provoke aggressive or unreasonable behavior in its occupant. Move a "fractious" child from this location.
1-4	Good for romance, artistic creativity, intellectual or academic success (a good combination to have in studio or study). In a career sense it predisposes to promotion and fame.
1-4-7	A specially good combination (taking into account the Period Star) up to February 2004. After this date 7-red becomes untimely and 4-green ceases to be a "usable" Star.
1-5	Illness, accidents, and disaster due to the malevolent 5-yellow Star. In terms of health it can portend ear and genital (including miscarriage) problems, bladder problems, or food poisoning and diarrhea (therefore it is a bad combination for marital bedroom, kitchen, or dining room).

(continued)

1-6	Brings wealth and financial intelligence. It is good for career, particularly in a martial occupation like the army or police. Good for learning: a good combination for a study. On the health front though, this combination can be associated with wounding and migraine headaches or head injury.
1-7	Favorable for wealth (but only during Period 7). It also predisposes to affairs of the heart and flirtation. Favorable for travel and good for salesmen or smooth talkers. Health indications include wounding with a knife or by animal attack and bleeding.
1-8	Good for wealth and career, during Period 7 and 8, but sometimes business partnership difficulties arise. Watch out for hearing, kidney, bladder, and genital health problems.
1-9	Financial difficulties, but good for promotion and academic achievements. Romance can be erratic. Health difficulties include heart or eye problems and venereal, fertility, and miscarriage problems.

2	A generally bad news Star! It is Earth-based and unlucky. It becomes much worse if combined with 5, the other unfortunate Earth Star. Use a red string strung with six traditional Chinese metal coins to help exhaust its ill effects.
2-2	Chronic illness and despair, especially if the Stars occur in a bedroom. Financially bumpy, but may generate windfall gains soon lost. Particularly pernicious if they occur in the SW Palace, which is their "home" Palace.
2-3	This combination causes gossip, arguments, legal entanglements, and aggressiveness. A bad combination for a politician. Tension between mothers and sons. Stomach, digestive, and abdominal problems are indicated. Try to keep this room very quiet and not activated.
2-4	This is an interesting combination and will stimulate romance (but sometimes with negative sexual encounters), particularly if the room is occupied by a young female. If the occupant is married, it may cause bickering between a mother and her daughter-in-law, with a suspicion of hidden agendas.

On the positive side, the 4 Star stimulates artistic creativity and intellectual or academic success, particularly for writers (and is a good combination to have in a studio or study). Health problems include abdominal, stomach, and spleen illnesses. |

(continued)

2-5	Very bad combination indeed. Health and financial disasters, illness, accidents, pain, even death. Try to totally avoid this area (best if it is located in a toilet area or in seldom used rooms). Total inactivity is the best remedy: shut up the room if you can. Health problems may include cancer, stomach problems, and miscarriages.
2-5-8	The 8 (which is also an Earth Star) helps to redeem the other two Earth Stars, especially when 8 is the Period Star (i.e., 2004–2024), leading to surprising prosperity.
2-6	Good for wealth (particularly from real estate, an Earth-based occupation), but bad for health, indicating pain, gastrointestinal problems, and possibly fever. Possibility of blockage and fire.
2-7	Metal Star 7 diffuses the problems associated with the 2 Star. Good for wealth during Period 7 (till February 2004), but after this it will be a case of easy come, easy go. After Period 7 this combination provokes damaging competition in business. Difficulties in conceiving and mother/daughter-in-law feuding a possibility. Illness specifically involving pain and bleeding wounds (which may be knife injuries) and diarrhea. Fire and divorce are also potential threats from this combination.
2-8	Wealth, fame, success especially in Earth-related real estate transactions. Potential illness includes digestive problems. This combination improves after February 2004, when Star 8 becomes Timely.
2-9	Business problems. Illness involving pain, eye, digestive, and particularly reproductive problems. Not a good location for a child's bedroom, as it threatens mental deficiency problems.

3	This Star, as it is now Untimely, provokes arguments, slander, and lawsuits. However when Period 8 is reached in February 2004 it becomes a "usable" Star, and so some of its worst excesses will be curbed.
3-3	A difficult combination resulting in cold-heartedness and disputes. Health issues may involve the feet, the lungs, or even hysteria and convulsions. Not a room to use for a newly married couple. Worse if it falls in the East Palace which is their "home" Palace.
3-4	Mental and emotional difficulties are often encountered with this combination (particularly in the case of female occupants). Male occupants may find they attract "crazy" girlfriends. Financially, embezzlement is a possibility.

(continued)

3-5	Financial difficulties, sometimes exacerbated by gambling, disputes over money, and difficulty with troublemakers. May bring bankruptcy. Illness, particularly infections, broken limbs, and cancer of the liver are threatened by this unfortunate combination. The eldest son is particularly at health risk in this location. Not as bad after February 2004, when 3-green becomes a "usable" Star.
3-6	Difficulties for teenagers. Health issues include accidental injury (particularly to the leg) and headaches.
3-6-9	A specially good combination (taking into account the Period Star) and the harmonic of 3.
3-7	Robbery, fraud (especially by a family member), and ruinous lawsuits. Injury by knives, and eye and leg problems. This combination will become much worse after February 2004, when 7 is no longer timely and returns to its typically unfavorable nature.
3-8	Bad for family, better for wealth and status or credibility. Difficulties for young children (particularly boys): not a good choice for a child's bedroom. Bad for family relationships. Reputed to stimulate homosexuality. Health issues with limbs, miscarriages, heart disease, and asthma.
3-9	Good for wealth promotion and fame (especially after February 2004 when 3-green becomes "usable"), but watch out that sharp practice does not provoke lawsuits. Possibility of fire-related injury. Good as the bedroom of a studious child. Heath concerns include the liver.

4	Good for academic and literary work. Don't forget that although this Star is usable in Period 7, it ceases to be so when we move to Period 8. So after February 2004, some of its better qualities need to be treated with caution.
4-4	Good for travel and romance. Also good for study and academics. Strengthened if they fall in the SE Palace, their "home" Palace. Bad for asthma and bronchial conditions.
4-5	Intimidation and gambling conspire to damage wealth. Bad for health, with potential for skin diseases, breast cancer, and infections.

(continued)

4-6	Bad for health and relationships. Good for fame, especially literary and academic. Possibility of eye and mouth disease, and miscarriages. Reputed to encourage suicides.
4-7	Good for romance till February 2004, after which there is the threat of divorce and litigation. Health issues include coughing, wounding, and miscarriage (the last two combinations would be bad rooms for a pregnant woman to use).
4-8	The Earth Star 8 brings potential for real estate earnings, but marital quarrelling. Improves in Period 8. Health concerns include gallstones, kidney diseases, mental or emotional problems, isolation, and rheumatism. A difficult room for children.
4-9	Possible fire risk, but excellent placement for a bright or gifted male child. Outside of Period 7 and 8, this combination can produce aberrant sexual liaisons.

5	Generally bad news! Earth-based and very unlucky Star. Worse if combined with 2 or 9. Use metal to exhaust its ill effects.
5-5	Serious illness except in Period 5. Causes family strife. Illnesses include bone cancer, injury, and impotence. (Very bad in a bedroom).
5-6	Can be good for money during Period 5 and 6. Otherwise not good for career. Bad for health including the threat of cancer and head-related problems.
5-7	Okay for money but only until February 2004. Relationship problems with bickering. Illnesses include food poisoning, heart, venereal disease, and mouth problems (bad in a kitchen or dining room location). Reputed to encourage prostitution and drug dependency.
5-8	Okay for money in Period 5 and 8, otherwise not good for money. Health issues include cancer, paralysis, mental illness, and rib and sinew problems, especially outside those Periods.
5-9	The 9 Star accentuates the already bad qualities of the 5-yellow Star. It encourages gambling, fire, accidents, and mental deficiency problems (best kept unused or as a "wet room").

(continued)

6	Although basically an auspicious Star, in the present Period it represents past prosperity, especially because of its link with the trigram Ch'ien, or Heaven, which is associated with Metal, specifically gold. This Star is only redeemed by a Timely number like 8 or 9.
6-6	Good for wealth only during Period 6 when it is Timely. Bad for family relationships. Lung diseases a problem. The effects are amplified if they occur in the NW Palace, the "home" Palace.
6-6-6	Indicates great wealth and children with illustrious careers. If at the front door, then the whole house benefits greatly.
6-7	A strong Metal combination. Good for wealth only during Period 6. Otherwise it promotes quarreling, jealousy, fighting, cheating, robbery. This gets noticeably worse after February 2004, when Star 7 ceases to be timely as does Star 6.
6-8	Two good Stars for wealth (particularly through real estate), good for career, fame, and reputation. Minor health indication such as mental instability.
6-9	Not good for family (especially rebellious sons) or health. Lung disease, brain and blood pressure problems are indicated.

7	Current prosperity till February 2004, when 7 reverts to being a non-beneficial Star. When it becomes Untimely, it is often associated with robbery. The 7-red Star is important to consider carefully because of its changing status as a Timely Star. A moving remedy like a grandfather clock or other regularly moving Metal machine will help activate this Star. Be sure to remove these activations after February 2004. The 8-white Earth Star will also help to tone down its worst excesses.
7-7	A good wealth combination till February 2004, after which it is an inauspicious combination, with the possibility of armed robbery and other troubles arising as Star 7 becomes Untimely. These effects are amplified if the 7-7 is found in the W Palace, the "home" Palace.
7-8	Good for romance, especially young adults (a good matrimonial bedroom). Good for wealth, and windfall gains, as 7 is redeemed by Star 8 after February 2004, especially success in competitive environments.

(continued)

| 7-9 | Good for flirting and seduction (a good combination for a bachelor's bedroom) but can cause relationship problems. Guard against heart problems and the possibility of fire. When the 7 is Untimely, the 9 helps to control its worst excesses. |

| 8 | Future prosperity. Acts as a beneficial modifier to other stars and comes into its own after February 2004, when it becomes the current prosperity Star. |

| 8-8 | Great for wealth, particularly in Period 8. This combination is particularly potent if it occurs in the NE, the "home" Palace. Good in the Southern Palace, where Fire contributes to its Earth strength. Produces illustrious children. |

| 8-9 | Well aspected for all sorts of joyful activities, family harmony, marriage, and wealth. |

| 9 | Distant prosperity, but will come more into its own as a wealth Star after February 2004 and very much so after 2024. The 9-purple Star accentuates the qualities of any other Star it may partner, for good or for ill. |

| 9-9 | Very favorable combination, increasingly so after February 2004 when it becomes future Timely, and superb after 2024. Particularly potent in its "home" direction in the South, where it is extremely favorable. Good for wealth, especially in the cosmetics and fashion industries. |

You may at first sight think that the above table is incomplete, as the 3-8 combination shows up, but not the combination 8-3. The reason is that in essence the result is the same. Some books list these as separate combinations, but this is not really necessary if you understand the Host and Guest principle (see later in this chapter). So if you can't for example find 8-3, look under 3-8.

It is helpful to know if the 3 is a Mountain Star (left hand top corner of each Palace, representing health and family) or a Water Star (right hand top corner of the Palace, representing wealth). From this you can refine your judgement as to the exact outcome, using your own common sense.

Often, because of the detailed nature of these combination effects, a good feng shui Master can predict specific health problems for specific members of the family residing in a particular room. This is a wonderful test of accuracy for the Flying Star analysis. If these turn out to be the case, this gives him an objective check on the correctness of the calculations (not to mention a situation that needs correcting). I have seen the look of sheer amazement, and in one case utter horror, as one such Master revealed the exact nature of medical conditions of family members who were not even present at the reading.

Such skill, however, takes a lot of practice, so when you are building up these skills just inquire if such and such a condition exists, don't ever presume to predict it.

Don't forget that good combinations can be enhanced and bad ones can be dissolved using the Elements, so that even the most horrible-looking combination can be worked with.

USABLE AND TIMELY STAR COMBINATIONS

In chapter 10 we looked at the Usable Star, and in chapter 5 we looked at the influence of Timeliness for ease of working. I have tabulated the Usable and Timely Water and Mountain Star combinations for the current and next Period. Make sure you use the correct table, then check the Mountain Star (across the top of the table) against the Water Star (down the left hand side of the table), showing where each combination is timely/untimely and usable/unusable. This will act as a rough and ready guide to which combinations may need remedial attention.

....

Table 11.3: *Summary of All Timely and Usable Star Combinations for Period 7*

For Period 7 (1984–Feb. 3, 2004)

Mountain Star		1 U	2 X	3 X	4 U	5 X	6 X	7 T	8 T	9 T
Water Star										
1	U	U,U	X,U	X,U	U,U	X,U	X,U	T,U	T,U	T,U
2	X	U,X	X,X	X,X	U,X	X,X	X,X	T,X	T,X	T,X
3	X	U,X	X,X	X,X	U,X	X,X	X,X	T,X	T,X	T,X
4	U	U,U	X,U	X,U	U,U	X,U	X,U	T,U	T,U	T,U
5	X	U,X	X,X	X,X	U,X	X,X	X,X	T,X	T,X	T,X
6	X	U,X	X,X	X,X	U,X	X,X	X,X	T,X	T,X	T,X
7	T	U,T	X,T	X,T	U,T	X,T	X,T	T,T	T,T	T,T
8	T	U,T	X,T	X,T	U,T	X,T	X,T	T,T	T,T	T,T
9	T	U,T	X,T	X,T	U,T	X,T	X,T	T,T	T,T	T,T

Table 11.4: *Summary of All Timely and Usable Star Combinations for Period 8*

For Period 8 (Feb. 4, 2004–2024)

Mountain Star		1	2	3	4	5	6	7	8	9
		T	X	U	X	X	U	X	T	T
Water Star										
1	T	T,T	X,T	U,T	X,T	X,T	U,T	X,T	T,T	T,T
2	X	T,X	X,X	U,X	X,X	X,X	U,X	X,X	T,X	T,X
3	U	T,U	X,U	U,U	X,U	X,U	U,U	X,U	T,U	T,U
4	X	T,X	X,X	U,X	X,X	X,X	U,X	X,X	T,X	T,X
5	X	T,X	X,X	U,X	X,X	X,X	U,X	X,X	T,X	T,X
6	U	T,U	X,U	U,U	X,U	X,U	U,U	X,U	T,U	T,U
7	X	T,X	X,X	U,X	X,X	X,X	U,X	X,X	T,X	T,X
8	T	T,T	X,T	U,T	X,T	X,T	U,T	X,T	T,T	T,T
9	T	T,T	X,T	U,T	X,T	X,T	U,T	X,T	T,T	T,T

* Timely=T; Untimely=X; Usable=U
** listed in the order "Mountain Star, Water Star"

You can see how radically the tides of luck change between one Period and another. Combinations that are both Usable and/or Timely are fine. Where one or both Stars are Untimely (X) or not Usable (U), then their bad qualities may prevail and a remedy may be worth considering. Of course this also depends upon real-world conditions such as the function and importance of a room. A summary of such Elemental remedies will be found at the end of chapter 15.

Host Stars and Guest Stars

When determining the outcome of various combinations, it is sometimes difficult to keep in mind which Star is the most important. There is a technique for identifying the most important Star of a pair of Stars (which can be used at all sorts of levels). It is usually only used in the Facing and Sitting Palaces, or where a Palace is affected by a real land-form feature.

This technique refers to the Stars as either Guest Stars (*ke hsing*) or Host Stars (*chu hsing*). This is just a handy way of working out your priorities in a systematic way when analyzing the Stars in a particular Palace. Because of the traditional Chinese respect for manners and detailed code of conduct in such things as hospitality, these terms (Guest and Host) convey a whole set of additional meanings. Some authorities refer to Host and Guest Stars simply as "Chief" and "Subordinate" Stars, but the concept goes much deeper than this.

In rough outline, the Host Star is the "one who arrives at the banquet first," or the one who is most important to the question being asked. For example, if we were concerned with the wealth prospects of a particular Palace, the Host Star would be the Water Star (in the top right hand corner of the Palace). If it was a question of health, then instead the Mountain Star would be the Host Star and the Water Star would become the Guest Star.

Take as a simple example, a Palace containing the Stars 6-9-8. We know that both 6-white and 8-white are both auspicious Stars, but we want to probe a little deeper. If you were examining the Stars in this Palace from the point of view of health prospects, then the Mountain Star (6-white) becomes the Host (i.e., the issue being considered), while the Water Star (8-white) becomes the Guest. The question you must now ask is, "Does the Guest Star support the Host?"

The Guest (8-white) is Earth, while the Host (6-white) is Metal. From the Productive cycle of the Elements, we know that Earth produces Metal. Therefore the Guest supports the Host. With the Host supported, it is a good combination for health.

If on the other hand the reverse was true (Host becomes 8-white = Earth; and Guest becomes 6-white = Metal) then the Guest does not support the Host (in fact the Guest drains the Host). This combination then suggests a minor health problem, in this case as it happens, in the form of mental instability. You can now see how the Guest and Host technique adds an additional dimension to the analysis of combinations.

In fact there are four possible relations between Guest and Host:

1. Enhancing or wang: The Guest supports the Host or both are the same Element. Beneficial and longer lasting.
2. Not moving: The Host supports the Guest. Not so beneficial, particularly in the Facing Palace.
3. Against inside: The Guest destroys the Host. Not beneficial for either Star.
4. Against outside: The Host destroys the Guest. The Host is weakened, so fortune comes quickly but only lasts a short time.

By applying this procedure for looking at Star relationships, the analysis will soon become second nature.

You can apply the Guest/Host procedure at many different levels. In the broadest sense Heaven ch'i can be seen as Guest affecting Host Earth ch'i. In terms of Flying Star the possible levels include:

1. The basic Lo Shu Palaces are the Host, while the Period Stars are the Guest.
2. The Period Stars as Host and the Mountain Star as Guest.
3. The Period Stars as Host and the Water Star as Guest.
4. For people questions, the Mountain Star as Host, the Water Star as Guest.
5. For wealth questions, the Water Star as Host, the Mountain Star as Guest.

In this chapter we have started to look at the interaction of the Stars, first just simple combinations like 2-5, and then a complete table of all 81 possible combinations of pairs of Stars. Then we looked at these combinations, in terms of Usability and Timeliness. The table of Timeliness and Usability makes it easy to check our basic conclusions about a particular combination. Finally the very important and very traditional concept of Host and Guest Stars allows us to give the right weighting to each Star.

Chapter 12

Visiting Stars

Some Stars literally visit or pass through a house after it has been built or occupied. These Stars make up the ch'i tides of smaller and smaller time cycles, plus the ones associated with the human occupants. The human occupants do affect the ch'i balance, especially in the rooms that they work and sleep in, and so it is important to figure in their ch'i. As for the Stars of the various ch'i tides, we have Annual Flying Stars, Monthly Flying Stars, Daily Flying Stars, and even Hourly Flying Stars. The first two of these are the most important, but we will also consider the others here.

ANNUAL FLYING STARS

So far we have looked at charts built up of 9 Palaces, each containing a Period Star (in the Center) with a Sitting (Mountain) and Facing (Water) Star. These charts cover 20-year periods. However there are also Annual Flying Stars for each year. These Annual Stars are less powerful than the 20-year Period Stars, but are a force that needs to be reckoned with.

To draw these charts, begin with the base Period Star chart. Then simply take the Annual Flying Star number from table 12.1 below and place it in the center Palace (write it below and to the right of the Period Star number). Then either copy out, or fly, the Stars in the normal manner. Annual Flying Stars always fly in a positive direction.

This will give you influences pertaining just to the year concerned. For example, for 2001 (or 2010 or 2119) simply use 8 as the center Palace Star. The table also shows the Annual Stars in all the other Palaces as well.

I have not shown Annual Flying Stars for years earlier than 2000, but it is an easy enough matter to extend the dates backwards using the same sequence.

Table 12.1: *The Annual Flying Stars*

Years			Annual Star in Palace								
			Center	NW	W	NE	S	N	SW	E	SE
2000	2009	2018	9	1	2	3	4	5	6	7	8
2001	2010	2119	8	9	1	2	3	4	5	6	7
2002	2011	2020	7	8	9	1	2	3	4	5	6
2003	2012	2021	6	7	8	9	1	2	3	4	5
2004	2013	2022	5	6	7	8	9	1	2	3	4
2005	2014	2023	4	5	6	7	8	9	1	2	3
2006	2015	2024	3	4	5	6	7	8	9	1	2
2007	2016	2025	2	3	4	5	6	7	8	9	1
2008	2017	2026	1	2	3	4	5	6	7	8	9

If you don't have this book on hand or prefer to work things out yourself, here is a quick way of calculating the Annual Star in your head:

Take for example the year 1976:

1. Add up all its digits: 1 + 9 + 7 + 6 = 23

2. If the resultant total is greater than 9 then add up its digits: 2 + 3 = 5

3. Subtract this total from 11: 11 - 5 = 6

4. This number is the Annual Star that should be placed in the Center of the Lo Shu.

5. Fly the rest of the Stars forward in the same order as usual:

Center	NW	W	NE	S	N	SW	E	SE
6	7	8	9	1	2	3	4	5

There you have it, the Annual Stars calculated without using the table.

Now that you know how to calculate them, how do you use them? Start by entering them into the existing Flying Stars chart. I suggest you mark them in the bottom right corner of each Palace smaller than the Period Star or the Mountain and Water Stars. You should now re-evaluate each Palace, taking the following into account:

1. Period Star and the Annual Star. Look out for Palaces where the Annual Stars particularly reinforce or reduce the strength of the existing Period Star.

2. Water (Facing) Star and the Annual Star, to check for changes in your wealth luck for this year. If you use the Host and Guest method, then the Annual Star is the Guest, which may or may not support the Host Mountain Star. If it supports the Host in key Palaces, then your wealth will be supported during that year. If it destroys its Host, then the reverse is true.

3. Mountain (Sitting) Star and the Annual Star, to check for changes in your health, family, and relationship luck for this year. If you use the Host and Guest method, then the Annual Star is the Guest, which may or may not support the Host Sitting Star. If it supports the Host in key Palaces, then your health, family, and relationships will be supported during that year. If it destroys its Host, then the reverse is true.

Remember that the 20-year Period, Water, and Mountain Stars are the strongest, but the Annual Stars will hold some sway for 12 months, and their influence should be checked at the beginning of each solar year, around February 4/5 to see if any defensive measures need to be taken. Particular Stars to pay attention to include the position of the Annual 5-yellow Star, at which we will look more closely in chapter 14.

YOUR PERSONAL STAR

Human ch'i is also a form of Visiting Star, and its calculation depends on the same arithmetic as that used for Annual Stars. The main Flying Star chart deals with the Period Star, which is rather literally set in stone when the building is built. There is one school of thought that maintains that this Period number may be *reset* at the point where a new family moves in, when the human ch'i changes. To analyze how the human ch'i changes the balance, we must understand how everyone's individual Star is calculated. Some readers will be familiar with this concept, which has been popularized under the label of "personal kua number," or *ming kua*.

One interesting sidelight on the calculation of the Annual Flying Stars (see example above) is that this calculation is exactly the same as that for calculating your personal *kua* number if you are male.

If you are male, your personal kua number is none other than the Annual Flying star of the year in which you were born. (If you were born before February 4/5, make sure that you subtract one from the year before calculating.)

If you are female, however, the calculation is slightly different (because yin, or female, Stars move in the opposite direction).

Take for example the same year 1976; to find out the kua number of a woman:

0. If her birthdate is before 4/5 February, deduct one from the year of birth

1. Add up all its digits: $1 + 9 + 7 + 6 = 23$

2. If the resultant total is greater than 9 then add up its digits: $2 + 3 = 5$

3. Add 4 to this total: 5 + 4 = 9

4. This number, 9, is the female kua number for a woman born in 1976.

There is one further refinement—personal kua numbers can never be 5, as 5 comes from the center and does not correspond with a kua or trigram. If either of the above calculations come out with a 5, then males are assigned a kua number of 2, while females are assigned a kua number of 8.

It is this kua or trigram number that the East House/West House feng shui system uses to determine your four best and four worst directions.

ROOTS OF THE EAST HOUSE/WEST HOUSE SYSTEM

In chapter 4 we listed the alternative names for the 9 Flying Stars. Among these names were the words for the 8 Traveling Stars, or best/worst directions, (like sheng ch'i, liu sha, etc.) whose roots lie in the Flying Star School. In the simplified East House/West House system of feng shui, your personal best/worst directions change according to your year of birth, as per the above calculation.

The reason for this is that these "directions" are actually the Annual Flying Stars. Once you know, for example, that sheng ch'i (or Generating Breath) is just another description for t'an lang, the beneficial 1-white Star, then it makes much more sense to think about these directions as your natal Annual Star configuration rather than as your kua number. Of course, "kua number" is still an accurate term, because the Annual Stars pass from one kua (trigram) Palace to another.

A more organized way to approach this is to consider the person's birth Annual Star as his or her Personal Star. In our example, the 7-red would be the Star that belonged to the person. Now, this should be checked against sleeping and working areas. Many practitioners treat the Personal Star (in this case 7-red) as a Guest Star. I suggest instead that you treat it as the Host Star in, for example, the bedroom, and look at how the Mountain and Water Stars of the room support it.

If the Star configuration in the bedroom is 1-1-8, then the Metal of the Personal 7-red Star will be drained by the Water of the 1-white Star (Metal is reduced by Water). On the other hand, the Personal 7-red will be supported by the 8-white Earth Star (as Earth produces Metal). Hence this bedroom will support the person's finances but will not encourage people support.

This means that one use for the Personal Star is to help select bedrooms for specific family members. To do this, check the Personal Star against the Mountain and Water Stars of each of the available bedrooms to select the room that most supports the individual being assessed. As a general rule, it is only areas that are personal to the individual that should be considered—basically the bedroom and office/study. Also check the main entrance against the head of the household Personal Star. Elsewhere in the building this Personal Star is not of any real account.

The use of the Personal Star (or kua number) to determine working and sleeping position has a long history and has been utilized by many powerful men. For example, Mao Tse Tung, who was born in 1893, apparently used 9 as his kua number, and hence

East as his sheng ch'i direction. Interestingly, it is 1892 that yields an Annual Star number of 9, and this suggests that Mao may have calculated his number from the previous year, or maybe from his conception date. It is not unheard of for people knowledgeable in these calculations to give erroneous birth dates to prevent their enemies drawing up an accurate 4 Pillar horoscope. Mao was a firm believer in feng shui (even though he banned the printing and reading of feng shui books and suppressed its use by his own citizens).

Wherever he went, Mao apparently insisted upon having his bed always aligned in an East-West direction so that his head would always point to the East while he slept. In fact further confirmation of this can be drawn from his given name "Tung," which means East. His father deliberately picked this name, as it corresponded with his son's most auspicious direction. In Mao's case it certainly seems to have worked!

MONTHLY FLYING STARS

One of the great Masters of the Form School, Wang Wei (AD 1323–1474) is the reputed author of the *Yellow Emperor's Siting Classic*, which says:

> Every year has twelve months, and each month has positions in time and space of vital and torpid ch'i. Whenever one builds on a sheng [vital] ch'i position of a month, wealth will come his way and accumulate. . . To violate a monthly position of ssu [torpid] ch'i will bring bad luck and calamities.

Checking the Monthly Flying Stars has its roots deep in antiquity. You should calculate Monthly Flying Stars to determine the quality of ch'i, and hence of luck, in any particular month of the year. These Stars are considerably weaker than either the Annual or 20-year Period Stars. But they have one very interesting aspect: they can be used to pinpoint the month when some drawn-out affair may be finally triggered or concluded.

If, for example, the Month Star and the Annual Star are the same in one particular month (or, that is, they support each other), then that is a month to watch out for, because relevant events are more likely to take a dramatic turn during that month than any other in the year.

You can usefully use the Guest and Host technique here by looking upon the Monthly Star as a Guest Star. If the Monthly and Annual Stars supporting each other are unfavorable and affect a key Water Star (wealth), then this may be the time to watch out for negative developments in a business venture, for example. If the Monthly and Annual Stars "gang up" to affect a significant Mountain Star (relationships, family, and health), then this may signal the breakup of a relationship, or an illness.

On the other hand, a beneficial conjunction of Annual and Monthly Stars at the main door or in the office might indicate that the time has arrived to implement new plans or to move ahead with a new project. Try to use the predictive quality of these Stars to both protect against and take advantage of the Monthly Stars.

Remember that here "month" applies to the Chinese solar month, which is tied in to the seasons and tides (appendix 9) not to the fairly arbitrary months of the Western calendar. It certainly does not apply to the Chinese lunar month.

Because there are only 9 Stars but 12 solar months, the last three months of the year reflect the pattern of the first three months of the year. There is no philosophical reason why this should be so, only a numerical one. I have always thought this is one of the minor defects in the Flying Star system.

To work out the Monthly Stars, use table 12.2 below. The theory is that the first Monthly Star of any year will be an Earth Star, and therefore either Star 2, 5, or 8 (all Earth Stars). To determine which of these three is the Monthly Star for the first month, you have to know what kind of year it is. This depends up the Earthly Branch assigned to the year: for simplicity we will use the animal signs (which equate with the Earthly Branches) to identify these years. The monthly cycle moves smoothly on to the next year without a break in the numerical sequence, but will always contrive to be 2, 5, or 8 on the first month.

For example, the four years corresponding to the animal signs that mark the 4 cardinal points (Rat-North, Rabbit-East, Horse-South, Cock-West) start the year with the 8-white Month Star. This and the other two groups, which start with a 5-yellow Star and 2-black Star respectively, are laid out below in the table.

Table 12.2: *The Monthly Flying Stars (with their relation to the Annual Stars)*

Solar Month	Month begins approx*	Rat, Rabbit, Horse, Cock Year	Ox, Dragon, Sheep, Dog Year	Tiger, Snake, Monkey, Pig Year
		Years (all 2000...)		
		08, 20, 32, 44	09, 21, 33, 45	10, 22, 34, 46
		11, 23, 35, 47	00, 12, 24, 36	01, 13, 25, 37
		02, 14, 26, 38	03, 15, 27, 39	04, 16, 28, 40
		05, 17, 29, 41	06, 18, 30, 42	07, 19, 31, 43
III***	Feb 5	8**	5	2
IV	Mar 6	7	4	1
V	Apr 5	6	3	9
VI	May 6	5	2	8
VII	Jun 6	4	1	7
VIII	Jul 7	3	9	6
IX	Aug 8	2	8	5
X	Sep 8	1	7	4
XI	Oct 8	9	6	3
XII	Nov 7	8	5	2
I	Dec 7	7	4	1
II	Jan 6	6	3	9

(continued)

* These dates fluctuate by plus/minus a few days between years.
** These Month Star numbers are those for the Center Palace only. You can then fill in the remainder of the Palaces by flying the Stars from the Center Palace in the usual order in a positive/yang direction.
*** An apparently awkward fact is that the first Month of the Chinese solar year starts with Branch III. (The reason for this is that the winter solstice of the previous year must always mark the beginning of Branch I.)

The Monthly Flying Star can be read from the table. I suggest that you write in Monthly Stars very small at the bottom left hand corner of each Palace. The Monthly Star is put in the Center Palace of the Lo Shu, and the rest of the Stars are filled in numerically sequentially in the usual *positive* or yang sequence:

Center, NW, W, NE, S, N, SW, E, SE

Although the Monthly Star is not given much weight, if it suddenly reinforces an Annual or Period Star, it might act as a trigger for the main action, so in a timing sense it might be the most important Star of all.

Fig. 12.1 *The Base Period 6 Chart*

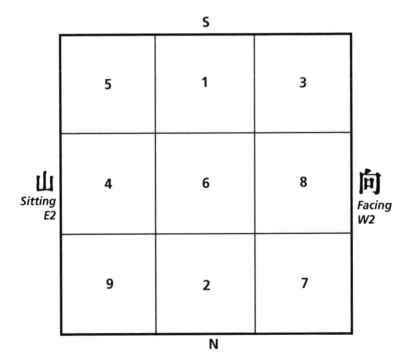

Fig. 12.2 *East-2 Sitting Period 6 House Chart*

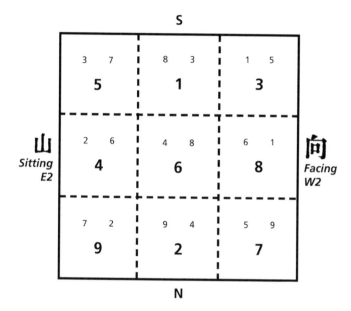

Let us do a worked example and look at the transformations of the Monthly star over the course of the year 2002 of an example house that sits in East-2 and was first built and occupied by its present owners in Period 6 (see figure 12.1). No major reconstruction has taken place since 1978.

Using the tables in appendix 1, and looking up East-2, we can fill in the Mountain and Water Stars, as shown in figure 12.2.

Now as we are checking the Monthly Stars for 2002, and this year is a Horse year, we can see from table 12.2 that the first month will have Star 8 in the Central Palace. Put that Star in, then fly the rest of the Monthly Stars in a positive direction. Write the Monthly Stars in the bottom left of each Palace, or cell (figure 12.3).

This might look a bit complex, but if you concentrate on the Monthly Stars it will become clearer. The first thing that you should notice is that the Monthly Star is coincidentally the same as the Water Star in each Palace. This will have the effect (for this month only) of considerably strengthening the Water Stars. As the Water Star is wealth related, you can expect a strengthening of wealth luck, especially in the SE Palace and Central Palace, where the beneficial Water Stars 7 and 8 are already located.

Let's generate the Monthly Star chart for the 2nd month (March 6, 2002 to April 4, 2002). Check table 12.2 and you will see that the Star in the Central Palace in the second month of 2002 is Star 7. When you fly the Stars you get the configuration in figure 12.4.

Here you can see that the already auspicious 6-8-1 combination in the West Palace is augmented by the 9-purple Star, which will increase both wealth and health and relationship benefits, as the 9-purple Star accentuates any other Stars it is with.

Fig. 12.3 *Monthly Stars for the First (Solar) Month of 2002 (February 4–March 5) for an East-2 Sitting House Occupied in Period 6*

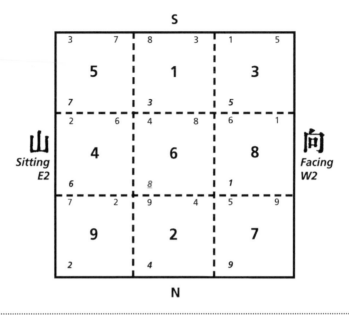

Fig. 12.4 *Monthly Stars for the Second (Solar) Month of 2002 (March 6–April 4) for an East-2 Sitting House Occupied in Period 6*

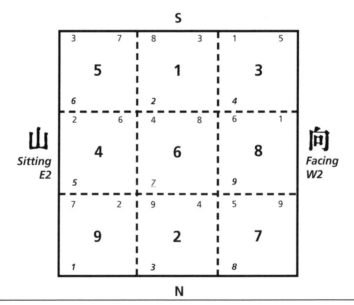

The reverse happens in the East Palace, where health and relationship luck will take a hit, as the Monthly Star 5-yellow flies in to reinforce the already troublesome 2-black Star.

You could continue to analyze the next 10 months to see the effect of the Monthly Stars, but for the moment these two examples should suffice. I suggest that, as an exercise, you draw up the next 10 months and try analyzing the likely trigger points yourself.

You should then stop and look back on what you have learned, summarized in figure 12.5, which brings together the various types of charts you can draw up to analyze the Flying Stars of a building.

1. Each chart has a Period Star that always flies in a positive direction.

2. Above and to the left of each of the Period Stars are the Mountain Stars, which may fly in either direction and which govern health, family, and relationships.

3. Above and to the right of each of the Period Stars are the Water Stars, which may fly in either direction and which govern wealth.

4. The second part of the illustration shows the Annual Flying Stars plotted with the Period Stars. These always fly in a positive direction.

5. The set of 12 charts that are the 12 Monthly Flying Star charts, one for each solar month starting on February 4/5. The Monthly Stars always fly in a positive yang direction. These allow you to spot the trigger times.

6. Personal kua numbers (or in other words the Annual Stars of their birth year) that can be used to help select the best bedrooms for specific family members.

DAILY FLYING STARS

We will not be considering the Daily Flying Star configurations in a lot of detail, as they are too weak to be of major significance.

The Daily Flying Stars are best looked up in one of the almanacs listed in the bibliography. If you want to calculate them yourself, then you should know that the Daily Flying Stars are keyed (as are all Flying Stars) to the solar calendar, specifically the mid-winter and the mid-summer solstices, which occur around the December 22 and June 2 each year. The Daily Flying Stars run in a positive direction (5, 6, 7, 8, 9, 1, 2 . . .) from the mid-winter solstice to the mid-summer solstice, at which stage they reverse and run in a negative direction (6, 5, 4, 3, 2, 1, 9, 8 . . .) until the next mid-winter solstice.

BEST DAY SELECTION AND KEY DIARY DATES

The Daily Flying Stars are mostly used for predicting what sort of day you are likely to have. This is important if you want to select a good day to get married, sign an important

Fig. 12.5 *Summary of the Different Types of Star Charts and How They Relate to Each Other*

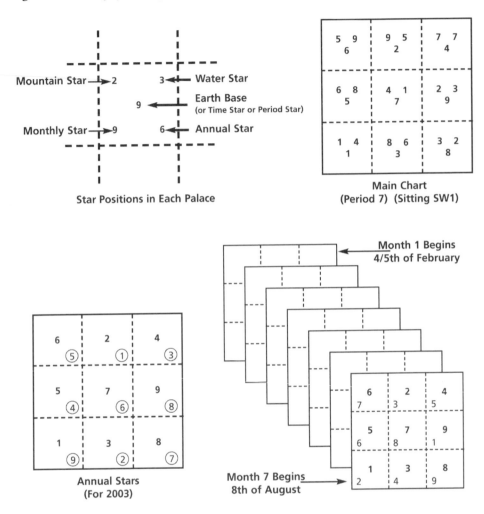

Mountain Star →2 3← Water Star

Earth Base
9 ← (or Time Star or Period Star)

Monthly Star →9 6← Annual Star

Star Positions in Each Palace

5 9	9 5	7 7
6	2	4
6 8	4 1	2 3
5	7	9
1 4	8 6	3 2
1	3	8

Main Chart
(Period 7) (Sitting SW1)

Month 1 Begins
4/5th of February

6 ⑤	2 ①	4 ③
5 ④	7 ⑥	9 ⑧
1 ⑨	3 ②	8 ⑦

Annual Stars
(For 2003)

6 7	2 3	4 5
5 6	7 8	9 1
1 2	3 4	8 9

Month 7 Begins
8th of August

Monthly Charts to Determine Timing
(12 charts, one for each solar month)

contract, move into a new house, or have a surgical procedure. Selection of such a good day will considerably improve your chances of success.

This selection is done by comparing your kua number (Personal Star) with the Flying Star of the day in question, using the compatibility of the 5 Elements. For example, say your Personal Star number is 7. The 7-red Star is Metal. We know that Earth produces Metal, therefore we can deduce that a Metal or an Earth day would be supportive for you.

These days are those that have Flying Stars 6, 7 (Metal) or 2, 5, 8 (Earth). Contrary days will be those with the Flying Star number 9, because this is Fire, and Fire destroys Metal. Water Star days are also not so good, as they deplete your Metal. Get the idea?

There are other related systems for calculating the general appropriateness or otherwise of individual days for different activities. This information appears in the *T'ung Shu*, but is also available in English translations such as that published by Raymond Lo and Ricky Than, or in the diaries published annually by Victor Dy at Renaissance in Manila (see the bibliography). All of these are excellent publications and their predictions of "day type" depend upon comparing the Earthly Branch of the day with the Earthly Branch of the solar month and with a special sequence of 12 days. Each of these types of day are suitable for a whole list of things (breaking ground, redecorating, going to the doctor, getting engaged, etc.) and not suitable for a range of other activities.

For example there are good days for signing a contract, and I think we all instinctively know that there are good days and bad days for that first date. There is even a day that the almanac says is not good for *any* applied activity, and in fact recommends you just indulge in wine or go fishing, as it were. I think we all have experienced that sort of day: the trouble is that we usually don't recognize it when it arrives, only after we have had a totally frustrating and fruitless day.

Perhaps this is a bit too black and white, but other days that are recommended for starting partnerships or opening stores, for example, are carefully observed by many Chinese businessmen, on the reasonable assumption that if a business arrangement is commenced on a beneficial day, it will continue to be fruitful, but if the same contract was signed on a "broken" day, it will only lead to friction, dissatisfaction, and little profit. Before anyone cries "superstition," I suggest you try it for yourself.

Hourly Flying Stars

Unfortunately the Hourly Flying Star is not simply allocated to the 12 double-hours of the day in order. Like the Daily Stars, the Hourly Flying Stars run in a positive direction (5, 6, 7, 8, 9, 1, 2 . . .) from the mid-winter solstice to the mid-summer solstice, at which stage they reverse and run in a negative direction (6, 5, 4, 3, 2, 1, 9, 8 . . .) until the next mid-winter solstice. In addition you need to know the Branch of the day to determine which Star starts the hours.

Table 12.3 below gives the Hourly Flying Stars.

The double-hour Flying Stars can also be utilized to decide the best time of the day to do something. For example, someone with a Personal Star number 1 (Water) would find a Metal hour supportive, as Metal produces Water. Metal hours have Flying Star numbers of 6 and 7.

We have covered a lot of ground in this chapter, but don't feel that you have to know it all immediately. You will now have an inkling of how some of the connections between the different formulas and schools of feng shui fit together.

Basically the Stars in this chapter are all Visiting Stars if we consider the Period, Mountain, and Water Stars as fixed Stars for a period of 20 years.

Table: 12.3: *The Hourly Flying Stars*

Day Branch Group (or Quadruplicity)

double hour	Rat/Horse Rabbit/Cock		Dragon/Dog Ox/Sheep		Tiger/Monkey Snake/Pig	
	yang flow*	yin flow**	yang flow	yin flow	yang flow	yin flow
23:00–01:00	1	9	4	6	7	3
01:00–03:00	2	8	5	5	8	2
03:00–05:00	3	7	6	4	9	1
05:00–07:00	4	6	7	3	1	9
07:00–09:00	5	5	8	2	2	8
11:00–13:00	6	4	9	1	3	7
09:00–11:00	7	3	1	9	4	6
13:00–15:00	8	2	2	8	5	5
15:00–17:00	9	1	3	7	6	4
17:00–19:00	1	9	4	6	7	3
19:00–21:00	2	8	5	5	8	2
21:00–23:00	3	7	6	4	9	1

* Yang flow is any date from winter solstice (circa December 22) to summer solstice (circa June 22), the warming or yang cycle of the year.
** Yin flow is any date from summer solstice (circa June 22) to winter solstice (circa December 22), the cooling or yin cycle of the year.

To summarize:
- The Annual Stars are an important indicator of the potential events of the year ahead, and you should place enhancers and cures for them on or about 4/5 February every year.
- The Monthly Stars will help you with timing, suggesting when to attempt something and when to hold back.
- The Daily and Hourly Stars are best looked up in a Chinese Almanac. Use them when you want to pick a date in the near future for a big event, marriage, and so on.
- The Personal Star (also known as your kua number) is useful in picking the best bedrooms for individual members of a household. They also help you predict events.

These calculations make the predictions and advice of a good feng shui *hsien sheng* (Master) worth paying for. When you have mastered them, you will also be able to predict and select the best timing for yourself.

Chapter 13

Special Star Patterns

We have looked at the generation of the different types of Star—the Period Star, the Mountain and Water Stars, and the Visiting Annual, Monthly, and Personal Stars. Now it is time to examine some of the overall patterns they make in the whole chart.

THE 4 TYPES OF FLYING STAR CHARTS

Let us take a closer look and single out significant charts, so when you come across one you will immediately recognize it. Despite the apparent complexity of the construction of Flying Stars charts, they all reduce to 4 types.

There is an interesting rule that arises from the structure of these charts, which can be used as a quick check on your calculations. It is this:

1. In any chart there will be three Stars with the same number as the Period Star; for example, if the Period is 7, then this Period number will of course be in the center.

2. The same numbered Mountain and Water Stars will fly to either the Sitting or Facing Palace and nowhere else in the chart.

These key Stars of the same number will (by definition) always be Timely during the period the house was built. In turn, they will then cause one of only 4 types of chart to be formed:

1. Favorable for wealth and for health, family, and relationships.

2. Unfavorable for health and for wealth, or reversed chart.

148

3. Favorable for wealth but unfavorable for health chart. This is a Double Facing chart, called this from the presence of both the Mountain and Water Stars in the Facing Palace.

4. Favorable for health but unfavorable for wealth chart. This is a Double Sitting chart, called this from the presence of both the Mountain and Water Stars in the Sitting Palace.

Statistically there are 216 possible chart configurations, that is 8 x 3 = 24 possible directions multiplied by 9 possible 20-year periods. But of these, the charts for subdivision 2 and 3, for each direction, are the same (e.g., SW2 and SW3 have the same chart), so the actual number of different charts is reduced to 144.

Let us look at just one Period. Of the 16 charts (2 possible in each of 8 directions) that apply to a house built (or first occupied) during Period 7:

4 are good for health and wealth
4 are unfavorable for both health and wealth, or reversed
4 are Double Facing charts
4 are Double Sitting charts
———
16 in all

Identifying which one of these 4 types of chart you have generated will immediately give you a general reading and indicate houses that you would not of choice purchase during the current Period.

Let us examine examples of each of these 4 types of chart for Period 7 (1984–2004). The rules apply equally well to other Periods. The key to identifying these charts at a glance is to *find the Mountain and Water Stars that have the same number as the Period Star.*

1. Favorable for Wealth and for Health, Family, and Relationships Chart

In Chinese this configuration is called a *wang shan wang shui* chart, literally "vigorous mountain, vigorous water" chart. It is also sometimes referred to as a Prosperous Sitting and Facing chart. This is illustrated in figure 13.1.

This occurs when the Period Star in the center (in this case 7, but the rule applies to all Periods) numerically matches the Facing Star *in the Facing Palace*, and the Sitting Star *in the Sitting Palace*. It is the *italics* that are important. In this chart the appropriate Facing Star (7) brings luck to the Facing Palace (W2). And the appropriate Sitting Star (7) brings luck to the Sitting Palace (E2). This is a very good chart, for both Stars are in the appropriate place and bring both kinds of luck.

This chart will be strengthened if there is real water outside the building on the Facing side and a good back support behind the building (on the Sitting side). This is the best of the 4 types of chart.

Fig. 13.1 *Favorable for Wealth and Health, or Wang Shan Wang Shui Chart*

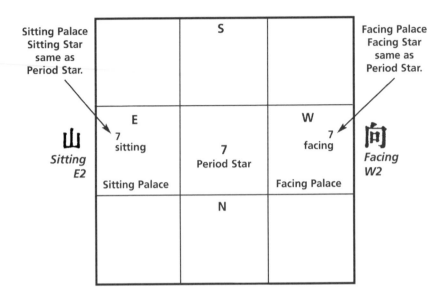

Fig. 13.2 *Reversed, or Shang Shan Hsia Shui Chart*

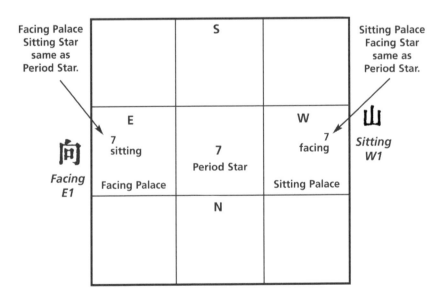

However, if the external Form is the reverse of this, then the chart bodes exceptionally bad luck, which is difficult to remedy.

2. Unfavorable for Health and for Wealth, or Reversed Chart

This is called a *shang shan hsia shui* chart, literally "up the mountain, down the river."

This occurs when the Period Star in the center (in this case 7) numerically matches the Facing Star *in the Sitting Palace*, and the Sitting Star *in the Facing Palace*, in other words, reversed (see figure 13.2). In this chart the Stars are in their opposite type of Palace, a very undesirable situation. The Facing Star (7) brings bad luck to the Sitting Palace, and the Sitting Star (7) brings bad luck to the Facing Palace. The result is unfavorable to both health and wealth, with ill health compounded by many financial ups and downs.

If the house naturally faces a mountain and is backed by a water feature, then it will bring its occupants better fortune. The placing of mountains in front of a house, with water behind, is totally contrary to the basic principles of Form School feng shui; nevertheless this is the rule according to Flying Star feng shui. Accordingly, the best correction (but not ideal) is to place Water in the form of a pond, swimming pool, or fountain behind the building (on the side of the Sitting Palace). And then to put something massive, mountainous, or Earth derived, like a wall, in front of the entrance or Facing side.

This category of chart also includes Combination of Three and Continuous Bead chart formations, which we deal with below.

3. Double Facing Chart

This is a favorable for wealth but unfavorable for health chart. It is called a Double Facing chart, from the presence of both of the same Star numbers in the Facing Palace (see figure 13.3). In Chinese this is called a *shuang hsing tao hsiang* chart, literally "double Star arriving at Facing."

Double Facing occurs when the Period Star in the center (in this case 7) numerically matches the Facing and Sitting Star both located *in the Facing Palace*. In this chart the appropriately placed Facing Star (7) brings wealth luck to the Facing Palace (S1), but the Sitting Star in the same Palace destroys health, family, and relationship luck.

The correction for the Sitting Star is to place an Earth or mountainlike feature, such as a wall, in the front of the entrance or Facing Palace. If the facing direction enjoys both Water and Mountain in front of it, then both kinds of luck will be supported.

4. Double Sitting Chart

This chart is favorable for health but unfavorable for wealth and is called Double Sitting from the presence of both of the same Star numbers in the Sitting Palace (see figure 13.4). This is called in Chinese a *shuang hsing tao tzuo* chart, literally "double Star arriving at Sitting."

Double Sitting occurs when the Period Star in the center (in this case 7) numerically matches the Facing and Sitting Star both located in the Sitting Palace. In this chart the appropriately placed Sitting Star (7) brings health, family, and relationship luck to the Sitting Palace (N2), but the Facing Star in the same Palace destroys wealth luck.

Fig. 13.3 *Double Facing, or Shuang Hsing Tao Hsiang Chart*

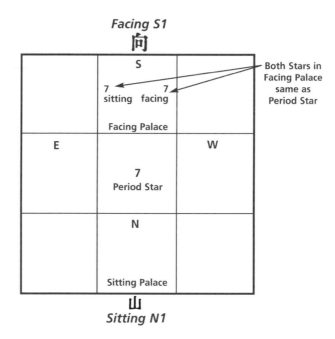

Facing S1
向

Sitting N1
山

The correction for the Facing Star is to place a physical Water feature such as a fountain or pool behind the rear or Sitting Palace. The presence of both a Mountain feature and a Water feature at the rear of the building will stimulate both kinds of luck. Some Masters recommend that in these circumstances the back door (on the Sitting side) is used as the primary entrance to the building.

Where there is only Water on the Sitting side, the expression is that "the Mountain falls into Water," thereby compromising family, relationship, and health luck.

Having identified the type of chart, and therefore derived an idea of the overall luck of the chart, you should now look at the Star patterns. By working out the meaning of the patterns in each of these Palaces you will have a much better feel for the chart: it will cease to be a sea of numbers. In your practice book, write down your conclusions about the Star patterns in each of these Palaces. Then you are ready to look for special patterns, some of which may overrule what you have already discovered.

SPECIAL CHART PATTERNS

We will now look at rarer types of chart. These charts depend on arithmetic symmetries of the Stars in each Palace. As before, these charts all need supporting exterior form structures to bring out their best qualities. Also note that these formations lose their

Fig. 13.4 *Double Sitting, or Shuang Hsing Tao Tzuo Chart*

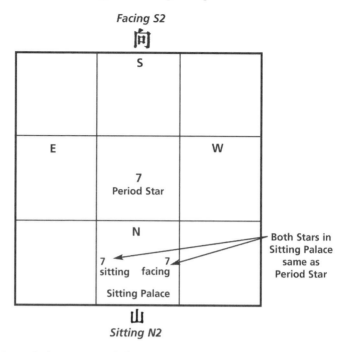

Facing S2

向

Sitting N2

山

power when their Period changes, as if the power of their ch'i has evaporated, except wherever explicitly stated to the contrary.

COMBINATION OF TEN CHART

The Combination of Ten chart (figure 13.5) is considered to be very favorable. The Chinese name is *he shih chu*, literally "Combination 10 configuration." You can find these by examining each Palace in a chart. In each Palace add the Period Star to either the Water or Mountain Star. If either of these additions come to 10 then you may have detected a Combination of Ten chart. Check that the same addition is also true in the other 8 Palaces to be sure. The theory is that addition summing to 10 shows a strong and smooth flow of energy to those Stars in every Palace, with support from the Period Star itself. The chart is totally beneficial.

Ten is considered to be a number of completion. The Chinese character for 10 is an equal armed cross showing balance in all directions. It is interesting to note that the Chinese had a decimal system of counting in the 14th century BC, during the Shang dynasty, some 2,300 years before the introduction of decimal arithmetic in Europe circa AD 976. Therefore it is not surprising to find that 10 is seen as a completion number by the Chinese.

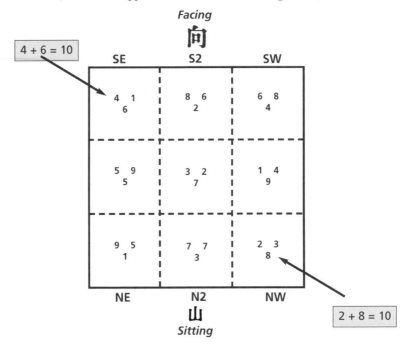

Fig. 13.5 *Sample Combination of Ten Chart from Period 7 (This also happens to be a Double Sitting chart.)*

An example of a Combination of Ten chart in Period 7 is the S2 Facing chart in figure 13.5 (which happens also to be a Double Sitting chart). To check this, take each Palace and add the Period Star to the Mountain Star. In each case this produces 10.

If you try the same for the Period Star and the Water Star, it only works in the North Palace. In each case of a Combination of Ten chart, one of the Stars in the addition must be the Period Star.

From an interpretation point of view, it is the Star that is part of this addition that is very much strengthened, some would say doubled, in efficacy. So in the case above, it is the Mountain Star that is strengthened in each Palace (not the Water Star). Some commentators go as far as to divide the Combination of Ten into two types: Facing Star Combination of Ten, and Sitting Star Combination of Ten. The first of these doubles the wealth luck of the chart, while the second doubles the health, relationship, and family luck of the chart.

There are only 20 occurrences of a Combination of Ten chart in 180 years. Like the other special charts, they need external Mountain or Water features to activate them, otherwise they remain just mathematical curiosities.

Another arithmetically extraordinary chart is the Combination of Three (sometimes called Parent String) chart (see figure 13.6) where *every* Palace has one of the combinations 1-4-7, 2-5-8, or 3-6-9. The Chinese name for this is *fu-mu san pan kua*, literally meaning "Parents of 3 Plate Trigram." It is not sufficient for one or two Palaces to have these combinations. Every Palace in the chart must have them. This configuration is very powerful and beneficial, but quite rare. This configuration overrules any unfortunate aspects of the chart to bring very good luck. Such a chart is associated with good health, great fortune, fame, respect, familial harmony, and respectful descendants.

This example (and indeed all Combination of Three formations) are also Reversed charts, with the Mountain Star at the Facing Palace, and the Water Star at the Sitting Palace. But this does not matter; it is nevertheless a very good chart. You can still do the same corrections as you normally would for a Reversed chart, although you should be careful how you mess with such a good configuration. The Combination of Three can be activated with a real Mountain feature on the Facing side, and a real Water feature on the Sitting side.

The power of this kind of formation may stem from the fact that every Palace has one Star from each of the 3 Primaries: Heaven, Earth, and Man. It is said to magnify the

Fig. 13.6 *Sample Combination of Three Chart from Period 8*

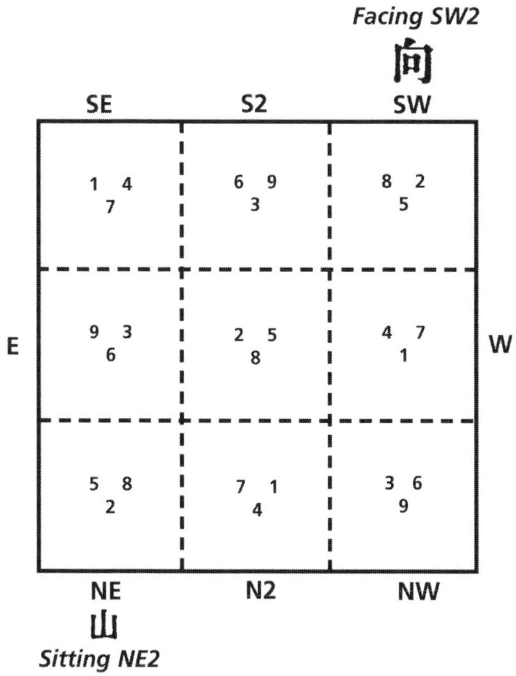

Facing SW2

向

	SE	S2	SW
	1 4 7	6 9 3	8 2 5
E	9 3 6	2 5 8	4 7 1	W
	5 8 2	7 1 4	3 6 9
	NE	N2	NW

山

Sitting NE2

inherent luck of the chart by a factor of three. It is also said to continue to work for its occupants during all Eras. Obviously if you find yourself living in such a structure, stay with it.

This kind of chart is quite rare and does not occur in the 1st, 3rd, 7th, or 9th Period, but appears 4 times each in the 2nd, 5th, and 8th Periods, but twice in the 4th and 6th, making a total of only 16 such charts in the whole 180 years of a Great Cycle.

Neither of these two special combinations will work if there is a missing Palace. In other words, if the house or building shape is not regular, and part of the building overlaps or underlaps the Lo Shu, then even with the presence of the right numbers, these special combinations do not work. In such a circumstance, serious consideration should be given to adding the missing area on to the building so that the Lo Shu is complete and these special combinations then come into play.

Continuous Bead Chart

The formation in figure 13.7 is called in Chinese *lien chu san pan kua*, which literally means "Continuous Bead 3 Plate Trigram." This formation occurs where the 3 Stars in every Palace follow each other successively, like beads on a string. It is also referred

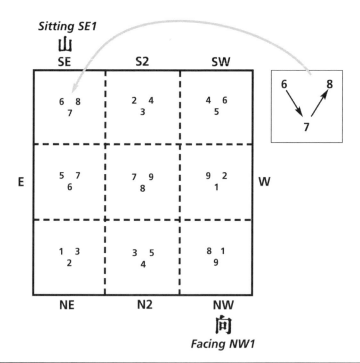

Fig. 13.7 *Period 8 Sitting SE1 Is an Example of a Continuous Bead Formation*

to as a Pearl String chart. For example, a Period 8, Sitting SE1 is an example of a Continuous Bead formation.

In the above figure, look in each Palace and you will see 3 numbers in succession, such as 6, 7, 8, or 2, 3, 4. This is why they are called a Continuous Bead. This condition must be true of every Palace. These charts reputedly have the potential to triple the good luck inherent in them, but they still need external physical support in the form of Mountain in front and Water behind. Without that external support they will not be as good a configuration.

You will have noticed that in this example the Stars in each Palace go sequentially Mountain Star-Period Star-Water Star, as in 6, 7, 8. As the ch'i flows *to* the Water Star this chart offers the potential to triple wealth luck. Conversely a chart whose stars in each Palace run sequentially Water Star-Period Star-Mountain Star will enhance the Mountain Star; in other words the family, health, and relationship luck would be tripled.

All Continuous Bead formations are also Reversed charts, but that does not matter.

PRISON, OR LOCKED, CHART

This is a type of chart that changes its quality radically from one Period to the next. Remember that (provided there is no Period resetting by roof renovation) a house's Flying Stars do not change as it gets older. The chart stays the same. What does change is the power and Timeliness of the Stars in that chart. So that from 1984 till 2004, the 7-red Star is powerful and good, but when this time is over it again becomes P'o chun, the "breaker of armies" and the "severer of fate." The numbers in the boxes don't change, but the qualities of those numbers certainly do.

Prison or Locked charts are a specific example of this change. They are sometimes called Trapped Prominent Star charts (see figure 13.8).

The theory behind them is as follows. If we have a chart whose Period number in the Central Palace is 7, for example, then the two Prominent Stars will be the Water Star 7 and the Mountain Star 7. In this chart, the Water Star 7 and the Mountain Star 7 can never be in the Central Palace.

However, it is possible for the Mountain Star 8 or the Water Star 8 to be in the Central Palace. This is not a problem during Period 7. But when we move into Period 8, the new Prominent Stars are Mountain Star 8 and Water Star 8. Guess what? If they are in the Central Palace, then they are considered Trapped.

So lets define that again. A Locked, or Prison, chart occurs when either the Sitting or Mountain Star with the same number as the *current* Period number is trapped in the Central Palace. This can never happen during the Period when the home was built (or occupied). But it can happen as soon as the next Period rolls around. Then the new Prominent Star changes and becomes trapped.

Lets look at an example: During Period 7, a Facing SE2 chart is OK. When, however, the magic February 2004 passes, the Mountain Star 8 becomes the Prominent Star and finds itself trapped in the Central Palace. The result is a Prison, or Locked, chart.

Let's just go over this critical concept one more time. Remember, once the chart has been set up, the Period, Water, and Mountain Stars don't move around at all. What happens, as the house ages and passes from Period to Period, is that the number of the

Fig. 13.8 *An Example of a Trapped Prominent Star 8 in a House Built in Period 7 (also happens to be a Continuous Bead Formation)*

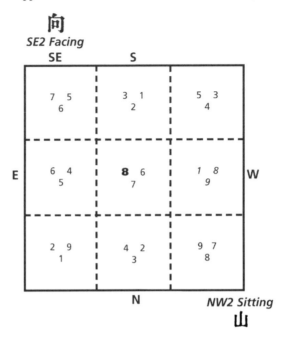

Prominent Star changes. In Period 7 the Prominent Stars are Water Star 7 and Mountain Star 7, but in Period 8 the Prominent Stars are Water Star 8 and Mountain Star 8. At this point, an ordinary Water Star 8 or Mountain Star 8 may be in the Central Palace. Suddenly they are promoted to Prominent Star (by the changing Period), and guess what? They are trapped in the quiet Central Palace where they can't spread their beneficial qualities.

If the newly Prominent Mountain Star is trapped in the Central Palace, then people and health luck will suffer, but if the newly Prominent Water Star is trapped in the Central Palace, then wealth luck will suffer.

This is because a trapped Prominent Star cannot effectively bestow its blessings on a house. If you think about it, you will see that there can never be a trapped Star formation at the time of construction or moving in because the current Period Star (being in the center) will not be able to generate a Mountain or Water Star of this number also located in the Center Palace. It is only when a house moves into a new Period that a trapped Prominent Star becomes a possibility.

For example a Period 6 house may have a 7 or 8 Mountain or Water Star in its Central Palace, but these only become of concern as the house moves into those Periods without any structural change. At this point in time, a house moved into during Period 7 with an 8 Star trapped in the Center Palace is of most concern. Examples of this configuration in Period 7 are NW1/NW2/NW3/SE1/SE2 and SE3 Facing properties. Anyone owning one of these properties should do the remedy designed to release the trapped Star just after the Period switches over to 8.

The classic cure for this condition uses the corresponding 5-yellow Star, on the grounds that the 5-yellow can work its release magic on its home turf, the Central Palace. The procedure is to introduce an exterior Water feature adjacent to whatever sector contains either the Mountain or Water Star 5-yellow. For example, to release a trapped 8 *Mountain* Star at the time a Period 7 changes to Period 8 in February 2004, place a Water feature adjacent and external to the sector that contains the 5-yellow *Mountain* Star.

However, messing with Water and the 5-yellow is fraught with danger, so some practitioners suggest the use of Water in a more symbolic sense. They say that the removal of walls or partitions between the Central Palace and the Palace holding the relevant releasing 5-yellow Star so that one can see the other is the correct cure. Let's look at the example in figure 13.9.

This is quite an interesting chart. It is a Double Facing chart built in Period 6 with both the Water Star 6 and the Mountain Star 6 in the Facing Palace. If you look at the Central Palace during the time of construction you can see nothing particularly wrong. However, come February 1984 and the Water Star 7 in the Central Palace becomes Prominent (now 7 is the Period) and is immediately trapped.

So what do we do? Using the last method you identify where the 5-yellow Water Star is located (as it happens in the West Palace). (Obviously the 5-yellow's Element is always

Fig. 13.9 *Fixing a Locked Chart (NW2 Facing Period 6 construction house in February 1984, just about to move into Period 7)*

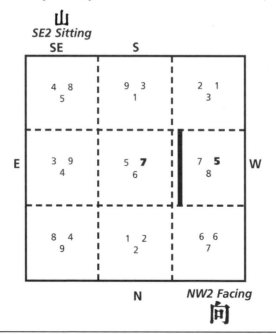

Earth. Here I am referring to the 5-yellow being in the Water Star position [top right] of the Palace.) Then you examine the wall between the center of the house (or it may be a hall) and the West Palace room. Is it possible to open a doorway or open up an unobstructed view between these rooms? If it is, then problem solved, by allowing the trapped Star to escape.

Some modern Masters, like Yap Cheng Hai, recommend this procedure only for yin houses (or grave sites), not the houses of the living. Instead he recommends the more radical route of changing the Period Star of the house altogether, which will give the house an entirely new chart. This route is expensive, as it involves either major renovations (including removal of the roof), or moving out and returning after the Period change, both of which are significant upheavals. Other suggestions have been made to release the trapped Star, but their implementation requires the services of a very experienced feng shui Master.

My recommendation is that you take action before you enter the Period where the Star becomes trapped. If you find that none of the above remedies are practical then you should consider the option of selling or renting the house and moving out.

Fu Yin and Fan Yin

These formations are concerned solely with the Central Palace or t'ai chi of the house. The Chinese for these two complementary types of formation is *fu yin* and *fan yin*. ("*Fu*" has the same meaning as "*fu*" in *fu wei*, which is associated with the Left and Right Assistant Stars. "*Yin*" means chant or song, and does not have the same meaning here as yin and yang.) These names literally mean "hidden song" and "contrary position song." These rather perplexing names are translated much more poetically by some commentators as "Hidden Siren" and "Inverse Siren."

The 5-yellow star is perhaps the most malevolent of all the Stars in the Flying Star system. Its natural home is in the Central Palace. When the 5-yellow Star flies back into the Central Palace, a special type of chart is formed (figure 13.10). By this I mean if either the 5-yellow Water or 5-yellow Mountain Star flies in a positive direction into the Central Palace, it creates a fu yin, or a Hidden Siren chart. When either of these flies backwards into the Central Palace, it is called a fan yin or Inverse Siren chart.

It is strange that the presence of the 5-yellow Star as a Mountain or Water Star in its home Palace should be a bad formation, and there is some doubt that it is always so.

Obviously neither of these charts will appear during the 5th Period, when the 5-yellow Period Star is at home in the Central Palace as the Period Star, because then it can't produce either a 5-yellow Mountain or 5-yellow Water Star in the Central Palace.

Despite the configuration being included in Master Shen's classic book on Hsuan Kung Flying Star, on the whole, I would not take too much notice of this particular special formation.

The effect of the Hidden or Inverse Siren depends on whether the Water Star or the Mountain Star is involved. If the former, then wealth may suffer; if the latter, then the more human side of things like family, relationships, and health are supposed to suffer.

But if we go back to first principles, we know that even bad configurations must be set off by physical or landform factors. How can we relate *any* external factors to the

Fig. 13.10 *A Mountain Star Hidden Siren Chart Facing W1 in Period 7*

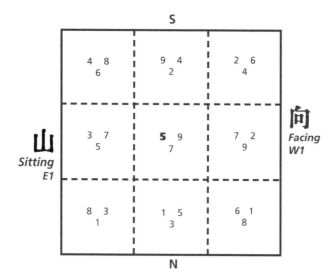

Central Palace? We can't, for we can only observe what is there internally in the house in this area.

This formation may be the real reason behind the general feng shui rule that you should not put water or clutter in the Central Palace. In other words, don't place too many things (especially water or any symbolic mountain feature) in the Central Palace area of a house, unless you want to run the risk of inadvertently activating a Hidden or Inverse Siren formation, which after all are fairly common. So keep the general precept, but don't worry too much about these two configurations in detail.

SUMMARY TABLE OF SPECIAL CHART PATTERNS

As a rapid way of checking if your chart has any special features, I have brought the key elements of this chapter together into one super-table in table 13.1. It acts as a quick summary, so that for Period 7 and 8 you can tell which are the overall best and worst Facing directions. You will then have to look at every chart in detail, but this will act as a good initial guide.

This table will also help in selecting land and the building direction of a new house. Instead of drawing up all 16 possible Facing directions, you can simply select from the best charts below, or at least eliminate the structurally bad ones. As you can only choose to build in the future, I have only used construction dates in Period 7 and 8 to simplify things.

This table will also be very useful in making a rapid diagnosis of the best and worst structures in these two very relevant periods, covering move-in dates from 1984 to 2024, if you subscribe to the theory that moving in resets the Period number.

Table 13.1: *Good and Bad Overall Chart Patterns in Periods 7 and 8*
(The directions shown are Facing Directions.)

Type of Chart	Facing in Period 7	Facing in Period 8
Good Charts		
Wang Shan Wang Shui (good for health & wealth)	W2/W3/NW1/E2/E3/SE1	SW1/NW2/NW3/NE1/SE2/SE3
Combination of Ten chart	S2/S3/N2/N3	SW1/NE1
Combination of Three chart	——	SW2/SW3/NE2/NE
Ho Tu 3 Number chart	W1/W2/W3/E1/E2/E3	S1/S2/S3/N1/N2/N
Continuous Bead chart	NW2/NW3/SE2/SE3	NW1/SE1
Mixed Charts		
Double Facing	S1/SW1/N2/N3/NE2/NE3	S2/S3/W2/W3/N1/E1
Double Sitting	S2/S3/SW2/SW3/N1/NE1	S1/W1/N2/N3/E2/E3
Potential Prison or Locked charts	NW1/NW2/NW3/SE1/SE2/SE3	NW1/NW2/NW3/SE1/SE2/SE3
Bad Charts		
Shang Shan Hsia Shui (Reversed)	W1/NW2/NW3/E1/SE2/SE3	NW1/SE1/SW2/SW3/NE2/NE3
Hidden/Inverse Siren chart	W1/W2/W3/E1/E2/E3	SW1/SW2/SW3/NE1/NE2/NE3

This table can act as a basic guide to the facing directions of good and bad charts during these two key Periods. Of course, "good" charts and "bad" charts are oversimplifications, and any chart can be improved with work, or even reversed. Using this table, you have an initial indication before you start detailed work.

Chapter 14

Wild Stars

Although the Flying Stars chart for each house differs according to its Period and orientation, there are some Stars that arrive at the same Palace in every house every year. As we saw in chapter 12, these are called the Annual Flying Stars. The Palaces affected by these are the same for every house. For example the Annual 5-yellow Star arrived in the East Palace in every house in 2002, and its Annual location is the same for everybody in any given year. The same is true of the Fate Stars, which fly around the Lo Shu, changing their position every year. So this chapter is effectively a checklist of the Flying Stars and Fate Stars, which you should check on at the beginning of each year, on or before February 4.

Instead of laboriously working out the position of all these more troublesome Stars every year, it is useful to have simple tables so that in any given year you can simply look up the tables in this chapter to see what needs immediate attention at the beginning of each new year.

THE ANNUAL 5-YELLOW TROUBLESOME STAR

We have already come across the nasty 5-yellow Star. Its annual location should be checked before you do any interior renovation or before doing structural feng shui changes. You should try not to disturb the 5-yellow Star. One of the reasons why the 5-yellow is considered so dangerous is that it is the one Star that does not have a corresponding trigram, and is therefore considered unpredictable.

Let's be clear. The Palace in the chart occupied by the 5-yellow should be attended to, but so should the Palace into which flies the Annual 5-yellow, which will change from year to year. So you need to look at 2 Palaces. Of course every 9 years these will be in the same Palace: and for that conjunction you really have to pay attention.

It is definitely a good idea to delay any renovation work in the Palace occupied by the Annual 5-yellow till the following year. For example, if you were planning in 2001 to renovate a guest bedroom that happened to be in the Southwest part of your home, you should have delayed it till the following year, when the troublesome annual 5-yellow Star had moved from the SW to the East sector.

In every case we are talking about the Chinese solar year, which begins on February 4 or 5, not the Chinese lunar year, which has a variable commencement date.

The location of the 5-yellow Star is important to observe for more than just redecoration timing. It may be a generally troublesome area. It is particularly bad if it coincides with your front door, because the constant traffic will stir up its malefic tendencies. If this is the case, siting a pair of heavy metal ch'i lin (*qirin*) there as door guardians is a traditional remedy. (Ch'i lin is often translated as "unicorn," but these hairy three-horned creatures are not at all like unicorns. The best place to see what they look like is to grab a bottle of Kirin beer and look at the label.) Try not to site important things (such as your office or your bedroom) in rooms affected by the Annual 5-yellow. How can you counter it? Total quiet is the best: if you have the luxury, shut up the room concerned.

An even more malefic combination than the straight 5-yellow Star is a combination of the two inauspicious Earth Stars, 5-yellow and 2-black. This combination can cause major illness, even fatalities, and on the wealth luck side, it can cause bankruptcy.

As you know from the chapter on the Annual and Monthly Stars, these can act as triggers or catalysts for the effects of this 5-2 combination. What you need to check is the annual and monthly arrival dates of either the 5-yellow or 2-black Stars in the Palace that is afflicted by the 2-5 combination. These are months to particularly guard against. During them you should be more circumspect in your dealings and not take the chances that you might ordinarily take. For example, don't put your health in jeopardy by forgetting any medication, don't take on court conflicts, and if you trade the markets, this is a good month to make sure your stop loss orders are all correctly in place. On the feng shui front, make sure that the room concerned is as quiet as possible, then apply the following cures:

As both Stars are Earth Stars, the traditional way of depleting them is to introduce Metal, which is produced by Earth (and therefore depletes Earth). The best kind of Metal is active metal—a metal chiming clock or a metal wind chime. See the next chapter for more about wind chimes. Be careful if you suggest a clock to a

Table 14.1: *The Location of the Annual 5-Yellow Star*

Year	Location
2000	N
2001	SW
2002	E
2003	SE
2004	Center
2005	NW
2006	W
2007	NE
2008	S
2009	N
2010	SW
2011	E
2012	SE
2013	Center
2014	NW
2015	W
2016	NE
2017	S

...and so on around the cycle again

client, because in a Chinese context a clock is often seen as inauspicious, as it marks the passing of time and has therefore an oblique association with death.

Another possible Metal cure is the 6 metal antique Chinese coins tied together with red thread. These represent the trigram Ch'ien, which is the trigram of Heaven and Metal. A refinement of this cure sometimes recommends the placement of 6 (antique) Chinese coins into or above a bowl of fresh water. Fresh water is important, because stagnant water does nobody any good. The coins introduce Metal, which will help to control the Earth of the 5-yellow. At the same time the Water will absorb the attention of the Earth ch'i, which will attempt to destroy the Water. As a refinement, some practitioners add salt to the water, which is partly to stop it from going stagnant. Salt also is symbolic of Big Water, or the sea.

For the sake of completeness it is worth mentioning the traditional symbolic image cures for the 5-yellow Star, although these will be disregarded by the purists. These include 4 or 9 bronze/gold fu dogs. If the 5-yellow is at the main door or a window or a bed headboard, then use an antique feng shui *lu ban* or bronze ruler. The bronze provides the necessary Metal Element. The calabash is a container made out of the shell of a hollowed-out bottle-shaped gourd. These were long used for carrying liquids and medicines, and so came to be the symbol of one of the three Chinese gods, Fu, Lu, and Shou, associated with health and long life. Another cure sometimes used is a *wu lou* calabash containing 8 pieces of white jade. The white jade is the color of Metal. The wu lou calabash is sometimes made of bronze, and referred to as a "6-8 curses-solving bronze wu lou calabash."

Table 14.2: *The Location of the Annual 2-Black Star*

Year	Location
2000	W
2001	NE
2002	S
2003	N
2004	SW
2005	E
2006	SE
2007	Center
2008	NW
2009	W
2010	NE
2011	S
2012	N
2013	SW
2014	E
2015	SE
2016	Center
2017	NW
2018	W

…and so on around the cycle again

THE ANNUAL 2-BLACK SICKNESS STAR

The same treatment can be used for the 2-black Star as it is also an Earth Star. This Star represents ill-speaking in its widest sense, particularly arguments, gossip, and slander. It also brings illness and other obstacles. In 2002, it was located in the South. As it is an Earth Star, it needed Metal to bring it under control.

Less crucial are the Annual visits of the 3-green and the 7-red Star.

THE ANNUAL 3-GREEN QUARREL STAR

This is the Star of quarrels, argument, and litigation. Although not nearly as virulent in its effects as the previous two Stars, it might need to be brought under control if it has been activated by a landform feature or a 9-purple Star. As it is a Wood Star, Metal can be used to cut it, or more subtle, Fire can be used to deplete it. So use bright reds and bright lights and candles to keep this argumentative Star in check. The location of this Star can simply be checked by doing the Annual Star chart of the year under investigation.

It is also traditionally thought possible to dissolve the effects of this Star by using a strongly symbolic sculpture such as a lion, tiger, or dragon; a fountain or aquarium; water with growing plants; a cactus; or an appropriate religious image. Go easy on using wild animal images inside the house, as these can often be too overpowering.

THE ANNUAL 7-RED ROBBERY STAR

This Star is not considered malefic until February 2004 when it ceases to be the beneficial Period Star and reverts to its true nature, which includes violence and robbery. As it is a Metal Star it may be satisfactorily drained by using Water (which it produces in the Production Cycle of the Elements). Some practitioners suggest a lamp to combat this Star, but that is using Fire and the Destructive Cycle, which is not as subtle as using Water and the Reductive Cycle.

Do not do this before February 2004 or you will reduce its *current* beneficial effect. The location of this Star can simply be checked by doing the Annual Star chart of the year under investigation.

The 7-red is said to be traditionally partly corrected by placing in its location a shrine or religious image or a thorny cactus plant (not flowers or succulent greenery).

THE 3 SHAS

Among the Fate Stars there are 3 particularly inauspicious Stars called the san sha. (The san sha were a San He (Three Combinations) School concept that was subsequently absorbed by the San Yuan Flying Star School in the late Ming dynasty.) This literally means the "3 killings," although it is sometimes translated as the "3 curses." In Cantonese you may see them spelled as *sam sart*. These negative ch'i energies move around from year to year.

Although they are often spoken about as one thing, they are in fact three separate Fate Stars and have their own names:

1. *Sui Sha*, the Year Curse (connected with T'ai Sui, Counter-Jupiter).
2. *Chieh Sha*, the Robbery Curse (associated with robbery and financial betrayal).
3. *Tsai Sha*, the Calamity Curse (indicating natural calamities such as flood and fire).

These three are all regarded as being malefic due to an excess of yin in each of these departments of life.

The good news is, however, that their negative effects will not be stirred up unless they are disturbed by renovation, ground breaking, or lots of noise. So do not renovate rooms corresponding to the location of this trio, nor do major landscape gardening here, or practice nearby with your rock band. It is perfectly all right to face them but not to sit on them.

Where are they located? In general terms they move round the 4 cardinal points:

In all Rat, Dragon, or Monkey years they are located in the South.
In all Rabbit, Goat, or Pig years they are located in the West.
In all Tiger, Horse, or Dog years they are located in the North.
In all Ox, Snake, or Rooster years they are located in the East.

But it is not quite as tidy as that, for the san sha cover three specific noncontiguous 15-degree Mountains each year as follows. This means they only affect 3 x 15 = 45 degrees, but the three parts of the san sha are spread out across a wider arc as shown in table 14.3.

Table 14.3: *The Location of the 3 Shas*

| Year | Mountain or Direction (covering 3 x 15 degrees) | | |
	Year Curse	Robbery Curse	Calamity Curse
2000	SE3	S2	SW1
2001	NE3	E2	SE1
2002	NW3	N2	NE1
2003	SW3	W2	NW1
2004	SE3	S2	SW1
2005	NE3	E2	SE1
2006	NW3	N2	NE1
2007	SW3	W2	NW1
2008	SE3	S2	SW1
2009	NE3	E2	SE1
2010	NW3	N2	NE1
2011	SW3	W2	NW1
2012	SE3	S2	SW1
2013	NE3	E2	SE1
2014	NW3	N2	NE1
2015	SW3	W2	NW1
2016	SE3	S2	SW1
2017	NE3	E2	SE1
2018	NW3	N2	NE1
2019	SW3	W2	NW1

How do you defend your home against the 3 Shas? Metal is the usual cure, often in the form of a metal ch'i lin (qirin) figure. Another traditional protection against the san sha is a figurine of Kuan Kung, who is god of war (and strangely also of wealth), and he is thought to be more than a match for them.

THE GRAND DUKE JUPITER

We met the Grand Duke Jupiter (Sui Hsing), and its shadowy mirror image, T'ai Sui, earlier in chapter 4. As Jupiter marks out the year, so his Star coincides with the direction of the Branch of the year. In other words, as 2002 was a Horse year, T'ai Sui was located in one of the 12 Earthly Branches. In this case, the Horse was located in the South (or to be more precise the S2 direction).

Once having located the Grand Duke Jupiter's position for the year, it is most important not to disturb him. Make sure that you do not dig the ground or carry out heavy construction work in this 15-degree sector.

In addition, the position directly opposite the Grand Duke Jupiter is often referred to as the clash position. This helps to remind you that you should not sit with your back against this clash position, because in doing so you will also be facing the Grand Duke Jupiter.

It is considered bad luck to habitually sit facing him directly in a confrontational manner. This applies to work and eating directions. It is fine to have the Grand Duke behind your back, as he will lend you strong support in this position. So what you have to check is the position of your desk chair and your dining room chair (so you don't also confront him while you are eating).

This positioning is quite precise, so that 5–10 degrees away from the exact bearing is quite enough to reduce the adverse influence. Table 14.4 lays out the position of the Grand Duke, so you can see that he cycles around the compass every 12 years and then comes back to the same position.

If you are doing a major total house renovation, then you should not concern yourself with the Grand Duke. However if you are just renovating a particular room or part of a room, check if that room coincides with the Grand Duke's position. If these renovations involve hammering, banging, or knocking down walls, then my advice is to delay this till the following (solar) year, so as not to disturb him, cause his none-too-friendly displeasure, and therefore bring about consequent bad luck for the occupants. If you are uncomfortable with the personification of this energy as a Duke, simply think of it as the direction of a particular energy flow that does not like to be interrupted! Other planetary/Element energies are not quite so picky! One supposed traditional remedy for the Grand Duke Jupiter is pieces of a bronze wu lou calabash.

I recommend that you list out these Wild Stars at the beginning of each year and deter-

Table 14.4: *The Location of the Grand Duke Jupiter*

Year	Grand Duke Jupiter
2001	SE3
2002	S2
2003	SW1
2004	SW3
2005	W2
2006	NW1
2007	NW2
2008	N2
2009	NE1
2010	NE3
2011	E2
2012	SE1
2013	SE3
2014	S2
2015	SW1
2016	SW3
2017	W2

mine what you need to put into place in the way of remedies. Don't be overly worried about the lesser ones, but do adjust for the 5-yellow and 2-black Stars, and make sure not to disturb the Grand Duke. Remember these are just personifications of energy situations—but they deserve the same attention you might give to putting up shutters when you hear a storm warning.

So there you have it: a run down on the Flying Stars and Fate Stars that you should check at the beginning of each year, on or before February 4.

Chapter 15

Remedies

There are three basic types of feng shui remedies:

1. Those using Element interactions to enhance or reduce an Element
2. Those using Form and alignment considerations, by blocking or deflecting incoming secret arrows, or sha ch'i, and
3. Those using more esoteric, religious, imagistic, or magical remedies.

Of these only the first category is specifically prescribed by Flying Star feng shui.

ELEMENTAL CYCLES

KEY GOVERNING CYCLES

Expressed simply, Flying Star cures are done via the Elements and how they relate to each other in their Cycles. Therefore we need at this point to revise our knowledge of the Cycles of Production, Destruction, and Reduction of the 5 Elements. These are explained below for the sake of clarity, but for simplicity you can deduce the remedies just by using the three circular diagrams shown in figures 15.1, 15.2, and 15.3.

Production

The Elements produce each other in the order shown in figure 15.1. Thus Wood burns to produce Fire, which results in ash (or Earth). Metal is also found in the veins of the Earth, from which (according to Chinese thought) sprang the underground streams (Water), which nourish vegetation and in turn produce Wood. In a sense each Element is the parent of the one following it in the Cycle. This order is the same as the order of the seasons and their Elements. Thus the Water of winter produces the new vegetation

Fig. 15.1 *The Production Cycle of the Elements*

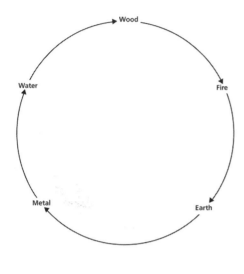

(Wood) of spring. This gives way to the heat (Fire) of summer until in autumn the crops are harvested by Metal instruments.

Use this Cycle to strengthen an Element by adding its parent.

Destruction

Each Element destroys another in the sequence shown in figure 15.2. Wood is destroyed by Metal implements, which are melted by Fire, which is quenched by Water, which is dammed by Earth, whose nutrients are extracted by Wood or vegetation. This is a grandparent relationship, because the destroyer is the parent of the parent of the Element being destroyed. For example Metal is the parent of Water which in turn is the parent of Wood. Metal is therefore the grandparent of Wood, but it also destroys Wood. This Cycle is sometimes called the Domination Cycle or the Controlling Cycle. Purists might say that no Element is ever destroyed, only transformed.

Fig. 15.2 *The Destruction Cycle of the Elements*

Use this Cycle to weaken an Element by adding its grandparent, but use it sparingly, as it is a disruptive way of achieving this objective.

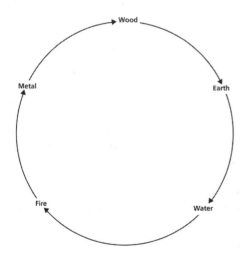

Reduction

This is the reverse of the Production Cycle, and will probably be the Cycle you most use when thinking out feng shui remedies. It exemplifies the child relationship. Each Element reduces its parent Element. For example Water produces Wood, as we all know water is necessary for vegetative growth. So Wood is the child of Water. But if you reverse this relationship, you can easily see how the child (Wood) wears out its parent by absorbing Water with its roots. Anyone who has ever been a parent will know the ability the child has to wear out the parent! This action is one of

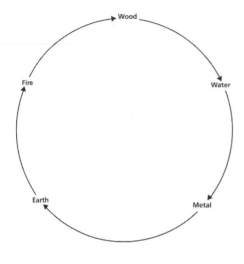

Fig. 15.3 *The Reduction Cycle of the Elements*

the Reduction Cycle. In full, Wood reduces Water which corrodes Metal which moves Earth, which smothers Fire which burns Wood. The old name for this Cycle is the Masking Cycle.

Use this Cycle to weaken an Element by adding its child, a more natural way of achieving your objective that the Destruction Cycle.

These Cycles provide the practical key to Flying Stars cures, and so it is very useful to know them by heart. Don't forget that the very physical examples given above are just one aspect of the Elements, which should be thought of as transitional phases rather than things. The strange thing about these phases is that they can be influenced by adding the relevant *physical* aspect of the Element. If this seems strange, then just think of acupuncture, where a very physical needle is inserted in the right place to effect a change in the intensity of the ch'i energy flowing at that point in the body. There is nothing hypothetical about Chinese feng shui or acupuncture medicine: the cures are very real and concrete.

By remembering the above Cycles you can easily work out the outcomes of various combinations. All this applies only to Stars interacting within one Palace. Water Stars tend to react to changes much faster than Mountain Stars, which are by their nature slower and quieter.

Remember that in almost every case it is better not to use the Destruction Cycle, as that promotes clash and opposition, giving opportunity for some of the ill effects you are trying to reduce. It is better to use the Reduction Cycle, where you are continuously occupying the destructive Element with its offspring, in the same way as you might distract a mother with many offspring rather than direct opposition. It is both a question of subtlety and of practicality. To give an example: suppose you want to reduce the effect of the 7-red Star after 2004 (when it becomes Untimely). This Star is Metal. The Destructive answer is that Fire destroys Metal. But the Reductive answer is that Metal produces Water. It is therefore more effective to add Water than to add Fire.

BIG ELEMENT, SMALL ELEMENT

We need also to consider the relative strength of each Element. The attribution of 5 Elements to 8 directions or 9 Flying Stars cannot be an even-handed or a symmetrical arrangement because 5 does not divide evenly into either 8 or 9. In fact there is only a one-to-one relationship between the Elements Fire and Water and the Stars/trigrams.

But there are 2 Stars/trigrams that partake of a Metal nature, and two that partake of a Wood nature. No less than 3 correlate with Earth (if you include the Center).

To distinguish between the two Metals, the two Woods, and two of the Earths, it is usual to refer to one as Small and one as Big. This has a very real and concrete meaning. For example, Big Wood might be a forest, as distinct from Small Wood, which might be a small plant. Big Water is the ocean while Small Water could be a garden pond. Big Earth can be a mountain, while Small Earth could be a boulder or maybe a stone fence. Big Metal might be a metal dome or metal ore contrasting with the Small Metal of a metal utensil. The way it works in terms of the 9 Stars is as follows. If you read table 15.1 from the outside to the center, you can see a certain symmetry.

Table 15.1: *Correlation between the Elements and the Stars: How the Big and Small Elements Relate to Directions and the Lo Shu Numbers.*

Star	Direction	Element
1	N	Water
2	SW	Big Earth
3	E	Big Wood
4	SE	Small Wood
5	Center	Earth
6	NW	Big Metal
7	W	Small Metal
8	NE	Small Earth
9	S	Fire

In using remedies that rely upon Elements it is important to check if you are dealing with the Big or the Small version of that Element.

USING THE ELEMENTS

By knowing precisely the interaction between the 5 Elements we can devise remedies or enhancements for particular situations. Suppose that the 5-yellow Star, which is a baleful Star at the best of times, had moved into a particular room. We know that the 5-yellow is an Earth Star. We ask what Element destroys Earth? The answer is Wood, but we should not use destruction, as it will stir up the vigorous opposition of the 5-yellow.

Instead we should deplete the Earth—a more subtle approach. So consider what Element is produced by Earth. The answer is Metal. So by hanging Metal wind chimes we help deplete the 5-yellow Star. Why use wind chimes instead of just a lump of metal? The reason is that passing breezes will stir the metal wind chimes, thus keeping the Metal activated: some of the effect is derived from the metallic *sound* of the chimes, and some from the passage of the ch'i through the wind chimes.

So what are the actual remedies, and where should they be placed? The answer is anything that truly represents the Element required, placed in the area of the house covered by the Palace under consideration. As a practical suggestion, don't choose locations too close to the theoretical borders of the Palaces because that increases the chance of an error if your calculations are slightly off. A second practical suggestion is to choose remedies as close as possible to traditional Elemental remedies. Feng shui is susceptible to deduction, but you need to guard against just using your intuition and making up remedies. Color is a useful reinforcing adjunct to placed remedies, but be wary of using it solely on its own.

When we understand which Element needs enhancing or diminishing, and in what Palace in the home or office this needs to be done, it only remains for us to select what to use to make these changes. In other words, we need to know exactly what to prescribe.

Table 15.2: *Objects Usable as 5-Element Remedies*

Element	Color	Sample Remedy	Preferred Shape
Water	Black (not Blue unless very dark)	Indoor fountains, fish tanks, humidifiers	Wavy or sinuous
Wood	Green	Indoor plants (especially hydroponics), bamboo flute	Tall and rectangular
Fire	Red (pink/purple)	Fire in the form of candles or lamps or faux flambeaux, red objects, a fireplace	Triangular, pointed
Earth	Yellow (beige/brown)	Crystals, large rocks, ceramics, pottery	Square
Metal	Gold, silver, metallic	Metal wind chimes, coins, clocks (especially striking), metal filing cabinets, metal objects, and sculpture	Spherical or domed

REMEDIES FOR EACH ELEMENT

There are two simple ways of activating an Element. First, add some more of that Element, or, less effectively, something symbolic of it. Remember that although you may be adding physical water, what you are really doing is stimulating Water energy.

Second, you could stimulate the Element that produces the Element you are trying to activate. For example, if you were trying to activate Wood energy, you could apply Water, as in the Production cycle of the Elements, Water produces (more) Wood.

The 5 Elements are considered to be a family, so that if you take a particular Element, then:

- The Element that produces it is its parent (logically enough)
- The Element it produces is its child
- The Element that controls (or destroys) it is its grandparent (isn't that often the way in an integrated family?)
- The same Element helps and supports it and is called its sibling (or brother/sister)

Let's take Wood as a concrete example.

- The Element that produces it is its parent—Water
- The Element it produces is its child—Fire
- The Element that controls it is its grandparent—Metal
- The same Element is called its sibling—Wood, of course

Get the idea? The Chinese are very family-minded and family structure often features in their metaphors.

What we are really doing here is assisting the inner processes of transformation, growth, and decay of the universe. By adjusting the family interaction of these energies we consequently adjust the "luck" environment behind the scenes.

Now let's say you have a situation where you want to strengthen a particular Element, or you need to tame one that is too strong. Table 15.3 shows how you would go about doing this. From this table you can easily choose which Element you need to introduce as a cure.

Now that you know which Elements to introduce, let's look at the sort of physical items you might use.

Water

To activate Water, you could add actual water, or things symbolic of Water, like the color black or pictures of waterfalls.

Typical Water enhancers are an aquarium or a small interior fountain. It is critical that the water is moving (or yang) water and definitely not stagnant. Hence if you use an aquarium, it must have an air bubbler to disturb the surface. Fish also help to keep the water moving.

Table 15.3: *Remedies Designed to Strengthen, Control, or Drain Each Element*

"Home" Palace	Element	TO STRENGTHEN		TO WEAKEN	
		Add Sibling to support	Add Parent to produce more	Add Grandparent to control/destroy	Add Child to drain/weaken
E, SE	WOOD	Wood	Water	Metal	Fire
S	FIRE	Fire	Wood	Water	Earth
SW, NE	EARTH	Earth	Fire	Wood	Metal
W, NW	METAL	Metal	Earth	Fire	Water
N	WATER	Water	Metal	Earth	Wood

The addition of fish, in fact, has three effects. First, their swimming helps to maintain movement. In the case of goldfish or koi carp their gold color is also symbolic of wealth (these fish were often placed in temple ponds). A stagnant fish tank, however, will produce stagnant ch'i and may be much worse than no remedy at all. Make sure the tank is not out of proportion to the room: you don't want to "drown" the room with too much Water. Such an outsized tank in a business environment might increase turnover to the point where staff were "drowning" in work, with no time to ensure increased profitability.

There is a lot of nonsense talked regarding the ideal number of fish. Enough for the tank is the right answer. But if you want to keep your symbolism correct, an odd number is best, as it is then a yang number.

If you are adding fish to the tank, nine would be a good odd number of fish, because it is the number of Palaces in the Lo Shu square. Some practitioners suggest a single black fish "to absorb the negative energies." The Chinese attitude to such fish, which might seem kind of heartless, is that if they die, that represents negative ch'i that has been absorbed by the fish rather than you, and is therefore a good thing!

A small fountain is also ideal, as it recycles the water and really stimulates the Element.

The traditional color for Water is black. Despite the desire by many Western decorators to avoid this color and go instead for blue, black is the traditional Chinese color for the Water Element. From a decorative point of view, it is far better to use dramatic black and then enhance it with silver or gold in filigree or detailing, producing a stunning result, than to merely depress an area by painting it dark blue. Incidentally, both these metallic detail colors generate Water, so they are useful.

Fire

To activate Fire, you could add actual fire or things symbolic of Fire. Live flame, like a fire in a grate, or candles, are excellent activators of Fire. Unfortunately, few houses or rooms are equipped with fire grates, and candles can be a fire hazard. Fortunately there are a lot of other Fire enhancers, such as light and red-colored things. Among the things now supplied by lighting specialists is a very interesting faux living flame light whose effect is created by illuminating twisting material that blows upwards and for all the world looks like a live flame.

The color to use for Fire is bright red. Maybe you can get away with dilutions of this color, but colors like salmon have strayed a long way from the archetypal red. Purple is also sometimes suggested as a Fire color, but is more appropriately used for Imperial purposes.

Light is yang and lifts ch'i. Lights that can be used to stimulate Fire include natural sunlight, electric lights, naked flames such as candles, or prisms and chandelier lusters that catch and refract light. Light can be effectively used to expel excessive yin from dark corners.

Earth

To activate Earth, you should add things symbolic of Earth.

Earth is a very interesting Element because it occupies three of the 9 cells of the Lo Shu. Enhancers can be literally Earth in the sense of crystals, or stones such as *lingbi* rocks—these are smooth but very interestingly shaped rocks that used to be collected by Taoist scholars. Some of these have been sold recently at auction in New York at prices around the $6,000 mark, showing that there are collectors who still take these lovely Taoist stones seriously. Larger rocks can also be used as they are in Chinese or Japanese gardens.

Of course crystals have a distinct part to play here. Not only do they come from the Earth but they also refract yang light. Many feng shui shops in the Far East now sell crystal geodes sawn in half, often amethyst, for feng shui purposes.

Some crystals are beautifully enhanced and made up into rolling crystal balls supported and rotated on a constantly flowing pad of water. These form elaborate and sometimes very expensive feng shui enhancers, but of course are not solely Earth in nature.

Colors for Earth include yellow, buff, faun, and beige.

Wood

To activate Wood, you could add growing plants or things symbolic of Wood.

Wood is, of course, growing vegetation, not just dead wood furniture. Virulent growers like bamboo are excellent as Wood enhancers. Bundles of vigorously shooting bamboo canes constitute an excellent Wood enhancer, and they will flourish in water without earth. Likewise other indoor plants can be utilized as Wood enhancers. Remember, like an aquarium, a moribund plant is worse than useless. Living plants also help to soften otherwise hard lines and sharp sha-producing corners.

It is said that artificial plants will do just as well, but I feel that plastic, cloth, and silk cannot embody the true nature of Wood, which is vegetative *growth*.

Dead or less-than-fresh-cut flowers are definitely out, as their potential for generating yin ch'i is much greater than any visual benefit they could confer. Anyone who has put their nose anywhere near the water from flowers well past their sell-by date will have no difficulty in understanding the meaning of ssu ch'i, or torpid ch'i!

Prickly plants like cacti or holly should also be avoided, except where they are specifically prescribed. Apart from any thought of tiny poison arrows, they are not comfortable plants to have around the house. Traditionally, a certain type of pond plant was also thought to be a Wood enhancer, and was in fact listed as one of the 12 imperial treasures.

The color for Wood is fresh green, the color of new spring vegetation.

Metal

To activate Metal, you could add things made of or symbolic of Metal.

Metal means several different things. It is literally the metal extracted from its "mother" the Earth. It is also symbolic of man-made things, particularly electronic items. Accordingly, good Metal enhancers include the television and the computer, with the added benefit that movement and electrical charge yields a yang bonus. Metal sculptures will also do, but watch out for poison arrows projected from sharp and spiky sculptures.

The color of Metal is a bit of a tricky one. White is acceptable, as it is the opposing color to the black of Water, which is generated from Metal. However, you can avoid white if you like, because there are all the metallic shades to choose from. Of course, as the Chinese root character for "metal" is the same as gold (perhaps reflecting the idea that all metals were just a corrupted form of gold), so the color of metallic gold makes the most appropriate color for Metal.

Wind chimes

A first-century BC Chinese scientific experiment used tubes of different lengths (derived from the pentatonic musical scale) filled with fine ash to measure the changing ch'i of the seasons. As each type of seasonal ch'i reached maturity, during the course of the year, so the ash was expelled by it from one of the pipes. Hence tubes (of specific lengths) have been known to conduct ch'i for some considerable time, and so it is no surprise that they are used as remedies.

The most commonly used tubular feng shui remedy is the wind chime. These have the same qualities as the flute, but since they are made of multiple tubes of varying but specific length, are more effective. Wind chimes are often used to regulate and slow down ch'i in positions like hallways. In more poetic feng shui texts, ch'i is personified as if it is seduced into stopping long enough to play with the wind chimes before passing on its way, rather than rushing straight through. Either way, wind chimes slow down ch'i.

Much has been written about how many tubes a wind chime should have, what they should be made of, and whether they should be solid or hollow. The archetypal wind chime should have five hollow metallic tubes, of specifically cut lengths tuned to the Chinese pentatonic musical scale. It can be made of metal or wood.

If you select a metal wind chime, moving Metal will help weaken any Earth Star such as the 5-yellow Star. It does not really matter how many chimes the wind chime has, except in a purely symbolic sense. If you are worried about symbolism then use a 6-chime version (rather than a 5-chime version) which does not repeat the number of the Star you are trying to neutralize. Use instead one of the two Metal numbers, 6 or 7; 6 corresponds to Big Metal so it is preferred to 7.

On the question of whether the tubes of the wind chime should be solid or hollow, my advice (contrary to the usual advice) is to use hollow chimes, as they are more effective at producing metal ch'i and the right sound than solid chimes.

In situations where metal would be a disadvantage (for example, where you want to accumulate Wood energy) a wood wind chime is a better choice. Solid metal wind chimes are often prescribed to press down on a negative energy, such as that generated by toilets. These will of course not be able to perform their ch'i conducting purpose in the same way as hollow tubes.

SHORTCUT ELEMENTAL CURES

Table 15.4 will give you a quick reference for Elemental cures for specific combinations. Don't rely upon it too much, but think each case through, using the knowledge you have built up about the interaction of the Elements. Just use the table as a quick check to see that you are on the right track. Make sure that you use the Period 8 table after February 4, 2004. Where the Stars are both either Usable (U) or Timely (T) no cure is necessary, so none is offered.

....

Table 15.4: *Summary of General Element Cures for Period 7 and Period 8 where either Star is Untimely and not Usable*

For Period 7 (1984–2004 Feb 3)

Mountain Stars→		1	2	3	4	5	6	7	8	9
		Water	Earth	Wood	Wood	Earth	Metal	Metal	Earth	Fire
		U	X	X	U	X	X	T	T	T
Water Stars										
1 Water	U	U,U	Metal	Fire	U,U	Metal	Water	T,U	T,U	T,U
2 Earth	X	Metal	Metal	F&Met	M&Wat	Metal	**Metal**	Metal	Metal	Metal
3 Wood	X	Fire	F&Met	none	Fire	Metal	Fire	Metal	Fire	Metal
4 Wood	U	U,U	F&Met	Fire	U,U	Metal	Water	T,U	T,U	T,U
5 Earth	X	Metal	**Metal**	F&Met	Metal	**Metal**	Metal	Metal	Metal	Metal
6 Metal	X	Water	Metal	Water	Water	Metal	none	none	Earth	Fire
7 Metal	T	U,T	Metal	Water	U,T	Metal	none	T,T	T,T	T,T
8 Earth	T	Earth	Metal	Fire	U,T	Metal	Fire	T,T	T,T	T,T
9 Fire	T	U,T	Metal	Metal	U,T	Metal	Fire	T,T	T,T	T,T

(continued)

Table 15.4 (cont.): *Summary of General Element Cures for Period 7 and Period 8 where either Star is Untimely and not Usable*

For Period 8 (Feb 4, 2004–2024)

Mountain Stars→		1	2	3	4	5	6	7	8	9
		Water	Earth	Wood	Wood	Earth	Metal	Metal	Earth	Fire
		T	X	U	X	X	U	X	T	T
Water Stars										
1 Water	T	T,T	Metal	U,T	Metal	Metal	U,T	Water	T,T	T,T
2 Earth	X	Metal	Metal	U,X	Metal	Metal	Metal	Water	none	Wood
3 Wood	U	T,U	Wood	none	none	Metal	U,U	Water	T,U	T,U
4 Wood	X	Metal	Metal	U,X	none	Metal	Metal	Fire	Fire	Fire
5 Earth	X	Metal	**Metal**	Metal	Metal	Metal	Metal	Metal	Metal	Metal
6 Metal	U	T,U	Metal	U,U	Metal	Metal	U,U	none	T,U	T,U
7 Metal	X	Water	Water	Water	Fire	Metal	none	none	Fire	Fire
8 Earth	T	T,T	none	U,T	Fire	Metal	U,T	Fire	T,T	T,T
9 Fire	T	T,T	Wood	U,T	Fire	Metal	U,T	Fire	T,T	T,T

Timely = T; Untimely = X; Usable = U
** listed in the order Mountain Star, Water Star

You will notice a preponderance of Metal cures in the table above. That is because Earth Stars (particularly Stars 2-black and 5-yellow) are a major cause of problems, and Metal effectively depletes the Earth in them. In addition, from the Production Cycle, you know that Metal generates Water, and Water is often needed, particularly to reinforce the Water Star. This is why Metal cures are more common than any other. This incidentally is why metal wind chimes have become almost synonymous with feng shui, while other remedies are less well known.

Don't overdo it. This table is not meant to promote the "let's put a cure in every room" approach to feng shui. Simple and balanced is best: sometimes a great Master will just make one or two key corrections to a building to make everything fall into place, while an obvious amateur will go round fussing about the color schemes, the potted plants, or the depth of tread on the stairs.

Obviously you don't have to introduce cures where the relevant room is seldom used, one of the "wet rooms," or an unimportant room. Likewise, some situations, like the threat of miscarriage in a bachelor's apartment, do not *necessarily* need to be rectified. So don't blindly apply the above table. Use your common sense first, and then check against this table to see if you have inadvertently prescribed an inappropriate Element cure, or forgotten a necessary one.

NUMERICAL CONSIDERATIONS

While a lot has been written about using, for example, 6 coins tied with ribbon, or a 6-chime wind chime, it is not always obvious that the numbers used are drawn from the Lo Shu square like so much else in feng shui. Remember that the 9 Flying Stars are correlated with the 5 Elements, and it is those numbers that suggest the numerical content of the cures. Typical examples of numerical considerations are shown in table 15.5.

....

Table 15.5: *Typical Numerical Considerations*

Lo Shu Number	Element
1	Water (as in one fish tank, never two)
2	Earth (as in 2 crystals, the double happiness sign, or the pair of Mandarin ducks)
3	Wood (as in three bamboos)
4	Small Wood (so not as strong as using 3)
5	Earth (in the unlikely event that you wanted to stir up the 5-yellow you might use five crystals)
6	Metal (as in 6-chime metal windchime, or 6 coins tied with red ribbon)
7	Small Metal (so not as strong as 6)
8	Small Earth (so not as strong as 2)
9	Fire (as in 9 candles)

There is some benefit, and no harm, in observing these numbers when constructing remedies, but don't be ruled by them to the point of inflexibility. One interesting notion which we already noted is the specification by some practitioners to use a 6-rod wind chime to suppress Earth, on the basis that 6 is a Metal number while 5 is the number of Earth. At first glance it make sense to use 6 rods. However the purpose of the wind chime is to allow ch'i to flow through its hollow rods and to produce metallic sounds. The original idea of the wind chime was to have one chime for each of the pentatonic notes of the Chinese music scale. The five chimes should be of a length that produces perfectly this range of sounds. Some would say that it therefore makes no sense to introduce a sixth jarring chime, simply to keep the numerical symbolism consistent. Others would point out that 5 perfect pentatonic notes are better than 6 chimes of haphazard length and pitch.

INACTIVITY

What is sometimes forgotten is that the 9 Flying Stars are energy. Energy feeds on energy. So if a Star combination in a specific room is energized by yang activity, sound, movement, or light, so its effects are magnified. This is good where it is an auspicious

Water Star or Star combination. But where it is a malevolent Star, one of the easiest ways to reduce its impact is to cut off its energy feed. This is why it is always advised, as a counsel of perfection, to locate storerooms or guest bedrooms where bad Stars are located. This is not to say that you wish your guests ill, but simply that guest bedrooms by their nature are seldom disturbed. The reason is that if the room is seldom used then the inauspicious Star is starved of energy.

If however, you don't have the luxury to redesignate the usage of your rooms each year, then apply the rule on a micro level. This means that if, for example, the troublesome 5-yellow Star is located in the East (as it was in 2002), make a point of removing all energizers from the East side of your main living and dining rooms. Shift the television, stereo, exercise bike, and anything else that makes noise or motion. Don't spotlight the area, and definitely don't work or eat here if you can help it.

That is the inactivity remedy, one that is often overlooked, but one that is very important. There is no point in putting up an Element remedy and then stimulating the area. So check out the inactivity remedy possibilities on a macro and a micro level first.

On the positive side, if you are trying to stimulate Fire, then lots of bright light helps, and the television and stereo fit nicely in a sector where you want lots of yang Metal.

Staunch traditionalists might say that only Element-related remedies are *real* Flying Star feng shui remedies. But light, sound, and movement can certainly help to correct or enhance feng shui. All these are yang cures and help counter an excess of yin, opposite of yang, darkness, silence, and stillness. Remember that the Mountain Star needs peace and quiet, but the Water Star can benefit from movement.

PROBLEM SOLVING

The key to solving feng shui problems is to know where to look. Don't just stare at the chart hoping something will jump out at you. You already know the Water Stars (top right of each Palace) are concerned with wealth. So if the problem is to do with finances, look first at each of the Water Stars in turn. Particularly look at the Prominent Water Star (the one with the same number as the current Period) and the Water Star at the front door (if it's not the same). Likewise if the problem is health, family, or relationship related, look at the Mountain Stars.

MONEY

Money is the province of the Water Star. So first check the Water Star of the current period, for example, 7 till February 2004, and 8 for the 20 years following that date. Assume it is the Host Star, and match it successively against the Guest Stars that enter that Palace, specifically the Mountain Star, the Annual Star, and maybe (if the problem is of short duration) the Month Star. Look for a lack of support from the Guest Star, or even Destruction of the Host's Element by the Guest's Element. Remedy this before going any further.

Check the adjacent external features. Sometimes a few physical changes are well worthwhile in the situation where money flow is the problem. Blocking off the sight line of a contraindicated or jagged Mountain feature is one route, and creating a supporting external Water feature is another route to go. It will be particularly beneficial to locate the Water Star of the current Period just inside the front door to welcome in the beneficial ch'i. It may well be practical to open a new front door to achieve this very situation.

Next look at the Water Star in the Facing Palace, and taking it as the Host Star, repeat the exercise in that Palace. (It is of course possible that you have already done this Palace when you attended to the Prominent Water Star.)

It is sometimes recommended that you check the micro feng shui of the door positions of the study/office and master bedroom to ensure that they are not sitting on an awkward Star like the 5-yellow. If so, remedy it with Metal: of course 6 coins tied with a red thread would be most suitable where the problem is money.

FAMILY

Arguments most frequently arise from the presence of the 3-green Star, particularly if it is found in conjunction with the 2-black Star. These Stars can either make one member of a family quarrelsome, by their presence in his bedroom, or they can make the whole family quarrelsome by their presence in the living or family room. Metal is the obvious solution to both these Stars, as Metal simultaneously conquers Wood (3-green) and depletes Earth (2-black). Maybe it's no coincidence that metallic chiming clocks were often seen as a feature in many living rooms before the universal ownership of personal watches!

MARITAL

Often argumentativeness or constant bickering (caused by the pressures of living closely with other human beings) is at the root of marital problems. In which case check for the same conditions as were discussed above under family problems, but look in the marital bedroom.

Then look at the location of the bed in this room. Check if it is cut or oppressed by any Form alignments. Then check the micro feng shui, and move it out from any 2-black, 3-green, and 5-yellow locations if at all possible. The micro feng shui will also show up these Stars if they are gathered near the internal door to the room, where they will need to be addressed.

Conception is another potential cause of marital discord. Look for sha ch'i lines immediately outside the bedroom window, and check that the micro location of the kitchen stove is not burning the Mountain Star of the current Period (Metal 7-red). When the 8-white becomes the Period Star this is no longer a problem, because the 8-white Star is an Earth Star (and benefits from Fire). Try also to ensure that the bread-winner is sleeping with his head pointing to his sheng ch'i direction.

Sometimes you will have to make changes that will in turn affect some other aspect of health, wealth, or happiness, and here the decision has got to be made in the knowledge that a trade-off will happen.

HEALTH

Problems are, the world over, remarkably similar and boil down to the same things, no matter where you are. One universal source of problems is health. Although I would be wary of anyone claiming that feng shui cures major health problems, feng shui is certainly able to indicate a position or location that will be more conducive to more rapid healing and better spirits in the patient. In the case of health problems your focus should be initially on the Mountain Star which corresponds to the current Period.

In Period 8, for example, you would locate the 8-white Mountain Star and take it to be the Host Star. Then look at the Guest Stars (the Water Star, the Annual Star, and maybe the Month Star) that fly into that Palace. Check to see if they support the Host Star. If they don't, set about introducing the Element that produces the Host Star, or counteracts any adverse Guest Star.

Then check the bedroom being used by the patient. Check that its Mountain Star is supported. If not, consider supporting it with the appropriate Element or moving the patient to a better bedroom. Then take the patients Personal Star (or kua number) as the Host and see if it is supported by the Guest Mountain Star.

Check that neither the Annual 2-black (Sickness Star) or 5-yellow Star fly into the room. If they do (especially if both fly in), then the patient should be moved forthwith to another room.

Don't forget to look outside at the Forms of the landscape. Remember that a large external Water feature immediately outside the Mountain Star you are considering can be very damaging and may need to be screened off. On the other hand, the addition of a Mountain feature here might help strengthen the Mountain Star under consideration.

On a micro level, the bed location and direction is very important where there are health issues, so next check, from a Form point of view, that the patient's bed is supported and not cut or oppressed by any sha ch'i. Then check the micro feng shui of the room to see if the bed needs to be moved away from any 2-black or 5-yellow Star or any other bad combinations.

Finally, it is worth considering the feng shui of the kitchen, especially if more than one member of the family is ill. Here the location of the stove is important. It is particularly important that the stove is not located in the micro Palace occupied by either the 2-black Sickness Star or the 5-yellow. Less obviously, the stove should not be placed where its Fire energy will destroy the Metal Star 7-red if this is the Mountain Star of the current Period.

Moving the patient under such circumstances has often seen a rapid improvement in their condition, particularly in situations like recurrent headaches or general loss of vitality. Feng shui must *never* be used instead of regular medical treatment, but it can provide a very useful adjunct.

CHILDREN AND STUDY

One of the recurring problems in any family is getting the children to study so that they can pass the exams necessary to the approach to a suitable career. In this the key Star is 4, which relates to literary and academic success. The selection of bedroom or study for the child should depend upon finding a room with a well-aspected 4-green Star. Be careful of a badly aspected 4-green as this is much more likely to promote unsuitable teenage affairs. As we all know, teen bedrooms can be the site of both study and early sexual exploration. Eight Mansions feng shui, which we are not covering in this book, suggests that the NE Palace is the most appropriate one for a study, which is okay as long as the Stars there are supportive. Check both Mountain and Water Stars.

A traditional remedy that has its roots deep in Chinese culture is the pagoda, which was often built in China as a feng shui device to control water and also to promote the success of local students in the imperial examinations. Consequently, the siting of a porcelain pagoda model in the child's study has also become a traditional remedy.

In this chapter we looked at Element remedies, which are considered by some to be the only remedies utilized by the Flying Star system. We revised the theory of the 3 key Cycles that enable you to prescribe the correct Element to enhance a beneficial Element, or mute a troublesome one. We then looked at how you can use this Element. The short-cut table can help you check your work and the deductions you've derived from the 3 key Cycles.

In addition to Elemental remedies, there is the inactivity cure, and a few of more traditional cures that can be found in the back streets of Hong Kong and Taipei but that require a more detailed knowledge of Chinese culture. Finally, we looked at remedies from the problem side, not just seeking to correct a chart, but to solve particular problems.

That concludes the book. I trust you will enjoy using and benefiting from the correct application of the 9 Flying Stars for many years to come.

Appendix 1

Table for Generating Instant Flying Star Charts

Earth Base Construction Cycle	Building Sitting Direction	Building Sitting Sub-Direction	Star (Base, Mountain or Water)	yin/yang Polarity i.e., Star Flies '+' or '-'	←——Star Numbers for You to Place in Lo Shu——→								
					Center	NW	W	NE	S	N	SW	E	SE
1			Base Cycle Star	1	1	2	3	4	5	6	7	8	9
	North	N1	Mountain	-1	6	5	4	3	2	1	9	8	7
			Water	1	5	6	7	8	9	1	2	3	4
		N2/N3	Mountain	1	6	7	8	9	1	2	3	4	5
			Water	1	5	6	7	8	9	1	2	3	4
	Northeast	NE1	Mountain	-1	4	3	2	1	9	8	7	6	5
			Water	1	7	8	9	1	2	3	4	5	6
		NE2/NE3	Mountain	1	4	5	6	7	8	9	1	2	3
			Water	-1	7	6	5	4	3	2	1	9	8
	East	E1	Mountain	-1	8	7	6	5	4	3	2	1	9
			Water	1	3	4	5	6	7	8	9	1	2
		E2/E3	Mountain	1	8	9	1	2	3	4	5	6	7
			Water	-1	3	2	1	9	8	7	6	5	4
	Southeast	SE1	Mountain	1	9	1	2	3	4	5	6	7	8
			Water	-1	2	1	9	8	7	6	5	4	3
		SE2/SE3	Mountain	-1	9	8	7	6	5	4	3	2	1
			Water	1	2	3	4	5	6	7	8	9	1
	South	S1	Mountain	1	5	6	7	8	9	1	2	3	4
			Water	-1	6	5	4	3	2	1	9	8	7
		S2/S3	Mountain	1	5	6	7	8	9	1	2	3	4
			Water	1	6	7	8	9	1	2	3	4	5
	Southwest	SW1	Mountain	1	7	8	9	1	2	3	4	5	6
			Water	-1	4	3	2	1	9	8	7	6	5
		SW2/SW3	Mountain	-1	7	6	5	4	3	2	1	9	8
			Water	1	4	5	6	7	8	9	1	2	3
	West	W1	Mountain	1	3	4	5	6	7	8	9	1	2
			Water	-1	8	7	6	5	4	3	2	1	9
		W2/W3	Mountain	-1	3	2	1	9	8	7	6	5	4
			Water	1	8	9	1	2	3	4	5	6	7
	Northwest	NW1	Mountain	-1	2	1	9	8	7	6	5	4	3
			Water	1	9	1	2	3	4	5	6	7	8
		NW2/NW3	Mountain	1	2	3	4	5	6	7	8	9	1
			Water	-1	9	8	7	6	5	4	3	2	1

Earth Base Construction Cycle	Building Sitting Direction	Building Sitting Sub-Direction	Star (Base, Mountain or Water)	yin/yang Polarity i.e., Star Flies '+' or '-'	←——Star Numbers for You to Place in Lo Shu——→								
					Center	NW	W	NE	S	N	SW	E	SE
2													
			Base Cycle Star	1	2	3	4	5	6	7	8	9	1
	North	N1	Mountain	1	7	8	9	1	2	3	4	5	6
			Water	-1	6	5	4	3	2	1	9	8	7
		N2/N3	Mountain	-1	7	6	5	4	3	2	1	9	8
			Water	1	6	7	8	9	1	2	3	4	5
	Northeast	NE1	Mountain	-1	5	4	3	2	1	9	8	7	6
			Water	-1	8	7	6	5	4	3	2	1	9
		NE2/NE3	Mountain	-1	5	4	3	2	1	9	8	7	6
			Water	1	8	9	1	2	3	4	5	6	7
	East	E1	Mountain	1	9	1	2	3	4	5	6	7	8
			Water	-1	4	3	2	1	9	8	7	6	5
		E2/E3	Mountain	-1	9	8	7	6	5	4	3	2	1
			Water	1	4	5	6	7	8	9	1	2	3
	Southeast	SE1	Mountain	1	1	2	3	4	5	6	7	8	9
			Water	1	3	4	5	6	7	8	9	1	2
		SE2/SE3	Mountain	-1	1	9	8	7	6	5	4	3	2
			Water	-1	3	2	1	9	8	7	6	5	4
	South	S1	Mountain	-1	6	5	4	3	2	1	9	8	7
			Water	1	7	8	9	1	2	3	4	5	6
		S2/S3	Mountain	1	6	7	8	9	1	2	3	4	5
			Water	-1	7	6	5	4	3	2	1	9	8
	Southwest	SW1	Mountain	-1	8	7	6	5	4	3	2	1	9
			Water	-1	5	4	3	2	1	9	8	7	6
		SW2/SW3	Mountain	1	8	9	1	2	3	4	5	6	7
			Water	-1	5	4	3	2	1	9	8	7	6
	West	W1	Mountain	-1	4	3	2	1	9	8	7	6	5
			Water	1	9	1	2	3	4	5	6	7	8
		W2/W3	Mountain	1	4	5	6	7	8	9	1	2	3
			Water	-1	9	8	7	6	5	4	3	2	1
	Northwest	NW1	Mountain	1	3	4	5	6	7	8	9	1	2
			Water	1	1	2	3	4	5	6	7	8	9
		NW2/NW3	Mountain	-1	3	2	1	9	8	7	6	5	4
			Water	-1	1	9	8	7	6	5	4	3	2

Earth Base Construction Cycle	Building Sitting Direction	Building Sitting Sub-Direction	Star (Base, Mountain or Water)	yin/yang Polarity i.e., Star Flies '+' or '-'	Center	NW	W	NE	S	N	SW	E	SE
3													
			Base Cycle Star	1	3	4	5	6	7	8	9	1	2
	North	N1	Mountain	-1	8	7	6	5	4	3	2	1	9
			Water	1	7	8	9	1	2	3	4	5	6
		N2/N3	Mountain	1	8	9	1	2	3	4	5	6	7
			Water	-1	7	6	5	4	3	2	1	9	8
	Northeast	NE1	Mountain	-1	6	5	4	3	2	1	9	8	7
			Water	1	9	1	2	3	4	5	6	7	8
		NE2/NE3	Mountain	1	6	7	8	9	1	2	3	4	5
			Water	-1	9	8	7	6	5	4	3	2	1
	East	E1	Mountain	1	1	2	3	4	5	6	7	8	9
			Water	1	5	6	7	8	9	1	2	3	4
		E2/E3	Mountain	-1	1	9	8	7	6	5	4	3	2
			Water	1	5	6	7	8	9	1	2	3	4
	Southeast	SE1	Mountain	-1	2	1	9	8	7	6	5	4	3
			Water	-1	4	3	2	1	9	8	7	6	5
		SE2/SE3	Mountain	1	2	3	4	5	6	7	8	9	1
			Water	1	4	5	6	7	8	9	1	2	3
	South	S1	Mountain	1	7	8	9	1	2	3	4	5	6
			Water	-1	8	7	6	5	4	3	2	1	9
		S2/S3	Mountain	-1	7	6	5	4	3	2	1	9	8
			Water	1	8	9	1	2	3	4	5	6	7
	Southwest	SW1	Mountain	1	9	1	2	3	4	5	6	7	8
			Water	-1	6	5	4	3	2	1	9	8	7
		SW2/SW3	Mountain	-1	9	8	7	6	5	4	3	2	1
			Water	1	6	7	8	9	1	2	3	4	5
	West	W1	Mountain	1	5	6	7	8	9	1	2	3	4
			Water	1	1	2	3	4	5	6	7	8	9
		W2/W3	Mountain	1	5	6	7	8	9	1	2	3	4
			Water	-1	1	9	8	7	6	5	4	3	2
	Northwest	NW1	Mountain	-1	4	3	2	1	9	8	7	6	5
			Water	-1	2	1	9	8	7	6	5	4	3
		NW2/NW3	Mountain	1	4	5	6	7	8	9	1	2	3
			Water	1	2	3	4	5	6	7	8	9	1

Earth Base Construction Cycle	Building Sitting Direction	Building Sitting Sub-Direction	Star (Base, Mountain or Water)	yin/yang Polarity i.e., Star Flies '+' or '-'	Center	NW	W	NE	S	N	SW	E	SE
4													
			Base Cycle Star	1	4	5	6	7	8	9	1	2	3
	North	N1	Mountain	1	9	1	2	3	4	5	6	7	8
			Water	-1	8	7	6	5	4	3	2	1	9
		N2/N3	Mountain	-1	9	8	7	6	5	4	3	2	1
			Water	1	8	9	1	2	3	4	5	6	7
	Northeast	NE1	Mountain	1	7	8	9	1	2	3	4	5	6
			Water	1	1	2	3	4	5	6	7	8	9
		NE2/NE3	Mountain	-1	7	6	5	4	3	2	1	9	8
			Water	-1	1	9	8	7	6	5	4	3	2
	East	E1	Mountain	-1	2	1	9	8	7	6	5	4	3
			Water	-1	6	5	4	3	2	1	9	8	7
		E2/E3	Mountain	1	2	3	4	5	6	7	8	9	1
			Water	1	6	7	8	9	1	2	3	4	5
	Southeast	SE1	Mountain	1	3	4	5	6	7	8	9	1	2
			Water	-1	5	4	3	2	1	9	8	7	6
		SE2/SE3	Mountain	-1	3	2	1	9	8	7	6	5	4
			Water	-1	5	4	3	2	1	9	8	7	6
	South	S1	Mountain	-1	8	7	6	5	4	3	2	1	9
			Water	1	9	1	2	3	4	5	6	7	8
		S2/S3	Mountain	1	8	9	1	2	3	4	5	6	7
			Water	-1	9	8	7	6	5	4	3	2	1
	Southwest	SW1	Mountain	1	1	2	3	4	5	6	7	8	9
			Water	1	7	8	9	1	2	3	4	5	6
		SW2/SW3	Mountain	-1	1	9	8	7	6	5	4	3	2
			Water	-1	7	6	5	4	3	2	1	9	8
	West	W1	Mountain	-1	6	5	4	3	2	1	9	8	7
			Water	-1	2	1	9	8	7	6	5	4	3
		W2/W3	Mountain	1	6	7	8	9	1	2	3	4	5
			Water	1	2	3	4	5	6	7	8	9	1
	Northwest	NW1	Mountain	-1	5	4	3	2	1	9	8	7	6
			Water	1	3	4	5	6	7	8	9	1	2
		NW2/NW3	Mountain	-1	5	4	3	2	1	9	8	7	6
			Water	-1	3	2	1	9	8	7	6	5	4

Earth Base Construction Cycle	Building Sitting Direction	Building Sitting Sub-Direction	Star (Base, Mountain or Water)	yin/yang Polarity i.e., Star Flies '+' or '-'	Center	NW	W	NE	S	N	SW	E	SE
					←——Star Numbers for You to Place in Lo Shu——→								
5													
			Base Cycle Star	1	5	6	7	8	9	1	2	3	4
	North	N1	Mountain	1	1	2	3	4	5	6	7	8	9
			Water	1	9	1	2	3	4	5	6	7	8
		N2/N3	Mountain	-1	1	9	8	7	6	5	4	3	2
			Water	-1	9	8	7	6	5	4	3	2	1
	Northeast	NE1	Mountain	-1	8	7	6	5	4	3	2	1	9
			Water	-1	2	1	9	8	7	6	5	4	3
		NE2/NE3	Mountain	1	8	9	1	2	3	4	5	6	7
			Water	1	2	3	4	5	6	7	8	9	1
	East	E1	Mountain	1	3	4	5	6	7	8	9	1	2
			Water	1	7	8	9	1	2	3	4	5	6
		E2/E3	Mountain	-1	3	2	1	9	8	7	6	5	4
			Water	-1	7	6	5	4	3	2	1	9	8
	Southeast	SE1	Mountain	-1	4	3	2	1	9	8	7	6	5
			Water	-1	6	5	4	3	2	1	9	8	7
		SE2SE3	Mountain	1	4	5	6	7	8	9	1	2	3
			Water	1	6	7	8	9	1	2	3	4	5
	South	S1	Mountain	1	9	1	2	3	4	5	6	7	8
			Water	1	1	2	3	4	5	6	7	8	9
		S2/S3	Mountain	-1	9	8	7	6	5	4	3	2	1
			Water	-1	1	9	8	7	6	5	4	3	2
	Southwest	SW1	Mountain	-1	2	1	9	8	7	6	5	4	3
			Water	-1	8	7	6	5	4	3	2	1	9
		SW2/SW3	Mountain	1	2	3	4	5	6	7	8	9	1
			Water	1	8	9	1	2	3	4	5	6	7
	West	W1	Mountain	1	7	8	9	1	2	3	4	5	6
			Water	1	3	4	5	6	7	8	9	1	2
		W2/W3	Mountain	-1	7	6	5	4	3	2	1	9	8
			Water	-1	3	2	1	9	8	7	6	5	4
	Northwest	NW1	Mountain	-1	6	5	4	3	2	1	9	8	7
			Water	-1	4	3	2	1	9	8	7	6	5
		NW2/NW3	Mountain	1	6	7	8	9	1	2	3	4	5
			Water	1	4	5	6	7	8	9	1	2	3

Earth Base Construction Cycle	Building Sitting Direction	Building Sitting Sub-Direction	Star (Base, Mountain or Water)	yin/yang Polarity i.e., Star Flies '+' or '-'	Center	NW	W	NE	S	N	SW	E	SE
6													
			Base Cycle Star	1	6	7	8	9	1	2	3	4	5
	North	N1	Mountain	-1	2	1	9	8	7	6	5	4	3
			Water	1	1	2	3	4	5	6	7	8	9
		N2/N3	Mountain	1	2	3	4	5	6	7	8	9	1
			Water	-1	1	9	8	7	6	5	4	3	2
	Northeast	NE1	Mountain	1	9	1	2	3	4	5	6	7	8
			Water	1	3	4	5	6	7	8	9	1	2
		NE2/NE3	Mountain	-1	9	8	7	6	5	4	3	2	1
			Water	-1	3	2	1	9	8	7	6	5	4
	East	E1	Mountain	-1	4	3	2	1	9	8	7	6	5
			Water	-1	8	7	6	5	4	3	2	1	9
		E2/E3	Mountain	1	4	5	6	7	8	9	1	2	3
			Water	1	8	9	1	2	3	4	5	6	7
	Southeast	SE1	Mountain	-1	5	4	3	2	1	9	8	7	6
			Water	1	7	8	9	1	2	3	4	5	6
		SE2SE3	Mountain	-1	5	4	3	2	1	9	8	7	6
			Water	-1	7	6	5	4	3	2	1	9	8
	South	S1	Mountain	1	1	2	3	4	5	6	7	8	9
			Water	-1	2	1	9	8	7	6	5	4	3
		S2S3	Mountain	-1	1	9	8	7	6	5	4	3	2
			Water	1	2	3	4	5	6	7	8	9	1
	Southwest	SW1	Mountain	1	3	4	5	6	7	8	9	1	2
			Water	1	9	1	2	3	4	5	6	7	8
		SW2/SW3	Mountain	-1	3	2	1	9	8	7	6	5	4
			Water	-1	9	8	7	6	5	4	3	2	1
	West	W1	Mountain	-1	8	7	6	5	4	3	2	1	9
			Water	-1	4	3	2	1	9	8	7	6	5
		W2/W3	Mountain	1	8	9	1	2	3	4	5	6	7
			Water	1	4	5	6	7	8	9	1	2	3
	Northwest	NW1	Mountain	1	7	8	9	1	2	3	4	5	6
			Water	-1	5	4	3	2	1	9	8	7	6
		NW2/NW3	Mountain	-1	7	6	5	4	3	2	1	9	8
			Water	-1	5	4	3	2	1	9	8	7	6

Earth Base Construction Cycle	Building Sitting Direction	Building Sitting Sub-Direction	Star (Base, Mountain or Water)	yin/yang Polarity i.e., Star Flies '+' or '-'	Center	NW	W	NE	S	N	SW	E	SE
7													
			Base Cycle Star	1	7	8	9	1	2	3	4	5	6
	North	N1	Mountain	1	3	4	5	6	7	8	9	1	2
			Water	-1	2	1	9	8	7	6	5	4	3
		N2/N3	Mountain	-1	3	2	1	9	8	7	6	5	4
			Water	1	2	3	4	5	6	7	8	9	1
	Northeast	NE1	Mountain	1	1	2	3	4	5	6	7	8	9
			Water	-1	4	3	2	1	9	8	7	6	5
		NE2/NE3	Mountain	-1	1	9	8	7	6	5	4	3	2
			Water	1	4	5	6	7	8	9	1	2	3
	East	E1	Mountain	1	5	6	7	8	9	1	2	3	4
			Water	1	9	1	2	3	4	5	6	7	8
		E2/E3	Mountain	1	5	6	7	8	9	1	2	3	4
			Water	-1	9	8	7	6	5	4	3	2	1
	Southeast	SE1	Mountain	-1	6	5	4	3	2	1	9	8	7
			Water	-1	8	7	6	5	4	3	2	1	9
		SE2/SE3	Mountain	1	6	7	8	9	1	2	3	4	5
			Water	1	8	9	1	2	3	4	5	6	7
	South	S1	Mountain	-1	2	1	9	8	7	6	5	4	3
			Water	1	3	4	5	6	7	8	9	1	2
		S2/S3	Mountain	1	2	3	4	5	6	7	8	9	1
			Water	-1	3	2	1	9	8	7	6	5	4
	Southwest	SW1	Mountain	-1	4	3	2	1	9	8	7	6	5
			Water	1	1	2	3	4	5	6	7	8	9
		SW2/SW3	Mountain	1	4	5	6	7	8	9	1	2	3
			Water	-1	1	9	8	7	6	5	4	3	2
	West	W1	Mountain	1	9	1	2	3	4	5	6	7	8
			Water	1	5	6	7	8	9	1	2	3	4
		W2/W3	Mountain	-1	9	8	7	6	5	4	3	2	1
			Water	1	5	6	7	8	9	1	2	3	4
	Northwest	NW1	Mountain	-1	8	7	6	5	4	3	2	1	9
			Water	-1	6	5	4	3	2	1	9	8	7
		NW2/NW3	Mountain	1	8	9	1	2	3	4	5	6	7
			Water	1	6	7	8	9	1	2	3	4	5

Earth Base Construction Cycle	Building Sitting Direction	Building Sitting Sub-Direction	Star (Base, Mountain or Water)	yin/yang Polarity i.e., Star Flies '+' or '-'	Center	NW	W	NE	S	N	SW	E	SE
					←——Star Numbers for You to Place in Lo Shu——→								
8													
			Base Cycle Star	1	8	9	1	2	3	4	5	6	7
	North	N1	Mountain	-1	4	3	2	1	9	8	7	6	5
			Water	1	3	4	5	6	7	8	9	1	2
		N2/N3	Mountain	1	4	5	6	7	8	9	1	2	3
			Water	-1	3	2	1	9	8	7	6	5	4
	Northeast	NE1	Mountain	-1	2	1	9	8	7	6	5	4	3
			Water	-1	5	4	3	2	1	9	8	7	6
		NE2/NE3	Mountain	1	2	3	4	5	6	7	8	9	1
			Water	-1	5	4	3	2	1	9	8	7	6
	East	E1	Mountain	-1	6	5	4	3	2	1	9	8	7
			Water	1	1	2	3	4	5	6	7	8	9
		E2/E3	Mountain	1	6	7	8	9	1	2	3	4	5
			Water	-1	1	9	8	7	6	5	4	3	2
	Southeast	SE1	Mountain	1	7	8	9	1	2	3	4	5	6
			Water	1	9	1	2	3	4	5	6	7	8
		SE2/SE3	Mountain	-1	7	6	5	4	3	2	1	9	8
			Water	-1	9	8	7	6	5	4	3	2	1
	South	S1	Mountain	1	3	4	5	6	7	8	9	1	2
			Water	-1	4	3	2	1	9	8	7	6	5
		S2/S3	Mountain	-1	3	2	1	9	8	7	6	5	4
			Water	1	4	5	6	7	8	9	1	2	3
	Southwest	SW1	Mountain	-1	5	4	3	2	1	9	8	7	6
			Water	-1	2	1	9	8	7	6	5	4	3
		SW2/SW3	Mountain	-1	5	4	3	2	1	9	8	7	6
			Water	1	2	3	4	5	6	7	8	9	1
	West	W1	Mountain	1	1	2	3	4	5	6	7	8	9
			Water	-1	6	5	4	3	2	1	9	8	7
		W2/W3	Mountain	-1	1	9	8	7	6	5	4	3	2
			Water	1	6	7	8	9	1	2	3	4	5
	Northwest	NW1	Mountain	1	9	1	2	3	4	5	6	7	8
			Water	1	7	8	9	1	2	3	4	5	6
		NW2/NW3	Mountain	-1	9	8	7	6	5	4	3	2	1
			Water	-1	7	6	5	4	3	2	1	9	8

Earth Base Construction Cycle	Building Sitting Direction	Building Sitting Sub-Direction	Star (Base, Mountain or Water)	yin/yang Polarity i.e., Star Flies '+' or '-'	Center	NW	W	NE	S	N	SW	E	SE
					←——Star Numbers for You to Place in Lo Shu——→								
9													
			Base Cycle Star	1	9	1	2	3	4	5	6	7	8
	North	N1	Mountain	1	5	6	7	8	9	1	2	3	4
			Water	-1	4	3	2	1	9	8	7	6	5
		N2/N3	Mountain	1	5	6	7	8	9	1	2	3	4
			Water	1	4	5	6	7	8	9	1	2	3
	Northeast	NE1	Mountain	1	3	4	5	6	7	8	9	1	2
			Water	-1	6	5	4	3	2	1	9	8	7
		NE2/NE3	Mountain	-1	3	2	1	9	8	7	6	5	4
			Water	1	6	7	8	9	1	2	3	4	5
	East	E1	Mountain	1	7	8	9	1	2	3	4	5	6
			Water	-1	2	1	9	8	7	6	5	4	3
		E2/E3	Mountain	-1	7	6	5	4	3	2	1	9	8
			Water	1	2	3	4	5	6	7	8	9	1
	Southeast	SE1	Mountain	-1	8	7	6	5	4	3	2	1	9
			Water	1	1	2	3	4	5	6	7	8	9
		SE2/SE3	Mountain	1	8	9	1	2	3	4	5	6	7
			Water	-1	1	9	8	7	6	5	4	3	2
	South	S1	Mountain	-1	4	3	2	1	9	8	7	6	5
			Water	1	5	6	7	8	9	1	2	3	4
		S2/S3	Mountain	1	4	5	6	7	8	9	1	2	3
			Water	1	5	6	7	8	9	1	2	3	4
	Southwest	SW1	Mountain	-1	6	5	4	3	2	1	9	8	7
			Water	1	3	4	5	6	7	8	9	1	2
		SW2/SW3	Mountain	1	6	7	8	9	1	2	3	4	5
			Water	-1	3	2	1	9	8	7	6	5	4
	West	W1	Mountain	-1	2	1	9	8	7	6	5	4	3
			Water	1	7	8	9	1	2	3	4	5	6
		W2/W3	Mountain	1	2	3	4	5	6	7	8	9	1
			Water	-1	7	6	5	4	3	2	1	9	8
	Northwest	NW1	Mountain	1	1	2	3	4	5	6	7	8	9
			Water	-1	8	7	6	5	4	3	2	1	9
		NW2/NW3	Mountain	-1	1	9	8	7	6	5	4	3	2
			Water	1	8	9	1	2	3	4	5	6	7

Note: The Mountain Star in each case is adjacent to its direction (column 3). The Water Star on the line immediately below it is located in the exactly opposite direction, but is not marked as such for the sake of clarity (as each chart is identified by its Mountain Star).

When you are placing the stars on the Lo Shu, the Base Cycle (Construction) Star goes in the middle of each square, the Mountain Star goes in the top left, and the Water (Facing) Star goes in the top right position of each square.

Appendix 2

The 24 Mountain Ring of the Lo P'an with the Flying Stars

Table A2: *The 24 Directions, Their Compass Readings, and Corresponding Flying Stars*

Direction	Compass Degrees	Chinese*	Stem/Branch/ Trigram	Flying Star
S1	157.5–172.5	*ping*	Stem	*Wu ch'u*
S2	172.5–187.5	**wu**	Branch	*P'o chun*
S3	187.5–202.5	*ting*	Stem	*T'an lang*
SW1	202.5–217.5	*wei*	Branch	*Chu men*
SW2	217.5–232.5	*k'un*	Trigram	*Lu ts'un*
SW3	232.5–247.5	*shen*	Branch	*Wen ch'u*
W1	247.5–262.5	*keng*	Stem	*Chu men*
W2	262.5–277.5	**yu**	Branch	*T'an lang*
W3	277.5–292.5	*hsin*	Stem	*Lien Chen*
NW1	292.5–307.5	*hsu*	Branch	*P'o chun*
NW2	307.5–322.5	*ch'ien*	Trigram	*Fu & Pi*
NW3	322.5–337.5	*hai*	Branch	*Chu men*
N1	337.5–352.5	*jen*	Stem	*P'o chun*
N2	352.5–7.5	**tzu**	Branch	*Wen ch'u*
N3	7.5–22.5	*kuei*	Stem	*Wen ch'u*
NE1	22.5–37.5	*ch'ou*	Branch	*T'an lang*
NE2	37.5–52.5	*ken*	Trigram	*Wu ch'u*
NE3	52.5–67.5	*yin*	Branch	*P'o chun*
E1	67.5–82.5	*chia*	Stem	*Fu & Pi*
E2	82.5–97.5	**mao**	Branch	*Chu men*
E3	97.5–112.5	*Yi*	Stem	*Lu ts'un*

Direction	Compass Degrees	Chinese*	Stem/Branch/Trigram	Flying Star
SE1	112.5–127.5	*chen*	Branch	*Wen ch'u*
SE2	127.5–142.5	*hsun*	Trigram	*Lien Chen*
SE3	142.5–157.5	*ssu*	Branch	*T'an lang*

The above table looks a bit complicated, so it is worth taking a bit of time to come to terms with its elegant structure. As you can see above, the 24 shan, or Mountains, are made up of:

    12 Earthly Branches
    8 of the 10 Heavenly Stems (omitting the Earth Stems)
    4 of the Trigrams (those that mark the "corner" points NW, SW, SE, NE)

Each Mountain covers 15 degrees out of 360 degrees of the compass. Let's analyze the structure, which is in fact very logical.

EARTHLY BRANCHES

The 12 Earthly Branches start at due North with Tzu and fill every second position around the compass.

Note that the Cardinal points are marked by the Branches Tzu (due North), Mao (due East), Wu (due South), and Yu (due West).

THE 4 TRIGRAMS

The four "corner" Trigrams of the Lo Shu mark the exact intercardinal points of the compass:

    Ken (NE)
    Hsun (SE)
    K'un (SW)
    Ch'ien (NW)

HEAVENLY STEMS

Eight of the 10 Heavenly Stems are divided according to their Element and follow the Production order in the 24 Mountains:

Water:	Jen (yang Water) and Kuei (yin Water)
Wood:	Chia (yang Wood) and Yi (yin Wood)
Fire:	Ping (yang Fire) and Ting (yin Fire)
Earth:	center (therefore invisible) Wu and Chi
Metal:	Keng (yang Metal) and Hsin (yin Metal)

The Stems are placed in order around the compass, in each case with the yang Stem first followed by the yin Stem.

Each pair of Stems flanks the Branch or trigram that marks the exact direction. Starting from the North it works like this:

Water Stems Jen and Kuei are placed either side of North.
Wood Stems Chia and Yi are placed either side of East.
Fire Stems Ping and Ting are placed either side of South.
Metal Stems Keng and Hsin are placed either side of West.

The resultant 24 Mountains have the following symmetries:

Note that the four directions NE, SE, SW, and NW each contain one of the four Earthly Brances: Chou, Chen, Wei, and Hsu. These appear as the first mountain in each of these four directions. The trigram is the center mountain of these intercardinal directions, and the third mountain is an Earthly Branch of the Element that relates to the season that follows.

This leaves each Cardinal point completely composed of one of the 4 Elements (the 5th Element, Earth, is in the center):

NE: Chou (Earth), Ken (trigram), and Yin (Wood)
The East is comprised entirely of Wood.
SE: Chen (Earth), Hsun (trigram), and Ssu (Fire)
The South is comprised entirely of Fire.
SW: Wei (Earth), K'un (trigram), and Shen (Metal)
The West is comprised entirely of Metal.
NW: Hsu (Earth), Ch'ien (trigram), and Hai (Water)
The North is comprised entirely of Water.

This reconfirms the basic Element/direction correspondences of basic feng shui:

E = Wood
S = Fire
W = Metal
N = Water

Appendix 3

Table of the 9 Periods

Table A3: *Flying Star Time Periods*

Era	Period or Yun 4/5 February in	Starting Year
Upper Era	Period 1	1864
	Period 2	1884
	Period 3	1904
Middle Era	Period 4	1924
	Period 5	1944
	Period 6	1964
Lower Era	Period 7	1984
	Period 8	2004
	Period 9	2024

Each Period is 20 years long. Each 60-year Era runs through the full 60 Sexagenary characters. Three Eras make one 180-year Great Cycle.

Appendix 4

The Lo Shu in Each Period

SE

3	8	1
2	4	6
7	9	5

Period 4

S

8	4	6
7	9	2
3	5	1

Period 9

SW

1	6	8
9	2	4
5	7	3

Period 2

E

2	7	9
1	3	5
6	8	4

Period 3

CENTER

4	9	2
3	5	7
8	1	6

Period 5

W

6	2	4
5	7	9
1	3	8

Period 7

NE

7	3	5
6	8	1
2	4	9

Period 8

N

9	5	7
8	1	3
4	6	2

Period 1

NW

5	1	3
4	6	8
9	2	7

Period 6

The *Lo Shu* for each of the 9 periods.

Appendix 5

Mountain Forms and the 9 Flying Stars

These formations are summarized in the feng shui classic, the *Han Lung Ching*, the "Classic of the Moving Dragon" by Yang Yun Sung (c. AD 888), who is often thought of as the patriarch of the Form School of feng shui. He goes into much more detail than we need to, but this is typical of the precision accorded a Form School feng shui diagnosis. For our purposes, it is sufficient to be able to simply identify which of the 9 possible Stars are represented by a particular landform as outlined in chapter 8. The following is an abridgement of his descriptions of the physical form of the Stars: it hints at further layers of interpretation.

1. *T'an lang*, the Covetous Wolf, has twelve characteristics. Of these, five are lucky and seven unlucky. The lucky forms of this Star are pointed, round, flat, straight, or small. The unlucky forms are absent in the middle, crooked, one sided, precipitous, inverted, broken, or empty. The pointed form is shaped like a bamboo sprout. The round form is complete on all sides. The flat form is perfectly level like a lying silkworm. . . The straight indicates absence of one-sidedness. The other characteristics of these formations are the appearance of instability, or of the breaking off of a water course, the hollowing of caves, and so on . . . Men say the Covetous Wolf is good. Its prevailing [external] Element is Wood.

2. *Chu men*, the Great Door, is the second flying star. The form loved by this shen is flat at the top and square on the sides. When a hill presents the appearance of a square or trapezium with the upper surface horizontal, this is caused by the presence of this Star. Wood is its prevailing [external] Element.

3. *Lu ts'un*, or Rank Preserved, is the third Star. Nine different shaped hills mark its presence. Its favorite shape has a flat top, a cylindrical body like a drum, and at the bottom it spreads into five (or sometimes four or three) branches like the toes of a human foot. Ordinarily it should be a malignant Star because its shape consists of a mixed nature. It is, however, able to adapt itself to conditions that secure good luck. It helps men to attain the lower ranks of the judiciary of second- or third-rate cities, and in certain circumstances gives the control of troops or success in literary (civil service) examinations. Earth is its ruling [external] Element.

4. *Wen chu*, or Literary Windings, belongs to the [external] Element of Water. It loves the shape of the snake and can be seen forming itself with three or four

bends in its body. The *lung chia* (feng shui practitioner) can detect its various shapes, such as, that of a thin snake, or if wider, a caterpillar. If wider still, it looks like a cast net. The points where it bends indicate the sources of water flow, and of the dragon's influence.

5. *Lien Chen*, Purity and Uprightness. Its [external] Element is Fire. The ancients valued it and called it "Red Flag" and "Brilliant Vapor." It likes to form a lofty range with rugged heights, umbrella-shaped folds, and sometimes the shape of a flattened ball. One form that it takes is that of a dragon tower, which is a conical shape, higher than anything around it. Another form it adopts is that of the "Palace of Precious Things," formed into several cones of equal height, or sometimes the form of a tortoise wrapped in a serpent, and guarding some precipitous gorge. The latter is considered to be the best indication, especially if accompanied by a mountain spring. (Note this is strangely the same as the symbolic animal of the North.)

6. *Wu ch'u*, Military Windings. Its Element is Metal. It is round at the top and broad at the bottom, like a bell or an inverted cooking bowl. In judging the hill shapes that make up this Star, it is easy to mistake the *kuei* (ghost or demon) for the dragon. This is especially the case when the shape is that of an inverted ladle. This is particularly so when the Ladle is like the shape of the tail of the Great Bear constellation, *Pei tou*, the Northern Ladle constellation [from which all the 9 Flying Stars derive]. The *kuei* and the dragon are both able to take the form of an inverted dust pan, an inverted spoon, or the inverted palm of a hand.

The skill of the feng shui Master is in distinguishing these, one from the other. Indeed the kuei may take the form of any of the 9 Flying Stars, and if each has four forms [square, round, crooked, and straight], there may be thirty-six shapes in all to be considered.

7. *P'o chun*, the Breaker of the Phalanx, is referred to the [external] Element of Metal. It has one normal and four peculiar shapes. The normal shape is that of three round-headed cones, seen raising one above the other like the folds of a flag. Below, it has ugly looking points like spears. Although it is a malignant Star, it can be quite serviceable in acquiring riches and rank. Upon high hills the heavenly essence of these Stars collects and becomes part of the six terrestrial or atmospheric Stars called *lu fu*, the six Palaces.

8. *Tso fu*, the Left Assistant, is under the influence of the [external] Element of Metal [this should be Earth]. Its normal shape is that of a head with a turban wrapped round it, in the front high, but behind lower. This Star is a servant of the great dragon who gives shape to the constellations. This Star, by its proximity to the Emperor [of the North Pole Star] can confer honors upon men well aspected by it.

9. *Yu pi*, Right Assistant, has no fixed shape at all. Its [external] Element is Water. Flatness is its favorite characteristic. It loves to be where hills break off and give place to the plain. It rules even surfaces and is therefore called "Hidden Glory." It is fond of narrow thread-like shapes and dim vestiges of form. It is like the snake which creeps through the grass, the fish leaping on the sand, the spider's thread, the traces of horses' hooves, the strings of a lyre. It likes that which is half real and half unreal, and which is scarcely visible to the eye. Even a few inches is enough to allow water to flow."

This free translation raises more questions than it solves, but in its poetry you can feel the power thought to reside in the landscape, a power that can activate the Flying Star residing inside the house. There are many feng shui hints woven into this text, which we do not have space here to unravel. One such hint is the nature of the Right Assistant, which suggests that it is just the unreal half of the Left Assistant, rather than a Star in its own right, and indeed that is how it is often treated, so that the 9 Flying Stars actually become eight.

Appendix 6

An Alternative Method of Dividing the Great Cycle

Most of the Flying Star feng shui that has made its way into English uses nine "average trigram dividing" Periods of 20-years each to make up the 180-year Great Cycle. There are other schools of Hsuan Kung feng shui that divide these 180 years unevenly, according to the "Early Heaven Sequence trigram dividing Periods." This was first brought to my attention by Abel Yeung many years ago in Hong Kong, who patiently explained to me that the exact length of these smaller Periods depends upon the trigram corresponding to the Period and their arrangement in the Great Cycle.

Each Period has a trigram attributed to it. The length of each Period under this system depends upon the value of this trigram. To work this out, you give the value of 9 to any yang line, and 6 to any yin line in a trigram. For example the K'un trigram is made up of three yin lines, so its value is 3 x 6 = 18. So its Periods should be counted as 18 years, not the standard 20 years. The Ch'ien trigram on the other hand is made up of 3 yang lines, so its Period length is 3 x 9 = 27 years. The length of each Period in this system is determined by adding up the value of these trigram lines. I recognized this system again in Master Chan's explanation of Hsuan Kung (Yuen Hom in Cantonese) feng shui.

Conventionally (using 20-year Periods), we entered Period number 7 in 1984 and will pass to Period 8 in 2004. But under this alternative system we are already in Period 8, with 1996 as the boundary year between Period 7 and Period 8. Both Schools agree, however, that the whole 180-year Great Cycle comes to an end in 2044. The alternative system, by the way, has no Period 5.

Under the alternative method, the Periods are as shown in table A.6.

Table A6: *Alternative Method for Dividing the Great Cycle*

Period	Trigram	Value of Trigram lines	Length Lines	Starting Year
Period 1	K'un	6+6+6	18	1864
Period 2	Hsun	9+9+6	24	1882
Period 3	Li	9+6+9	24	1906
Period 4	Tui	6+9+9	24	1930
Period 5 [not used]				
Period 6	Ken	9+6+6	21	1954
Period 7	K'an	6+9+6	21	1975
Period 8	Chen	6+6+9	21	1996
Period 9	Ch'ien	9+9+9	27	2017
			——	2044

Total Great Cycle = 180

Having said that, we use the fixed 20-year Period division system throughout this book.

Appendix 7

Main Schools of Feng Shui

Leaving aside the many New Age varieties of intuitional and faux feng shui that have sprung up in the West in the last 20 years, let's concentrate on authentic Chinese Schools with a history counted in centuries rather than decades. There are roughly 9 main Schools, with many variants. With some subdivisions this expands to 14 Schools. Of these the most basic distinction is that some Schools concentrate upon external landforms, the so-called Form School or *luan tou*, while others attempt to "detect the pulse of the dragon" by utilizing the numerology of the trigrams, Elements, and other factors like the "Fate Stars." These are the so-called Compass Schools, or *li ch'i*.

This is possibly the first time this list has been published in full in English. From it you can seen how few of the Schools have actually made their way into popular English feng shui literature.

1. *San He* (3 Harmony) School. The basic Form School often referred to as *hsing shih* or *luan tou*. This School teaches the use of mountains and dragon veins to draw in ch'i, and Water Dragon formulas designed to retain and accumulate it.

The following Schools are often referred to as *li ch'i*, or ch'i pattern or Compass School feng shui:

2. *Pa Kua* (8 trigram) School. Concerned with the 8 trigrams related to 5 Elements and 8 directions.

3. *Wu Hsing* (5 Element) School. Concerned with Production and Destruction Cycles of the Elements.

4. *Chi Men Tun Chia* (Mysterious Gate and Hidden Time) School. This has just begun to be taught in the West, usually under the pinyin spelling of *Qi Men Dun Jia*. It is based on the 8 Gates and 9 Palaces.

5. *Hsuan Kung Ta Kua* (Dark Palace Hexagram) School. Makes use of the 64 Hexagrams on the lo p'an. Also the *Cheng Kua* School. Hsuan Kung is often translated as "Mysterious Void" but is closer in meaning to "Dark Palace" (where kung is understood as a pun). The Dark Palace is, of course, that of the Pole Star around which travel the 9 Flying Stars of *Pei To u*.

6. *Hsuan Kung Fei Hsing* (Dark Palace Flying Star) School. The subject of this book, which is part of the *Hsuan Kung* (or Xuan Kong) School. Hsuan Kung used to be called *Yuan Kung*, which refers specifically to Cycles and Palaces.

7. *Pa Chai* (8 Mansion) School. Popularized during the 1990s by Lillian Too, amongst others. It allocates fixed sectors to a house/office according to compass directions, and correlates these with the *pa kua*.

7a. Black Hat Sect (BTB) feng shui, promoted by Thomas Lin Yun in the U.S. since 1986, is modeled on a very simplified fixed *pa kua* version of Pa Chai.

8. *Tzu Wei Tou Shu* (Purple Star) School. This is a form of Chinese astrology (quite different from 4 Pillar astrology) that uses sitting and door directions and several hundred fate stars.

9. *Fan Kua* (Flipping Trigram) School. Looks at mountain/water relationships and uses the transmutation of one kua into another by systematic line changes. We touch briefly on this in chapter 4.

I have not included *Ming Kua* (Life kua) or *Pa Tzu* (8 Character or 4 Pillar) astrology in the list because although the latter is often taught as part of feng shui (by such excellent teachers as Raymond Lo) it is really personal astrology rather than feng shui. Undoubtedly I will have omitted some Schools, and I would be pleased to hear from any readers who wish to draw my attention to any other significant Schools. On the whole, however, almost every School calls upon one or another of the above methods to judge the feng shui of any site.

Appendix 8

Chinese Dynasties and Feng Shui Chronology

Traditional Emperors		**Significant feng shui event**
	BC	
	4000	Neolithic grave containing feng shui symbolism.
Fu Hsi	2852–2737	Invented the 8 trigrams. Discovered the *Ho t'u* and Early Heaven Sequence of the trigrams.
Shen Nong	2737–2697	
Huang Ti (the Yellow Emperor)	2697–2597	Reputedly invented the compass and a primitive calendar based on 60-year cycles of Stems and Branches that began in the year 2637 BC
Shao Hao	2597–2513	
Chaun Hsu	2513–2435	
Ti Ku	2435–2365	
Ti Chi	2365–2356	
Yao	2356–2255	Set up astronomical observatories to help regulate the calendar.
Shun	2255–2205	Attempted to regulate the rivers.
Yu	2205–2197	Discovered the Lo Shu and Later Heaven Sequence of the trigrams, and succeeded in regulating the floods.

Historic Dynasties

Hsia (Xia)	2150–1557	Hsia solar calendar devised.
Shang	1557–1027	60-day cycle devised from 10 Heavenly Stems and 12 Earthly Branches

Historic Dynasties		Significant feng shui event
Chou (Zhou)	1027–221	King Wen discovered the 64 hexagrams and wrote the *Chou I*, part of the *I Ching*.
Spring and Autumn Period	770–476	Confucius edited the *I Ching*. Lao Tzu wrote *Tao Te Ching*. Feng shui formed from combining the Compass + *I Ching* + calendar.
The Warring States Period	476–221	Chou Yen (350–270 BC) mentions the 5 Elements
Ch'in (Qin)	221–206 BC	Burning of the books by Emperor Chin Shih Huang Ti.
Han	206 BC–AD 220	Kan-yu (one old name for feng shui) becomes a profession. Many books on feng shui known, e.g., *Golden Kan-yu Thesaurus*. Ching Wu, Master Blue Raven.
Three Kingdoms (Wei, Shu, Wu) feng	220–265	Kuan Lo (209–256) writes classic feng shui text. Chu-kuo Liang or Chu Kok Liu (the military strategist) invents *Chi Men Tun Chia* style shui.
Chin (Jin)	265–420	Kuo P'o (276–324), "father of feng shui," writes the *Burial Classic*.
Southern & Northern dynasties	420–589	Wang Wei (415–443)
Sui	589–618	
T'ang	618–906	Feng shui flourishes. Yang Yun Sung (849–c. 888) brings Form School together.
5 Dynasties & 10 Kingdoms	906–960	
Sung (Northern)	960–1127	Wang Chih founds the Fukien Compass School based on trigrams, Stems and Branches. *Lo p'an* established with 17 rings. Flying Star calendars common.
Northern Kin & Southern Sung	1127–1279	Chen Hsi-I founded *Tzu wei tou shu* Astrology/feng shui
Yuan (Mongol)	1260–1368	Chao Fang writes about the compass or *lo ching*.

Historic Dynasties		Significant feng shui event
Ming	1368–1644	First Ming Emperor (Chu Yuan Chuan 1368–1398) kills many Taoist feng shui Masters and issues false feng shui books. Establishment of *San Yuan* feng shui. *Lo p'an* expanded to 36 rings. Chiang Ta Hung writes important Hsuan Kung texts.
Ch'ing (Qing) (Manchu)	1644–1911	Use of 4 Pillar horoscope integrated with feng shui. Master Shen Chu Reng (1850–1906) writes classic book of Hsuan Kung Flying Star.
Republic of China	1912–1949	Feng shui suppressed in mainland China (1927).
People's Republic of China	1949–present	The Cultural Revolution (1966–76) closes down most of feng shui in People's Republic of China. First 20th-century English book on feng shui written by the present author (1976). First book on feng shui published in Chinese in People's Republic of China (1989) since its suppression. First worldwide full-color feng shui magazine *Feng Shui for Modern Living* published (1998–2000) in English and Chinese.

Appendix 9

Chinese & Western Calendar Concordance

Dates of Beginning of Chieh or Ch'i*	Ch'i No.	Name of 24 Ch'i, or Solar Seasons	Name in English	Earthly Branch***
4-Feb	1	Li Ch'un	Spring commences	III - yin
19-Feb	2	Yu Shui	Rain water	
5-Mar	3	Ching Chih	Insects waken	IV - mao
20-Mar	4	Ch'un Fen	Spring Equinox	
4-Apr	5	Ch'ing Ming	Clear brightness	V - ch'en
20-Apr	6	Ku Yu	Corn rain	
5-May	7	Li Hsia	Summer commences	VI - ssu
21-May	8	Hsiao Man	Corn sprouting	
5-Jun	9	Mang Chung	Corn in ear	VII - wu
21-Jun	10	Hsia Chih	Summer Solstice	
7-Jul	11	Hsiao Shu	Little Heat	VIII - wei
22-Jul	12	Ta Shu	Great Heat	
7-Aug	13	Li Ch'iu	Autumn commences	IX - shen
23-Aug	14	Ch'u Shu	Heat finishes	
7-Sep	15	Pai Lu	White Dew	X - yu
23-Sep	16	Ch'iu Fen	Autumn Equinox	
8-Oct	17	Han Lu	Cold Dew	XI - hsu
23-Oct	18	Shuang Chiang	Frost Descends	
7-Nov	19	Li Tung	Winter commences	XII - hai
22-Nov	20	Hsiao Hsueh	Little Snow	
7-Dec	21	Ta Hsueh	Great Snow	I - tzu
21-Dec	22	Tung Chih	Winter Solstice	
5-Jan	23	Hsiao Han	Little Cold	II - ch'ou
20-Jan	24	Ta Han	Great Cold	

This particular year is 2000, hence
* plus 1 day in some years
** plus or minus 1 or 2 days in some years

Ruling Planet	Element (Excluding Earth)	Season	Date* Season Begins	Date** of Mid-Season
Jupiter	Wood	Spring	4-Feb	
		Spring Equinox		20-Mar
Mars	Fire	Summer	5-May	
		Summer Solstice		21-Jun
Venus	Metal	Fall/Autumn	7-Aug	
		Autumn Equinox		23-Sep
Mercury	Water	Winter	7-Nov	
		Winter Equinox		21-Dec
		Spring next year	5-Feb	

*** Note that the year starts with the 3rd Branch, yin.
NB: The solstice and the equinox are the mid-points of each season, as shown above, not the beginning of the season as is commonly thought in the West

Appendix 10

The Water Forms
of the 9 Flying Stars

There are also Water forms that correspond to each of the 9 Flying Stars. One set of correspondences between the Flying Star and Water configurations give a hint as to how the relevant Water feature should be supplied with Water. There is also an interesting correspondence with parts of the human body (which seems to be listed simply as a way of remembering the possible Water flow than for any other reason).

Table A10: *The Nine Flying Stars with Their Corresponding Water Feature Flow Directions*

Star	Chinese Name Shape	Meaning	Body part	Water flow
1-White	T'an lang	Covetous Wolf	mouth	water can enter but not exit
2-Black	Chu men	Great Door/ Gate	nose	water can enter and also exit
3-Green	Lu ts'un	Rank (Salary) Preserved	penis	water can exit but not enter
4-Jade	Wen ch'u	Civil Career ("Windings")	ear	water may not enter or exit
5-Yellow	Lien chien	Honesty, Purity, Uprightness	eyes	water can exit but not enter
6-White	Wu ch'u	Military Career ("Windings")	navel/belly	water can enter but not exit
7-Red	P'o chun	Broken Army	anus	water can exit but not enter
8-White	Tso fu	Left Assistant	nose	water can enter and also exit
9-Purple	Yu pi	Right Assistant	navel/belly	water can enter but not exit

We won't go into great detail, but the above table gives some hints as to how to engineer Water features to support these Stars where they arrive in the form of Water Stars. Of course you should only support the Star if it were auspicious and advantageous.

Appendix 11

Feng Shui Practice

When you come to using your skills with Flying Star feng shui, the first thing you need to buy is some kind of practice book. It could be loose leaf with photocopied sheets or a large format lined notebook, whichever suits you. The thing you must avoid is doing various feng shui diagnoses on sundry bits of paper that may soon get lost. Keep it all in one book where you can refer back to it, to see what you found in the past, and to check on results in a year's time. This way you can be sure what worked and what didn't.

Initially you should just do your own Flying Star feng shui, then that of friends, resisting the temptation to prescribe cures or remedies until you have had enough practice to be confident and fluent in drawing up correct charts. Then you need to do a few feng shui changes and watch and record the results. That kind of experimentation is invaluable, but it is not kind to do it at the expense of strangers. You should be ready to say when you are wrong or when it does not appear to have worked. You can only learn by your mistakes. Many of you will not want to go beyond working on your own feng shui and perhaps doing an occasional reading for immediate friends.

But if you do go beyond this and actually do consultations, then at this point you have an ethical dilemma. You are not trained sufficiently to practice professionally, but on the other hand you don't want to spend hours of your time working without recompense. I suggest the way round that is to suggest a donation in proportion to the perceived benefits of any formal reading that recommends remedies or a course of action. Certainly this will result in a few "no fees," but on the other hand you will get some measure of client satisfaction. When you have started to have noticeable success, and perhaps spent some time doing charts with an acknowledged teacher or Master, then and only then, should you think of a fee scale.

Appendix 12

Typical Analysis Sequence

It is helpful initially to have a checklist of the order in which to do things. The checklist below is not exhaustive, merely a suggested way of working.

You need an accurate ground plan of the building you are working on, a blank Lo Shu, and a lo p'an.

1. Record details of:
    Date of reading/consultation
    Name of owner
    Address
    Date and time of owner's birth
    Date of construction of building
    Date of present owner's move in

2. From this you should be able to calculate:
    Construction Period (Period Star or Earth Base) of building
    Period Star of present owner's move in date (if required)
    Personal Star (kua number) of the owner and from this the owner's 4 best/worst directions, sheng ch'i, etc.

3. Use your lo p'an to determine and write down the building's
    Facing Mountain direction (and exact degrees)
    Sitting Mountain direction (and exact degrees)
    (which should be 180 degrees greater/lesser than the Facing direction)

4. Draw up the chart with Period, Mountain, and Water Stars.
    Mark in the Period Star (construction or move in Period) in the central Palace.
    Mark the Sitting and Facing directions.
    Use appendix 1 Shortcut Method to fill in all Palaces with Sitting and Facing Stars, and then move on to Step 5, or use the Full Method as follows:

    Fly the Period Star
    Move the Sitting and Facing Star numbers into the Central Palace (sitting Star to the top left, and Facing Star to the top right)
    Fly the Water and Mountain Stars

5. Relate the chart to reality:
    a) Place the chart next to the ground plan of the house.
        Identify the Facing direction of the house and the Facing Palace on the chart. Turn the chart Facing direction to coincide with the ground plan Facing direction.
    b) Draw in the 9 Palaces, using a ruler (either 8 Pie Wedges or 9 Palaces).
    c) Mark in the Stars on the ground plan.
    d) Note down any significant visible landform features and mark their position adjacent to the correct Palace, such as:
        Mountains, hills, or buildings;
        Water, rivers, ponds, streets, the driveway, gates.

6. Check overall combinations:
Determine which of the 4 types of chart pattern it is.
    a) Good for Wealth and Good for Health
    b) Double Facing
    c) Double Sitting or
    d) Reversed chart

Check if the chart forms one of the standard combinations, and interpret accordingly:
    a) Combination of Ten
    b) Combination of Three
    c) Continuous Beads
    d) Hidden & Inverse Siren

7. Interpret Key Palaces
    Facing Palace
        Especially interaction between Period Star and Water Star
    Sitting Palace
    Palace containing the main door, if not the Facing Palace
    The Palace containing the kitchen
    The Palace containing the master bedroom
    The Palace containing the home office or study
    Any Palace that adjoins a significant landform feature

For each Palace, consider the following Star Combinations and meanings in descending order of importance. In each case designate the most relevant Star as the Host Star:
    a) The Facing Star and its relationship with the Mountain Star
    b) The Facing Star with the Period Star
    c) Mountain Star with the Period Star

8. Do small t'ai chi or micro feng shui, applying the Lo Shu to key individual rooms to place furniture, particularly:

> Bedrooms: to determine the position of the bed and room door
> Kitchen: to determine the position and the orientation of the stove and its "fire mouth"

9. Check the Annual Visiting Stars:

> Annual Star arriving in the Facing and Main Door Palace.
> Which Palace the Annual 5-yellow, the 2-black, t'ai sui, and san sha fly to, and what cures should be put in place.
> Interaction of the Annual Star with the Period Star and Water Star in each Palace

10. Check the Monthly Visiting Stars:

> Check the interaction of the Monthly Stars with the Annual Stars
> Check for trigger months when Monthly Stars fly into key Palaces that have sensitive combinations.

11. Check the human ch'i:

> Calculate the Personal Star (or kua number) of all key occupants (especially the head of the family) and judge if they are supported by the Stars located in their bedrooms and workrooms.

12. Ascertain and instigate appropriate remedies:

> a) Place Form School deflectors of inauspicious external structures.
> b) Place Elemental enhancers and adjustments indicated by the Flying Stars.

Remember to concentrate on one Palace at a time, and for each Palace make notes on each of the above considerations. It is most important to write down your conclusions, recording position, birth dates of main occupants, chart, and conclusions Palace by Palace, plus any recommendations. It helps to have a well-organized practice book so that you can go back and check your work later when you have greater ability. If you are working for clients, then it is useful to refer back when the feng shui assessment needs to be done again at the next New Year.

That way your work will not look to you like a hopelessly complex mass of figures. You can't expect to figure out something as complex as luck without going to a bit of trouble first. Remember that rarely used rooms and wet rooms will nullify whatever Star combination comes into their areas, so these can be almost immediately written off.

Glossary

The terms in this book are rendered in Wade-Giles transliteration. To help readers who are more familiar with pinyin transliteration, some of the pinyin equivalents have been cross-referenced in this glossary. See the note at the beginning of the book for an explanation of these two methods of transliteration.

You can see immediately that pinyin uses "q" to represent "ch" as in ch'i which is a bit confusing to say the least. Pinyin also uses both "zh" and "j" to represent what sounds like "j" to Western ears.

24 Mountains: The most important Ring on the lo p'an compass, which consist of the 12 Earthly Branches, 8 of the Heavenly Stems, and the 4 corner Trigrams. There are 6 Water, 6 Fire, 6 Wood, and 6 Metal Directions on the 24 Mountains ring.

Almanac, Chinese: an annual Chinese publication that includes all kinds of advice, including Flying Star locations for the year and the best/worst activities for every single day of the year.

Ba Zi: see *pa tzu.*
Bagua: see *pa kua.*
Bazhai: see *pa chai.*
Bird, Red: A Form School low hill formation at the front of a house or site.
Book of Changes, see *I Ching.*
Branches: see Earthly Branches.
Bright Hall: see *ming tang.*

Calendar, lunar: A calendar based on "months" measured by Moon cycles.
Calendar, solar: a calendar, like the standard Western one, based on the Earth's revolution round the Sun, but more precisely aligned to the seasons.
Cardinal points: North, South, East, and West.
Cash: the name for old round Chinese coins with a square hole in the middle.
Celestial Animals: Green Dragon, White Tiger, Black Tortoise with snake, Red Bird.
Ch'ien trigram: the trigram of Heaven and late Autumn.
Chai: house.
Chen trigram: trigram of thunder and Spring.
Ch'i kung: a martial art which concentrates ch'i energy in the body.

Ch'i: the vital energy of the universe, in man, the heavens, and earth, sometimes referred to as "cosmic breath." Ch'i in the human body, is considered a yang counterpart to blood: it forms and circulates blood.

Ch'ing Dynasty: AD 1644-1911.

Chor sin, see Mountain Star.

Chou Dynasty: 1027-221 BC.

Chou I: an old name for the *I Ching*.

Chueh ming: severed fate or total loss location in house.

Compass School: the Fukien School of feng shui, which uses the lo p'an to locate and diagnose ch'i flows. More correctly called the fang wei (Directions and Positions) School.

Compass, Chinese: see lo p'an.

Daoism, see Taoism.

Destructive Cycle: the cycle of the Elements that is ordered: Metal, Wood, Earth, Water, then Fire.

Devil's Door: the northeast, sometimes considered a bad direction to face a front door.

Direction: one of the 8 main compass points, or in a more specialized sense, the 24 Mountain ring on the lo p'an.

Dragon Gate: the gate through which successful scholars are supposed to pass, metaphorically turning from a mere carp into a dragon.

Dragon, Green: the Form School hills to the left of a house or site (looking out from the front door).

Dragon, Yellow: the Celestial Animal associated with the Central Palace.

Early Heaven Sequence: or *hou t'ien*, a circular arrangement of the 8 trigrams, such that the trigram Ch'ien is in the South. Used on defensive pa kua mirrors and for the feng shui of exterior landforms.

Earth Base: When a house is built it is thought that the act of building encapsulates the Earth energies of that Period or Time into the structure. This Period number is the Earth Base.

Earthly Branches: (*ti kan*), the 12 divisions of the day, or the year, which are combined with the 10 Heavenly Stems to form the 60 Sexagenary characters.

East Group: the directions SE, N, S, E.

East/West system: the system that divides people and houses into two types, the East Group and the West Group.

Eight House formula: see Eight Mansion formula.

Eight Mansion formula: the feng shui division of a room or building into 8 fixed sectors that are attributed to aspirations such as Career, Wealth, Marriage, etc.

Elements, Five: the *wu hsing:* Water, Fire, Earth, Metal, and Wood.

Facing direction: The front side of building; often, but not always, the side on which is the front door.

Facing Star, see Water Star

Fan Yin: also known as Reverse Chant, when the 5-Yellow Star, flying in a yin (backward) direction, occupies the Mountain or Water Star position of the Central Palace.

Fang shih: a master of Taoist magic.

Fang wei: see Compass School.

Fei Hsing: Flying Star.

Fei Sin, see *Fei Hsing*.

Feng sha: a noxious ch'i-destroying wind.

Feng shui hsien sheng: a professional practitioner of feng shui.

Feng shui: the Chinese system of maximizing the accumulation of beneficial ch'i to improve the quality of life and luck of the occupants of a particular building or location. Literally "wind water."

Feng: wind.

Five Elements, see Elements.

Floating Stars, see Flying Stars.

Flying Stars: the subject of this book.

Form and Configuration School: *hsing shih*, feng shui practice that uses landform structure to determine positions of maximum beneficial ch'i accumulation. Its most famous Master was Yang Yun Sung (AD 840-c.888).

Four Pillars: your personal Chinese horoscope, specifically the 8 Chinese characters and their associated Elements generated by determining the Stem and Branch of each of the year, month, day, and hour of your birth date.

Fu Hsi: an early ruler of China said to have discovered or invented the trigrams.

Fu wei: house location that has mild good fortune

Fu Xi, see Fu Hsi.

Fu Yin: known as Reiterative Chant (or Hidden Siren), when the 5-Yellow Star, flying in a yang (forward) direction, occupies the Mountain or Water Star position of the Central Palace.

Ganzhi system, see *kan shih* system

Geomancy: an old *mis*-translation of feng shui. In reality Geomancy is a completely different Arab system of divination by dots and sand, originating in North Africa in the 9th century AD.

Great Cycle of 180 years: 9 cycles of 20 years. The current Great Cycle begun in 1864.

Green Dragon, see Dragon.

Hai huo: the accidents and mishaps or mild bad luck location in a house.

Heavenly Stems (*t'ien shih*): the 10 characters that represent the cycle of the 5 Elements in both their yin and yang form. They combine with the 12 Earthly Branches to form the 60 Sexagenary characters.

Heaven's Heart: the Central Palace of the Lo Shu.

Hetu: see *ho t'u*.

Hexagrams: the 64 figures formed by placing one trigram on top of another in every possible combination. A figure made up of 8 lines on top of one another, either broken or unbroken. The basis of the *I Ching*.

Ho hai, see *hai huo*.

Ho T'u: a square, like the Lo Shu, used with the Former Heaven Sequence feng shui.

Hsia Calendar: the traditional Chinese agricultural and solar calendar.

Hsuan: dark, obscure, rather than profound, secret, mysterious.

Hsing, see Elements.

Hsiu: the 28 Chinese (uneven sized) constellations often found marked on one of the outer rings of a feng shui compass.

Hsuan Kong: a School of feng shui that includes Flying Star feng shui. Literally "Dark Palace."

Hsüeh: the lair, or site, of the maximum concentration of beneficial ch'i. Can also apply to an acupuncture point.

Hsun: the trigram of wind and early Summer. Sometimes spelled "Sun."

Huo: Fire.

I Ching: the Chinese *Classic of Changes*, a philosophical and divinatory book based on the 64 hexagrams.

Intercardinal points: NW, SW, NE, SE.

Jin, see *chin*.

K'an: the trigram of Moon and water and mid-winter.

K'un: the trigram of Earth and late Summer.

Kan shih system: the 60 combinations of 12 Earthly Branches (*t'ien kan*) and 10 Heavenly Stems (*t'ien shih*).

Kan yu: an old name for feng shui.

Ken: the trigram of mountain and early Spring.

Killing Breath: see *sha ch'i*.

Kua number: really the Personal Star number derived from the Annual Flying Star of your year of birth (in the case of males).

Kua: means both trigram (3 lines) and hexagram (six lines).

Kuei: see *kwei*.

Kwei: ghosts, has also been translated "demons."

Landscape feng shui, see Form School feng shui.

Later Heaven Sequence (*hsian t'ien*): a circular arrangement of the 8 trigrams, such that the trigram Ch'ien is in the NW. Used in assessment of the interior layout of homes or offices.

Li Chun: the commencement of Spring, the day the Annual Stars change, the beginning of the Chinese Solar New Year, which begins on February 4th or 5th each year.

Li: the trigram of fire and the South.

Liu sha: the six curses or six imps location in a house.

Lo p'an: the feng shui compass. The primary tool of feng shui.

Lo shu: the magic square with 9 chambers (or Palaces), whose numbers add up to 15 in every direction.

Luck: is considered to be comprised of three components known as Heaven Luck (fate), Earth Luck (feng shui), and Man Luck (your own efforts).

Lui sha, a common incorrect spelling of liu sha.

Lunar Calendar: see Calendar, lunar.

Lung Ho T'u: Dragon and Tiger Map.

Lung Mei: Dragon Veins, but *not* the same as ley lines. They are the channels that ch'i follows through the Earth.

Lung: the Chinese dragon, a water creature.

Luo Pan: See *lo p'an*.

Luoshu: see *Lo Shu*.

Ming Dynasty: AD 1368-1644.

Ming gua, see *Ming kua*.

Ming kua: destiny trigram, or personal kua number. Actually the Annual Flying Star of the year of birth, in the case of males.

Ming Shu: fate calculation, a form of Chinese astrology.

Ming tang: bright hall, the courtyard, or the open space in front of a building where beneficial ch'i can accumulate.

Ming: life, fate, destiny.

Mountain Star: the Sitting star in Flying Star feng shui.

MPW: Mountain-Period-Water order of stars.

MTW: Mountain-Time-Water order of stars.

Mu: Wood.

Nien yen, see *yan nien*.

Pa chai, see Eight Mansion formula.

Pa kua mirror: a mirror (flat, concave, or convex) surrounded by the 8 trigrams in the Former Heaven Sequence designed to reflect sha ch'i.

Pa kua: literally "8 trigrams," or more specifically, the octagonal arrangement of the 8 trigrams.

Pa tzu: translates as Four Pillars, but literally means 8 (Chinese) Characters.

Palace: This is one of the 9 Lo Shu cells that a building is divided into for the purposes of a feng shui diagnosis. Each Palace (except the Central Palace) corresponds to one of the 8 trigrams. Palaces are usually referred to by their trigram, i.e., the K'un Palace, or more simply by their compass direction.

Period: 20-year Period, nine of which make up a 180-year Great Cycle.

Poison arrows, see Secret arrows.

Productive Cycle: the cycle of the 5 Elements which progresses: Wood, Fire, Earth, Metal, Water.

Qi Gong, see *ch'i kung*.

Qi, see *ch'i*.

Qing Dynasty, see Ch'ing Dynasty.

Reductive Cycle of the Elements: the 5 Elements reducing each other in the cycle order Wood - Water - Metal - Earth - Fire.

Sam Sart (Cantonese), see *San Sha*.
Sam, Master, see Shen Chu Reng.
San Ban Gua, see *San Pan Kua*.
San Bao, see *San Pao*.
San He: Three Combinations, a major traditional School of feng shui.
San Pan Kua: a configuration where all Palaces of the Flying Star chart contain the Mountain-Period-Water combinations of 147, 258, and 369. Reputedly, this structure is auspicious under all circumstances.
San Pao: the three Treasures: *jing (essence)*, *ch'i (vitality)*, *shen (spirit)*, which have no Western counterpart.
San Sha: Fate Stars called the three Evils or Three Killings, or literally, the "three *sha*."
San Yuan: Three Cycles, a major traditional school of feng shui.
San Yuan Chiu Yun: the three sub-cycles and nine periods.
Seam Needle: one of the directional needles on a San He lo p'an. The seam needle reads 7.5 degrees behind the correct needle. The seam needle was originally used in yin house feng shui as the guideline to locate the sha "sands" and "water."
Secret arrows: cutting ch'i generated by a straight alignment of roads, trees, poles, or adjacent buildings.
Sector: an area of a room or building corresponding to one of the cardinal or inter-cardinal points, i.e., N, S, E, W, NW, SW, SE, NE.
Sexagenary combinations: The 60 combinations of 12 Earthly Branches and 10 Heavenly Stems.
Sha: There are more than 15 distinct and separate words/characters in Chinese, with different meanings, all of which can be transliterated into English as *sha*. Even when they are pronounced with 4 different tones, many cannot be distinguished except by writing the Chinese character. There are three different *sha* relevant to feng shui:
Sha: [1st tone] killing, murder, slaughter, hence sha ch'i, killing ch'i.
Sha: [1st tone also] sand, (also small hills used as a geographical term), hence "the sha in front of a site."
Sha: [4th tone] an evil spirit, as in the Fate Stars, the "three shas."
Sha ch'i: cutting or killing ch'i.
Sha qi, see sha ch'i.

Shan: mountain in the geographical sense, but also the term for the 24 directions on the major lo p'an compass ring.
Shang Shan Hsia Shui: literally "up the mountain and down the water," a reversed house chart.
Shang: to ascend, up, above.
Shar, see *sha*.
Shen Chu Reng: a feng shui Master, author of the work *Shen Shih Hsuan Kung Hsue*.
Shen: spirit. the governing force that enlivens the flesh.

Sheng ch'i: strong or generating ch'i. Success and great prosperity location in house.

Sheng qi, see *sheng ch'i*.

Sheng: life, growth.

Shui: water, also a general term for a river.

Siang sin, see Water Star.

Sitting direction: where a house sits, the opposite of the Facing Direction.

Sitting Star see Mountain Star.

Solar calendar: see Calendar, solar.

Ssu ch'i: stagnant or torpid ch'i.

Stems, see Heavenly Stems.

Sui Hsing: the planet Jupiter.

Sui Po: the Branch known as the Year Clash, diametrically opposite the Branch of the Year.

Sun, see Hsun trigram

T'ai chi: the Great Ultimate from which every thing else came. The "tadpole" symbol showing its division into yin and yang.

T'ien I: the Heavenly Doctor or health location in house.

T'ien Yi, see *T'ien I*.

T'ien: heaven, or in one sense literally the sky.

T'ung Shu: the Chinese Almanac.

T'ung Sing, see *T'ung Shu*.

Tai Ji, see *t'ai chi*.

Tai Sui: Counter-Jupiter, or the Grand Duke Jupiter. It is the direction related to the year, i.e., Tiger direction in a Tiger year.

Taiji, see *t'ai chi*.

Tao: the Way, the essence of Taoism.

Ti: Earth.

Tiger, White: the Celestial Animal of the West.

Tong Shu: see *T'ung Shu*.

Tortoise: see turtle.

Trigrams: the 8 possible figures made of combinations of 3 yin (broken) and yang (whole) lines.

Tu: Earth.

Tui: the trigram representing lake and mid-Fall.

Turtle or Tortoise: one of the 4 Celestial Animals, associated with the North. A yin creature often accompanied by a snake.

Tzu Wei Tou Shu: Purple Star system of Chinese Polar astrology system that has 12 Palaces and hundreds of Fate Stars.

Wang: prosperous, vigorous.

Wang Shan Wang Shui: a Flying Star configuration meaning "prosperous mountain and prosperous water" chart, good for people and good for money.

Water Star: the Star that corresponds with the Facing direction or front of a house.

West Group: the people or houses who best locations are NW, SW, W, NE.

Wu Hsing, see Elements, Five.

Wu kuei: the "five ghosts" location in house.

Wu Xing, see *Wu Hsing*.

Wuxing, see *Wu hsing*.

Yan nien: the longevity location in house.

Yang: the active male principle. Yang is the complimentary opposite of yin.

Yang chai: the houses of the living.

Yang Yun Sung: perhaps the greatest early Master of the Form School of feng shui (AD 840-circa 888).

Yellow Emperor: Huang Ti (2697-2597 BC) perhaps the greatest of the legendary emperors. Not to be confused with Chin Shih Huang Ti (the first Ch'in emperor who "burnt the books" (c. 221 BC).

Yi Jing, see *I Ching*.

Yin chai: literally "dark house," meaning tomb or grave site.

Yin/Yang symbol, see *t'ai chi*.

Yin: female passive energy, the opposite of *yang*. Yin is used to characterize qualities such as dark, inside, negative, female.

Yu: space, geographical space.

Yuan: Period of 60 years.

Yun: literally "luck," the 20-year Periods that repeat 9 times in each 180-year Great Cycle; the Periods are called *ta yun*, the big luck; the annual cycles are called *hsiao yun*, the small luck.

Zhou Dynasty: see Chou Dynasty.

Zhou yi: an old name for the *I Ching*.

Zi wei, see *tzu wei tou shu*: a form of Chinese astrology, different from 4 pillar astrology.

Bibliography

Dy, Victor. *The 4 Pillars of Fortune Analysis for Everybody*. Renaissance, Makati, Manila, 2001.

Lo, Raymond. *Feng Shui and Destiny*. Tynron Press, Lutterworth, 1992.

Lo, Raymond. *3 Period and 3 Harmony Combined Lo Pan Interpretation*. [A manual accompanying Raymond's excellent *lo p'an*]. Thompson House, Hong Kong, 2001. www.fengshuicentre.com.hk.

Moran, Elizabeth and Val Biktashev. *The Complete Idiot's Guide to Feng Shui.* www.aafengshui.com (With chapters by Master Joseph Yu and Foreword by Stephen Skinner.) Alpha Books, New York, 2002.

Sherrill, W. A. and Chu, W. K. *An Anthology of I Ching*. RKP, London, 1977.

Skinner, Stephen. *Living Earth Manual of Feng-Shui: Chinese Geomancy.* Penguin/Viking, London, 1982.

Skinner, Stephen. *Feng Shui, the Traditional Oriental Way*. Parragon, Bristol, 1997.

Skinner, Stephen. *Feng Shui for Modern Living (the book)*. Cima/Cico Books, London *and* Trafalgar, New York, 2000.

Skinner, Stephen. *Feng Shui Before and After: Practical Room-by-Room Makeovers for Your House.* Tuttle Publishing, Boston, 2001. www.tuttlepublishing.com

Skinner, Stephen. *K.I.S.S. Guide to Feng Shui*. Dorling Kindersley, London & New York, 2001. www.dk.com

Skinner, Stephen and Kwok, Man-Ho. Article on "Chinese Almanac" in *Feng Shui for Modern Living* magazine, Issue No, 1,2, London, April, May 1998. www.fengshui-magazine.com

Skinner, Stephen. Article on "Flying Stars" in *Feng Shui for Modern Living* magazine, pp. 80-81, Issue No. 22, London, February 2000. www.fengshui-magazine.com

Too, Lillian (with Grandmaster Yap Cheng Hai). *Flying Star Feng Shui*. Konsep Lagenda, Kuala Lumpur, 1999. [exactly the same book was also published as *Chinese Numerology* 1994].

Twicken, David. *Flying Star Feng Shui Made Easy*. Writers Club Press, San Jose, 2000. www.chineseastrologynow.com [The most succinct book on Flying Star].

Walters, Derek. *Chinese Astrology*. Aquarian Press, London, 1987, reissued 2002. [The most complete book on Chinese astrology in English].

Walters, Derek. *The Feng Shui Handbook: A Practical Guide to Chinese Geomancy*. Aquarian Press, London, 1991.

Wong, Eva. *Feng Shui, The Ancient Wisdom of Harmonious Living for Modern Times*. Shambhala, Boston & London, 1996.

Wong, Eva. *A Master Course in Feng-Shui*. Shambhala, Boston & London, 2001. [Basically an expansion of the previous book.]

Wu Jing-Nuan. Yi Jing. (The *I Ching*). Taoist Center, Washington, 1991.

Yap, Joey. *Flying Star Charts for All the 9 Periods and 24 Directions*. Yap Cheng Hai Feng Shui Center of Excellence, Kuala Lumpur, 2001. www.ychfengshui.com.

Yap, Joey. *An Advanced Feng Shui Home Study Course in Xuan Kong*. Yap Cheng Hai Feng Shui Center of Excellence, Kuala Lumpur, 2000. Order through www.dragon-gate.com or email: xuankong@ychfengshui.com. [Probably the most comprehensive text on Flying Stars feng shui available in English.]

Yu, Master. Feng Shui Correspondence Course. www.astro-fengshui.com

LOOKUP CARDS SHOWING SUMMARY FLYING STAR TABLES:

Alvarez, Juan M. *Feng Shui Tables*. Feng Shui Cultural Center, Florida, 2001. www.fengshuicom.net.

Tanzer, Elliot. *Feng Shui Master Formulas*. Distributed by Feng Shui Warehouse, 2001. www.fengshuiwarehouse.com.

[Both sets of cards are packed with summary information. Unfortunately both of these cards omit Period 1 Flying Stars charts for some reason.]

Versions of the Chinese Almanac Useful for Flying Star Calculations:

Alvarez, Juan M. *Feng Shui: The Thousand Year Manual, Tables and Formulas*. Feng Shui Cultural Center/Fairy's Ring, Florida, 2001. www.fengshuicom.net.

Goh Kee Seah. *The Comparative Solar & Lunar Calendar (1864-2043)*. Landmark Books, Singapore, nd.

Koh, Vincent. *Hsia Calendar 1924 to 2024*, Asiapac, 1998. www.asiapacbooks.com. [Probably the first, and one of the clearest, Almanacs in English.]

Lo, Raymond. *The Thousand Year Calendar for Feng Shui and Destiny*. Hong Kong, nd. [In Chinese except introduction, for years 1900 to 2050.]

Than, Ricky and Lo, Raymond. *Chinese Almanac (T'ung Shu) for the Year of the Great 2003*. Thompson House, Hong Kong, 2001. www.fengshuicentre.com.hk.

Flying Star Software

Software for Feng Shui. www.fengshui-magazine.com.

Sources of Lo P'ans

You can purchase the Chinese compass, or *lo p'an*, in most large Chinatowns in cities like London, San Francisco, and Sydney, or order via the internet from:

Dragon Gate, Kuala Lumpur, Malaysia. www.dragon-gate.com.

Thompson House, Hong Kong. www.fengshuicentre.com.hk.

Other Relevant Web Sites for Flying Star:

www.168fengshui.com
www.aafengshui.com
www.amfengshui.com
www.astro-fengshui.com
www.chineseastrologynow.com
www.fengshui.net
www.fengshuiliving.com
www.fengshui-magazine.com
www.fengshuinetwork.net
www.fengshuiqueen.com

www.fengshui-school.co.uk
www.feng-shui-school.com
www.fengshuiseminars.com
www.fengshuisociety.org.uk
www.fengshuisos.com
www.geomancy.net
www.houseoffengshui.com
www.iffs.net
www.imperial-fengshui.com
www.raymond-lo.com
www.ychfengshui.com

Index

Note: page numbers in *italic* refer to illustrations.

children, 86-87, 184-85.
　　See also auspicious and inauspicious
　　　　combinations of Stars
Chinese Almanac (*T'ung Shu*), 48-51,
　　145
Chinese architecture, 72-74, 81, *82*
Chinese calendar. *See* lunar calendar;
　　solar calendar
Chinese compass. *See* lo p'an
Chinese dynasties, 24-26, 209-11
Civil/Literary Career (Windings). *See*
　　Star 4-green
"Classic of the Moving Dragon" (Yang),
　　202-4
clocks, 164-65
closets, 87
coin swords, 47, *48*
colors of Flying Stars, 60-62
Combination of Ten chart, 153-54, *154*
Combination of Three chart (Parent
　　String chart), *155*, 155-56
combinations of Stars, 119-33
　　basic auspicious, 120-21
　　basic inauspicious, 120
　　health implications of, 121-22
　　Host and Guest, 131-33, 137, 138,
　　　　182-83, 184
　　in key Palaces, 118
　　significance and potential outcome
　　　　of, 123-29
　　Usable and Timely, 130-31
Compass Directions
　　4 cardinal, 3-5
　　4 intercardinal, 7, *7*
　　and the Lo Shu, *12*, *13*, 30-31
　　See also lo p'an (Chinese compass)
compasses. *See* lo p'an
construction dates, 69-71, 104-5
Continuous Bead charts, *156*, 156-57
Counter-Jupiter (T'ai Sui), 48-49, 168
courtyards, 73, *74*
Covetous Wolf. *See* Star 1-white
crystals, 177
Cycles, 20-26

60-year, 20-22
180-year (Great Cycle), 23-27, 205-6
　　and Chinese dynasties, 24-26
　　historic, 26
Cycles of the Elements, 5-6, *6*, 170-72

D

Daily Flying Stars, 143-45
Dark Warrior, 43
dens and studies, 86-87
desk placement, 93
Destruction Cycle of the Elements, 5-6,
　　6, *171*, 171
dining rooms, 85
Directions, 24 (24 Mountains), *32*, 32-
　　34, 197-99
diseases, 121-22, 183-84
doors
　　apartment buildings, 89
　　main entrances, 41, 84-85, 89, 114,
　　　　164, 183
　　room, 91, 183
Double Facing chart, 151, *152*
Double Sitting chart, 151-52, *153*
Dy, Victor, 145
dynasties, Chinese, 24-26, 209-11

E

Earth (Three Primes), 3
Earth Base Stars. *See* Period Stars
Earth Element, 4-6, 172-73, 177
Earth Plate, 28, 39
Earthly Branches (Ti Chih)
　　described, 18-19
　　60 Sexagenary combinations, 20-23
　　and the 24 Directions or
　　　　Mountains, 32-34, 198
East House/West House system, 58,
　　137-38
8 Traveling Stars, 59, 137-38

8 Trigrams. *See* Trigrams
Elements, 5 (wu hsing), 4-6
    Cycles of, 5-6, 6, 170-72
    Flying Star correspondences, 62-63,
       173
    in key Palaces, 117-18
    relative strengths of, 172-73
    remedies for each, 175-81
    and seasons, 4, *5*, 17
    and Trigrams, 8, 9
entrances. *See* doors
extensions. *See* renovations and
    additions

F

Facing Direction, 37-38, 40-42, 89-91,
    106-7, 108
Facing Palace, 114
Facing Stars. *See* Water Stars
family problems, 183
family rooms, 85
fan yin (Inverse Siren), 160-61
Fate Stars, 48-51, 166-67. *See also*
    Northern Ladle (Pei Tou)
favorable and unfavorable nature of
    Stars, 67-69
Favorable for Wealth and for Health
    chart, 149, *150*, 151
fei hsing. *See* Flying Stars
feng (wind), 2
feng shui chronology, 209-11
feng shui schools, 207-8
feng shui theory, 1-14
    definition, xiii-xiv
    8 trigrams, 7-10
    5 Elements, 4-6
    geography and, 1-2
    Lo Shu (*see* Lo Shu square)
    Three Primes, 3
    yin and yang, 2-3
Fire Element (huo), 4-6, 176-77
fire mouth, 94

fish, 175-76
5 Elements. *See* Elements
Flipping Trigram, 52-53
floor plan analysis, 72-83
    8-sector pie wedge method, 75-78,
       78
    included and excluded areas, 72-75
    9-Palace Lo Shu method, 78-83
flowers, 177
Flying Star Charts (flying the Stars)
    Annual, 134-36, 163-66
    basic types, 148-52
    Combination of Ten, 153-54, *154*
    Combination of Three, *155*, 155-56
    combinations (*see* combinations of
      Stars)
    Continuous Bead, *156*, 156-57
    Double Facing, 151, *152*
    Double Sitting, 151-52, *153*
    example, 108-12
    Favorable for Wealth and for
      Health, 149, *150*, 151
    full method, 105-7
    Hidden Siren (fu yin), 160-61, *161*
    Hourly, 145, *146*
    identifying and interpreting key
      Palaces, 113-18
    Inverse Siren (fan yin), 160-61, *161*
    Monthly, 138-43
    Prison, or Locked, 157-60, *158*
    shortcut method, 107-8
    special patterns, 161-62
    summary table of chart patterns,
      161-62
    tables for generating, 187-96
    types of, summary, *144*
    Unfavorable for Health and for
      Wealth (Reversed), *150*, 151, 155
Flying Star feng shui
    analysis sequence, 216-18
    described, xiii-xiv
    practice of, 215
Flying Stars (fei hsing)
    basic nature of, 67-69

I

I Ching, 8 trigrams of, 7-10
inactivity, 118, 181-82. *See also* activation
inauspicious and auspicious combinations of Stars, 120-29
Individual Stars (Personal Stars), 136-38, 143-45
Inverse Siren charts (fan yin), 160-61, *161*

J

Jupiter, 21, 48-49, 168

K

kitchen god (Tsao Chun), 94-95
kitchens, 86, 93-94, 95, 184
koi carp, 176
kua. *See* Trigrams
Kuan Kung, 167

L

landscape, 96-100, 114, 118, 184, 202-4, 214
Later Heaven Sequence, *9*, 9-10, *10*, 63
lien chu san pan kua (Continuous Bead charts), *156*, 156-57
lights, 177
lingbi rocks, 177
living rooms, 85
lo p'an (Chinese compass), 28-43
    24 Directions or Mountains, *32*, 32-34, 197-99
    buying, 34
    Chinese characters on, 39
    described, 28-30
    homemade, 34-36, *35*, 37-38

Lo Shu and, 30-31
    magnetic interference, 38-39
    reading, 36-40
    substitutes for, 36, 37-38, 39-40
Lo, Raymond, 145
Lo Shu square
    basic, with directions, *104*
    described, 11-14
    9 Palaces of, 78-83, 101-5
    and traditional Chinese architecture, 73-75
    use in apartment buildings, 89-91
Lo Shu Turtle, 11, *11*
lu ban, 165
luck, definition of, xiii-xiv
lucky and unlucky stars, 56-59
lucky numbers, 66-67
lunar calendar, 15, 16, 102

M

macro feng shui, 89-91
magnetic interference, 38-39
Man (one of Three Primes), 3
Mao Tse Tung, 137-38
marital problems, 183. *See also* auspicious and inauspicious combinations of Stars
Metal Element (chin), 4-6, 178-79
    and Annual 5-yellow Star, 164-65
    Big and Small, 172-73
micro feng shui. *See* rooms
Military Career (Windings). *See* Star 6-white
military compass. *See* trekking compass
ming kua, 136
mini-seasons (Ch'i Chieh), 16-17, 212
money problems, 182-83
Monthly Flying Stars, 138-43
Mountain Forms of the Flying Stars, 99-100, 202-4
Mountain Stars (Sitting Stars), 41, 42, 65, 96-100, 106-7, 136.

"Books to Span the East and West"